Early Childhood Systems

Transforming Early Learning

D1516491

Early Childhood Systems

Transforming Early Learning

Sharon Lynn Kagan
Kristie Kauerz

EDITORS

Teachers College, Columbia University
New York and London

Published by Teachers College Press, 1234 Amsterdam Avenue, New York, NY 10027

Library of Congress Cataloging-in-Publication Data

Early childhood systems : transforming early learning / edited by Sharon Lynn Kagan, Kristie Kauerz.
    p. cm.
  Includes bibliographical references and index.
  ISBN 978-0-8077-5296-8 (pbk.)—ISBN 978-0-8077-5297-5 (hardcover)
  1. Early childhood education—United States--States. 2. Child care services—United States--States. I. Kagan, Sharon Lynn. II. Kauerz, Kristie.
LB1139.25.E28 2012
  372.21—dc23
                                                            2011045772

ISBN 978-0-8077-5296-8 (paper)
ISBN 978-0-8077-5297-5 (hardcover)

Printed on acid-free paper
Manufactured in the United States of America

19 18 17 16 15 14 13 12   8 7 6 5 4 3 2 1

We dedicate this book to our sisters.

To our blood sisters,
Betty Doris Goldberg
and
Amy McIntosh and Jennie Dawe,
who frame our family systems and
who continually surround us with their fierce loyalty, deep
compassion, and the sense of knowing what is truly important
in life.

And to our countless professional sisters who aim high and
work hard to bring to fruition an early childhood system for
America's children and families.

Contents

Acknowledgments

Many people have contributed to the development of this volume. Foremost among them was Luba Lynch, whose quiet, thoughtful, and supportive stances have made this foray into the systems work possible and pleasurable. We are deeply indebted to the A. L. Mailman Family Foundation, whose generosity made this work doable. Their support of this, and so many efforts, makes them a treasure in early childhood's very fiber. To the contributors who put up with our seemingly endless edits and queries, we give thanks. We strongly applaud the work they each put into their chapters, making this a compendium that hopefully will make a real difference.

In our work, we were supported by others. At Teachers College, we would like to acknowledge the fine editorial work of Jocelyn Friedlander. With a constant smile and a tough red line, she helped to keep this volume organized and make it readable. Penina Braffman and Samara Wallace-Noyola offered considerable organizational and fiscal supports to us and to the contributors. In the end, this is our work; we take joy in having done it and responsibility for its contents. Fervently, we hope that it propels forward the existing and yet-to-be-imagined efforts that focus on early childhood systems.

Sharon Lynn Kagan, Ed.D., New Haven, Connecticut
Kristie Kauerz, Ed.D., Cambridge, Massachusetts

Part I

CONTEXT FOR EARLY CHILDHOOD SYSTEMS

CHAPTER 1

Early Childhood Systems
Looking Deep, Wide, and Far

Sharon Lynn Kagan and Kristie Kauerz

Incontestably, the past decades have witnessed remarkable changes to the provision of services for young children and their families. Although remaining limited in quantity and quality, inequitably dispersed, and organizationally fragmented, early childhood has risen in priority on many parental, political, and practice agendas. Across the United States, there is growing understanding of the importance of the early years as fundamental to the well-being of children, families, and society in the short and long term. Supported by compelling data from the biological and social sciences, early childhood has moved from a barely recognized service to the center of much policymaking, with governments at local, state, and federal levels regarding it as a necessary panacea for a host of social ills.

For parents and families, as well, the impact of early education has become apparent. Some parents worry as much about and invest as much in their child's preschool education as they do their child's college education. Cascades of parenting books, DVDs, and websites populate libraries, bookstores, and the internet. Courses in parenting, infant reading kits, and parenting newsletters flock the market. Whether in Minnesota, Kentucky, or South Dakota; whether located in elegant and expensive early childhood centers or in church basements; whether using polished toolkits and colorful toys or pebbles, stones, and mud; and whether staffed by BA-level teachers or volunteers, early childhood education is taking hold as both a public and private priority.

As with any movement that grows organically and comparatively rapidly, challenges exist. Written about elsewhere by countless experts, the nature of services for young children and families varies dramatically. Many are concerned about their inequitable distribution, suggesting that if not done well, early childhood education may fuel the divide between particular groups of children (Kagan, 2006). Cognizant of tight budgetary conditions, others lament the costs of providing high-quality services and question both the replicability and the sustainability of such efforts (Finn, 2009). Still others are concerned about accountability and seek to document proven social and academic outcomes caused by children's participation in early childhood programs (Ackerman & Barnett, 2006). Perhaps most important, many are concerned about the nature and quality of the services rendered, noting that the high expectations levied on early childhood programs will not be realized unless quality provisions are secured (Kagan & Cohen, 1996). Equity, replicability, sustainability, accountability, and quality are all critically important to consider and to address thoroughly and thoughtfully so as to maximize both the current early childhood political momentum and the contemporary investments being made on behalf of young children.

Indirectly, this book addresses these challenges, but they are not its focus. Although emanating from the same sociopolitical context, another cadre of issues has emerged over the past 40 years. Interest in early childhood *systems* has crescendoed as the plethora of investments, programs, and services has increased. Layered on top of an already inchoate array of services distributed among the public and private sectors and multiple departments and levels of government, new early childhood efforts make both service delivery and policy administration more complex and disorganized. Hence, as new efforts emerge, early childhood leaders and policymakers beckon for coordination, linkages, partnerships, and effective and accountable use of resources. They beckon for thinking that transcends the provision of any individual program and considers early childhood service delivery broadly and comprehensively, as a system. They note that early childhood is at a developmental juncture, moving from a scattered array of programs to a recognized service sector, replete with needs for legitimacy and cogency. As in so many other service sectors—including health, education, and transportation—that began as small, idiosyncratic efforts, the early childhood field's expansion demands management, organization, and the development of systems.

Within early childhood, the need for systems and systems work is not new. Recognizing fissures in the field and their detrimental effects, scholars have proposed the development of an early childhood education system for decades (e.g., Kagan & Cohen, 1996; Sugarman, 1991). These calls were based not on theoretical hypotheses, but on acknowledged and reflected reality: Early childhood has been a splintered field since its emergence. Responsibility for programs and services has been episodic and divided across different political and administrative jurisdictions. With the federalist political system of the United States, for example, early childhood has been partitioned vertically, with the federal government holding responsibility for some programs (e.g., Head Start, Child Care and Development Block Grant, and Medicaid), state governments responsible for other programs (e.g., state-funded prekindergarten, the administration of child care subsidies, and state children's health insurance programs), and local communities for still others (e.g., resource coordination and referral services for parents). Early childhood also is split horizontally, with different departments overseeing different components of services. Often departments of human or social services administer child care efforts, while departments of health administer early intervention and home-visiting programs. Not surprisingly, education departments usually administer early childhood services more directly related to education, including family literacy efforts and education services for children with disabilities.

Given these realities, calls for coordination, collaboration, and systems development have gained prominence in the lexicon and literature of early childhood education. Whether dubbed systems efforts, partnerships, linkages, coordination, or collaboration, such efforts are designed to stimulate new thinking and new actions that will expand services, improve their quality and outcomes, and reduce inequities in access. The goal of such efforts is to institutionalize programs and policies into durable systems. Although the precise efforts vary, those engaged in them share the recognition of the burdens of an incoherent nonsystem of early childhood services and seek to redress them. Increasingly, systems are seen to be essential goals for the early childhood field. The widespread adoption of early childhood system building as both a day-to-day undertaking and a long-term goal underscores some of the field's enduring issues (e.g., equity, quality, sustainability, and accountability), while simultaneously introducing a myriad of new issues (e.g., the potential leverage of subsystems and the best use of limited resources when faced with the simultaneous needs of expanding programs *and* building system infrastructure).

As this volume goes to press, President Barack Obama's Administration announced that $500 million from Race to the Top funds will be used to support the Early Learning Challenge, to be administered jointly by the U.S. Department of Education and the U.S. Department of Health and Human Services, funded through Race to the Top. The competitive grant program calls on states to take a comprehensive approach to developing integrated, high-quality early learning systems, which in turn will help ensure that more children, especially high-need children, enter school ready and able to succeed. This is an unprecedented time for thinking comprehensively about the needs of young children. Consequently, this volume addresses both the old and the new issues, looking backward and forward at early childhood systems and system building in the United States.

BACKDROP FOR THIS BOOK

Colloquially, contemporary efforts to build an early childhood system have been likened to "constructing a house without a foundation" or "building a plane while flying it." Aptly, these analogies capture the urgency of the situation, suggesting that industrious, real-time action is underway. However, where these descriptions vary from reality is that in the case of building a house or a plane, there are clear design strategies and plans to guide actions and to orchestrate construction. In the case of system building, there is no such clarity. As this volume will highlight, definitions of what a system is vary, as do the visions of what such a system should accomplish. The pathways that are understood to be necessary for implementation vary and continue to evolve, as do the strategies that demarcate these pathways. For example, throughout this volume, some authors refer to the "four-oval" graphic for a comprehensive early childhood system. First developed in 2005, this is the prevalent conceptual model for the system of systems approach in early childhood. As this volume went to press, the Early Childhood Systems Working Group revised the graphic in order to clarify some of the concepts, to incorporate lessons learned from field-based users of the graphic, and to reflect the evolving understanding of system-building work.

Despite a somewhat unclear vision, indistinct strategies, and perpetually evolving thinking, numerous system-building efforts are in progress and many more are being launched every year. Across these system-building efforts, there is growing consensus around some issues and lingering uncertainty around others. Both the certainties and the uncertainties provide a backdrop to this volume. In this chapter, we attempt to tease out and preview some of the themes that weave throughout the remainder of the book.

General Agreements

We identify some of the general agreements emerging around early childhood systems development work and then delineate some of the different definitions and inconclusive issues raised by others in this volume and elsewhere.

The Pervasiveness of Change. There is wide acknowledgment that we live in an era of rapid change and that change is inevitable. No exception, the field of early childhood is experiencing remarkable changes. Throughout this volume, authors reflect on changes caused by the increased scientific understanding of young children's brain development, as well as changes caused by the scope and scale of government involvement in programs that support children's learning and development. Some of the contributors emphasize change that is external to the early childhood field, such as broad societal shifts in population demographics, while others call attention to change from within the field itself, such as expansion in the size and number of programs delivering services in both the public and private sectors. Change is both pervasive and having a profound impact on the early childhood field.

The Need for More Change and a New Think. What all of the contributors to this volume can agree on is that old policy approaches to early childhood education, with their focus on unitary programs, are no longer enough. The early childhood field needs to continually change and adapt its thinking and strategizing to meet the context of current trends. Indeed, there is growing acknowledgment that a focus on the direct services that children and families receive, in the absence of simultaneous attention to the infrastructure, is an inefficient policy strategy. We must move from asking narrow questions related to just one program or funding stream to framing overarching, integrative questions that transcend programs. This profound shift gets to the essence of a new way of thinking about service delivery and policy formulation by focusing on how the systems impacting children intersect and how they work together more effectively and efficiently.

The Need to Plan and Act Simultaneously . . . Now. The early childhood field as a whole, as well as states and local communities, are replete with strategic plans for how to improve services for young children. While plans are important, there is an emerging sense of urgency to begin to enact new thinking and to develop a more systemic approach to early childhood services—now. While not eliminating a focus on the quality of early childhood programs, advancement for equity and sustainability will demand a refocus on diverse elements of the infrastructure. Exhausted by both "here today, gone tomorrow" funding support and intransigent policy regulations established decades ago but not modernized to meet today's imperatives, policymakers and practitioners recognize that long-term commitments and planned investments must be coupled with short-term action and incremental policy reform. Throughout this volume, contributors highlight promising possibilities for both planning and action, as well as for both the short and long term. To balance these, accountability, governance, and capacity building are crucial—and these issues are addressed extensively herein.

The Need for Multiple Models/Approaches and Their Evaluation.
While the call for systems thinking and development is loud and clear, there is no unified call for a single approach to achieving a functional early childhood system. More than a matter of mere collegial politeness and acceptance of diverse strategies, the lack of consensus no doubt is predicated on the

freshness of systems work. Indeed, lacking any thorough and independent evaluations of systemic effectiveness, there is no single model that reigns supreme. Moreover, given postmodernist thinking that acknowledges the role of context and change, as noted above, it is unlikely that any single systems approach will work uniformly well in all contexts. States and communities differ in their political apparatuses, in their approaches to collaboration, in their resources, and in the ways that they structure public and public/private engagements. As such, there is a strong need for multiple well-documented systems efforts, with the goal of discerning what works well (not best) under what conditions.

Multiple Terminologies and Definitions

Practice and literature are awash with various definitions of systems generally and with different labels for and definitions of early childhood systems specifically. Even in this chapter and throughout this volume, "early childhood," "early care and education," "early childhood education," and "early childhood development" are used interchangeably in the discussions of systems that impact services for young children. Some of the contributing authors (and others in the field) envision a system that serves children from birth to school entry, others from birth through age 8, and still others something else. Some focus on systems that coordinate and align the variety of programs and services related specifically to early education (e.g., prekindergarten, child care, Head Start, early childhood special education). Some discuss comprehensive systems that encompass not just children's early education settings, but also family support, and pediatric health and mental health. Some scholars and practitioners describe seven elements to a system (see, for example, Bruner, this volume), while others describe eight elements (see, for example, Kagan, Tarrant, and Kauerz, this volume).

This multiplicity of terms and definitions reflects the complexity of the work and the breadth and depth of creative energy engaged in its conceptualization. It also, though, can be confusing to policymakers and practitioners alike. Goffin (this volume) notes that defining a coherent and functioning system demands that the early childhood field first define itself before it comes to grips with a definition of the system that will contain its practices and policies. In posing a set of critical questions, Goffin asks the field to define its intent, the chronological age span represented by the field, and its scope (e.g., the degree to which it incorporates allied disciplines of health, mental health, family support).

Given all of the creative and productive systems work underway across the country, and exemplified in this volume, establishing agreement on a single common definition of a system may be premature. As an interim step, we argue that more precision in how terms are used will serve the field well by clarifying who is doing what, for which purposes, and with what effects. To that end, we offer some provisional definitions that guided the construction of this volume.

Early Care and Education System. An early care and education system includes only those programs that explicitly address the early care and education needs of young children from birth to age 5. An early care and education system embraces the full scope of early childhood care and education settings that children encounter prior to kindergarten, including child care, family child care, preschool, prekindergarten, Head Start, early childhood special education, and nursery schools.

Early Learning System. An early learning system includes the above-listed early care and education programs and services, but its scope extends into the early elementary grades (kindergarten through 3rd grade), addressing the education of children from birth to age 8 (including before- and after-school care).

Early Childhood System. An early childhood system includes early care and education and the early elementary grades and also extends to embrace comprehensive services for young children, including health and mental health services. Early childhood systems usually address the needs of young children from birth to age 8. This is the most comprehensive of the three types of systems and, because of its scope, encapsulates the other two types of systems just defined. In general, throughout this chapter we default to using the term "early childhood system" when we intend to encapsulate all three types of systems defined herein.

While these three system definitions differ in important ways, they share early childhood education—not child health or family support—as the locus, emphasis, or entry point for system building. We recognize that there are many other systems defined within the broad field of early childhood services. For example, there are critical efforts underway to establish comprehensive health systems for children, addressing issues such as health insurance, medical homes, and complex funding streams (such as Medicaid, State Children's Health Insurance Program [S-CHIP], and private insurance). While they are crucial to children's overall well-being, this volume does not address these systems efforts; rather, it focuses on the above three system definitions, those that use early childhood education as their primary vantage point.

Multiple Challenges

Beyond different definitions, there are multiple issues that characterize the discourse regarding early childhood systems. As the reader delves into the chapters herein, these issues will be explored in greater depth, with some being addressed by many contributors. The following issues are presented below as a preamble to the challenging work of system building in early childhood.

What Is Lost. Inherent in much of the work on systems is the assumption that systems work is constructive and will yield positive consequences for the delivery of services to young children and their families. However infrequently, some scholars have raised considerable concern regarding negative effects of systems work. It is our stance that these issues should not impede systems work, but should inform it. Four such issues merit attention.

First, in developing a system, does the early childhood field stand a chance of homogenizing its services too much? One of the hallmarks of high-quality early education is the flexibility accorded to individual programs and states. Because system building requires alignment and coordination, how much of that diversity will be compromised? How much compromise in terms of flexibility is necessary and how much is too much? Second, and related, to what extent will a systems approach curtail options for parents? In other words, is there a way to develop a systemic approach that honors the diversity of family needs and desires? Third, and also related, is to what degree will such systematization curtail the field's historic commitment to cultural diversity and multiculturalism? Fourth, given that much of the focus of system building is on government structures and strategies, will systems efforts honor the place of nonpublic providers and nonpublic strategies?

Inherent in this set of issues are the potential drawbacks of constructing too tight and prescriptive a system for early childhood. Such questions are quite real and come up throughout this volume. While the reader will be interested to discern different ideas about these questions and his or her own conclusions, we suggest that such issues get to the core of systems work, which is what makes it interesting and necessary. Given the numerous examples that are discussed herein, we suggest that there are thoughtful approaches underway that are cognizant of these "loss" issues and are provisioning for them.

Home-Based Child Care. Throughout this volume and throughout much of the systems work that is underway, very little attention is accorded family child care and family, friend, and neighbor care. Cordoned off as though an entirely separate universe, home-based child care is an essential element of any early childhood system. In the United States, home-based providers serve cascades of children, more than are served in center-based programs. Just how home-based child care will and should fit into the emerging early childhood system needs sustained attention. Too little is being done in this essential service delivery area.

Indicators, Data, and Evaluation. The development of early childhood systems will take time, energy, and funds. Accordingly, the field needs to be ready to address questions regarding the effectiveness of, and benefits derived from, systems work. To date, there are only embryonic efforts underway to determine indicators of effective systems and to document the success of a systems approach to early childhood service delivery. While it is difficult to mount randomized trials, there are scores of ways that data can and should be collected so as to attest to the gains (or losses) that accrue as a result of systems work. Concomitantly, standards for effective systems should be developed.

Readers will discover a host of other cross-cutting issues throughout this volume. Is there a "best" starting point for systems work? Is there a necessary sequence of systems development? Are there non-negotiables in system building—people, organizations, or strategies that are inherently and absolutely necessary to successful system building? Is there a price tag for what it will cost to build an effective system?

LOOKING FORWARD

With burgeoning attention being accorded early childhood, given the mounting interest in systems work, and given the lack of attention to early childhood systems work in the literature, it seemed appropriate to develop this volume. As editors, we have longstanding interest in systems work, with each of us writing about, studying, and implementing systems efforts. Despite our interests and experiences, we felt that an edited volume would be the best way of capturing the diversity of ideas and issues facing system builders; we believed that an edited volume would deftly portray multiple perspectives on the research, policy, and practice of systems work; and finally, we knew that an edited volume would be an appropriate and engaging vehicle to incorporate "voices from the field" to share their current successes and challenges.

To that end, this volume was designed to be a contemporary compendium on early childhood systems. As a whole, it addresses issues such as why systems have emerged, what they hope to accomplish, what some have accomplished, and the challenges they face. From various perspectives, the volume elaborates on the strategies employed in these diverse efforts, stressing the similarities and variations among them. As an edited volume, the book chronicles different interpretations of the nature of an early childhood system as well as different interpretations regarding how systemic effectiveness can be conceptualized and assessed. Its contributors are well-known thinkers and doers in systems work. Consequently, the volume represents an up-to-date chronicle of the status of systems thinking and systems work. Intentionally, as a first goal, the volume is organized to present foundational thinking coupled with concrete examples of work in progress. In so doing, it aims to honor and incorporate the work of practitioners, policymakers, and scholars alike.

As a second goal, we aimed to have the volume advance the collective thinking of the field. Recognizing the diversity of thoughts and opinions that surround systems development, we hoped that the volume would provide a forum for reflection by many of those working on systems. We aimed to have this work be an action-driven springboard. The volume, then, was designed to serve as a catalyst not only for identifying common issues but also for addressing common visions and definitions. To that end, we took some of the key themes and issues raised in the volume and worked to achieve some consensus around them, using a Delphi methodology. The final chapter of the volume describes the process and outcomes that were derived from these efforts. We hope that this volume advances both individual and collective thinking about early childhood systems and serves as a platform to inform government at federal, state, and local levels, as well as private and nongovernmental organizations engaged in work that benefits young children and their families.

Finally, our third goal in constructing this volume was to raise the tough issues. Because systems are being constructed as this volume goes to press, it is important that systems leaders and thinkers have the benefit of their colleagues' thinking and writing (Goal 1), have the benefit of consensual thinking that exists (Goal 2), and have a no-nonsense understanding of the issues that systems work evokes. Not for the faint of heart or for those who seek quick fixes, system builders deserve to have potential stumbling blocks and sinkholes identified as they move forward. To that end, this volume raises the important issues—both those that show great promise and those that confound and confuse—that systems work needs to address.

With these three goals in mind, we, the editors, have attempted to amass a set of seasoned authors and practitioners, a set of integrity-driven issues, and a glimpse into the possible ways diverse ideas about early childhood systems might coalesce.

ORGANIZATION OF THIS BOOK

The book is divided into five parts and 21 chapters. Following this chapter, the remainder of the first part, "Context for Early Childhood Systems," presents the opinions and ideas of six prominent early childhood systems leaders who cross the bounds of research, policy, and practice (Chapter 2). We asked them to share their visions of a high-functioning early childhood system. A collection of short essays, together they reveal interesting and sometimes stark contrasts in systems conceptualization and operationalization. There is no singular notion of what a system is, whom it should serve, or how to go about building it. Contributors vary in their conceptions of the scope of the system. Bruner suggests that a system should address the comprehensive needs of children and essentially be a "system of systems"; Traylor asserts that a system might do well to focus aligning its mission with the goals of public education. While one hopes that the overall system will align service systems (Bruner), another hopes that it will concentrate on aligning programs (Ponder). Yet another (García) calls for systems to align the work and intentions of research, policy, and practice.

The contributors vary in their ideas of the age range of children that should be served by a system, with some asserting an early childhood system should focus on programs and services for children from birth to age 5 (Ponder, Klein); others extending the age range to embrace birth (or prenatal) through 3rd grade (Bruner, García, Hill Scott); and one asserting that the focal age range should be children from ages 3 to 8 (Traylor). One perspective highlights the importance of a system meeting the needs of dual language learners (García), while another highlights the importance of vulnerable children (Klein). One highlights the importance of the federal government (Klein); one the importance of state government (Ponder); one the importance of school districts (Traylor); and another the importance of families (Hill Scott).

In short, the collection illuminates the diverse approaches to systems thinking that exist. Although the various opinions and perspectives are not mutually exclusive, they do raise the question of both the need for and viability of achieving a coherent vision of a system. The essays herein are not presented as competing paradigms in a zero-sum game. Rather, they are included as exemplars of the rich diversity of perspective and priority that currently, albeit often uncomfortably, co-exist in the early childhood field.

Contributors to the second part, "Essential Subsystems," address the fact that system building requires attention to the underlying infrastructure that supports the work's alignment, coherence, and sustainability. This part provides a set of five chapters, each devoted to an element of the infrastructure: (1) early learning standards and accountability; (2) program accountability and quality rating and improvement systems (QRIS); (3) governance; (4) professional development; and (5) data systems. These structures and processes transcend, cut across, or sit above existing program and sector boundaries. More specifically, in Kagan's chapter on early learning standards and accountability, she recounts the evolution of the standards movement for what children should know and be able to do in elementary and pre-primary education. She presents an approach that has been followed internationally as a vehicle for using standards to coordinate a systemic approach to early education. Schaack, Tarrant, Tout, and Boller provide a thorough and up-to-date analysis of the role that QRIS can have in the development of an overall early childhood system. They present three provocative conceptual frameworks—functional analysis, institutional analysis, and adaptive systems analysis—that illustrate how QRIS may produce a more integrated early care and education system. Kauerz and Kagan underscore the importance of governance to building the early childhood system, suggesting that there are two essential functions of governance (authority and accountability) that are manifest in two compatible approaches to governance (within-government and cross-sector). This chapter takes a fresh look at how the structures and processes of governance can and should be conceptualized differently, while still adhering to the same essential functions, depending on a system's definition and scope. In their chapter, Hyson and Vick Whittaker present a rich discussion of professional development for teachers, highlighting its evolution and how changes in policies, contexts, and research have affected the construct of an early childhood professional development system. To illustrate their work and subsystem efforts, the authors provide a detailed analysis of professional development efforts in Delaware, New Mexico, and Pennsylvania. Gruendel and Stedron assert that an early childhood data system, at the state agency level, is one of the essential core infrastructure components of a coordinated, durable early childhood system and that its design and functionality deserve significant attention and ongoing investment. They discuss how such data systems are evolving and how federal and state governments are supporting this element of the early childhood system.

Taken together, this part provides deep insights into how elements of the infrastructure of an early childhood system, often called subsystems, are evolving. The strength of these chapters is that they provide a look backward at why and how these subsystems were developed, while also providing prospective thoughts about the future of the work. Common to all of the chapters is the pervasive challenge of how to link and integrate these efforts so that, in concert, they establish a firm infrastructure for an early childhood system.

Because system building is not simply a theoretical undertaking, but a very practical one requiring translating hypothetical visions into real-world efforts, the third part, "Transcendent System-Building Processes," addresses processes, frameworks, and mechanisms that contribute to the building of systems. In five chapters, each one integrating the subsystems discussion above, the part addresses: (1) identifying the state policies that matter; (2) developing systems supports at the local level; (3) financing the building of systems; (4) estimating the costs of the system; and (5) evaluating system-building initiatives. Kagan, Tarrant, and Kauerz describe a planning process to identify the state-level policies and principles that must guide system development. The chapter delineates a process that states can use to simultaneously gain a big picture understanding of a system's various components and identify practical, action-oriented, near-term policy changes to pursue. Clifford explores the relationship between state and local systems work, bringing explicit attention to the roles and responsibilities of local governance structures and processes. Stebbins highlights an often-overlooked, yet absolutely necessary, system finance issue—how to finance the system-building activities of strategic planning, coordination, leadership development, and technical assistance. Brodsky then turns to a different sort of financing issue, focusing on a means to quantify the costs of the system (i.e., services and infrastructure) itself. He argues that cost estimation is vital as a framework to ensure that early childhood systems are comprehensive, high-quality, logistically feasible, and politically viable. Finally, Coffman addresses the complex issue of how to evaluate system-building efforts. The chapter offers a framework to guide states in clarifying goals for evaluating five areas of their system-building work: context, components, connections, infrastructure, and scale.

These five chapters provide an invaluable glimpse at some of the innovative thinking that has gone into creating processes and frameworks that guide states and localities in their system-building efforts. These chapters are both innovative and practical, presenting accessible ways to support comprehensive visions and incremental action at the same time.

To illustrate how pieces of early childhood system building come together in the real world, the fourth part, "Snapshots of System Building in Action," provides seven examples of different states' efforts. While each state snapshot highlights a different approach, each represents substantive progress toward the development of an early childhood system. In these chapters, the reader will find reflected themes presented in earlier sections of the volume. Each chapter offers perspective on how one or more of the visions (presented in Part I), infrastructure elements (discussed in Part II), or transcendent processes (discussed in Part III) is serving as an avenue for meaningful progress toward building an early childhood system.

Coleman and Hardin present their exemplary work in Colorado and delineate the development of a framework that led to a common vision, shared across sectors and among stakeholders, for early childhood system building. Froelicher describes how Washington State is using its Early Learning and Development Benchmarks (early learning standards) as a centerpiece for system building. Thornburg and Mauzy present their work in Missouri on the development and implementation of a quality rating system. This chapter is strikingly honest in its evaluation of the successes achieved and the challenges faced in the process. It also provides a strong example of how a focus on one subsystem can be pivotal in addressing other subsystems. Kershaw and Reale were involved in the development and implementation of the Massachusetts governance system; their chapter delineates the work that has been accomplished and points, like the following chapter, to the importance of a coordinated governance mechanism. While they focus on legislative approaches, Dichter presents the Pennsylvania experience with a focus on the key role played by the executive branch of state government. Russell presents North Carolina's landmark work where she and colleagues use professional development as a cornerstone of system-building efforts; the chapter provides clear explication of the various elements that served as the foundation for the work. Finally, Nagle presents Louisiana's approach to developing an early childhood budget as a crucial means for defining and implementing policy priorities.

What these chapters reveal is that different states embark on system-building efforts in different ways and from different vantage points. They all share wise lessons about their past efforts and provocative ideas about the future of their work. No single state has achieved the creation of "*THE* system"; indeed, this volume suggests that system building is an ongoing process without a definitive endpoint. Each state herein (and many others not represented in this volume) has made significant progress toward building "*A* system." These chapters establish concrete roadmaps for how incremental efforts contribute in essential ways to the development of a comprehensive early childhood system.

The concluding part, "Looking Toward the Future: Finding Common Ground on System Building," looks ahead to the future. In her thoughtful and provocative chapter, Goffin delineates a set of polemics that she feels are essential to address. Not only fundamental to systems work, these issues weigh heavily on the field and need attention as it attempts to move forward in an integrated and systematic fashion. Goffin challenges the reader to think hard and long before leaping into action for action's sake.

The concluding chapter in the volume, compiled by the editors, reflects the results of a Delphi process that was developed to discern the level and nature of consensus that could be achieved around systems efforts. This section suggests that early childhood system building is a frontier deserving of increased attention and more explicit discernment of definitions and evaluation of approaches.

REFERENCES

Ackerman, D. J., & Barnett, W. S. (2006, July). Increasing the effectiveness of pre-school programs. *Preschool Policy Brief, 11*. New Brunswick, NJ: NIEER. Retrieved from http://nieer.org/resources/policybriefs/11.pdf

Finn, C. E. (2009, Fall). The preschool picture. *Education Next, 9*(4), 13–19. Retrieved from http://educationnext.org/files/fall09-preschool-pictures.pdf

Kagan, S. L. (2006). *American early childhood education: Preventing or perpetuating inequity?* (Research Review No. 1). New York: Teachers College, Campaign for Educational Equity.

Kagan, S. L., & Cohen, N. (Eds.). (1996). *Reinventing early care and education: A vision for a quality system.* San Francisco: Jossey-Bass.

Sugarman, J. M. (1991). *Building early childhood systems: A resource handbook.* Washington, DC: Child Welfare League of America.

Chapter 2

Perspectives on and Visions of Early Childhood Systems

Vision vs. Reality: The Real Challenge of Large Systems Development

Karen Hill Scott

The field of early care and education has made amazing progress on all fronts since the mid-20th century. Whether the measure is public perception of preschool or funding levels for child care, early education is better off and better understood today than ever before. However, the field is so highly decentralized that few system-building advantages have accrued from the progress. In fact, *THE* system is not *A* system and this hinders program effectiveness for current users and stymies efficiencies for future implementation.

CREATING A VISION

The definition of a comprehensive early childhood system used in this book involves multiple public agencies and goes way beyond the limits imposed by current public policy structures. Let's examine the components of the definition:

An early childhood system provides comprehensive services for children from birth to age 8 and includes early care AND early education AND K–3 education, AND also embraces health AND mental health.

The above definition requires the engagement of six or more service delivery sectors (represented by multiple bureaucracies), eight age cohorts (which could be consolidated into three age groups), and, if the system is universal, about 36 million children and their parents (U.S. Census Bureau, 2008).

Creating a conceptual scheme for such a system requires a strong, broad, and shared vision that can be meaningfully embraced by divergent stakeholders.

The Superordinate Goal

A shared vision must provide an inspiring, compelling, and visual image of a desired future. Taken at face value, it states noble and just aims, and incites little dissent or controversy. A sample vision statement that could work at the national, state, or local level might be: "Every child in this country will have the opportunity to experience a secure, healthful, and learning-filled childhood that will set the foundation for a productive and successful life."

The words "secure, healthful, and learning-filled" are all within the responsibility of existing public agencies (Departments of Health, Human Services, Education, Higher Education, Agriculture) at all levels of government. So the statement above could be adopted by an inter-agency collaborative or an appointed advisory committee charged with system building, or embedded in a legislative or executive directive reflecting public policy. Ideologically, the statement is simple, benign, not overwrought, and not prescriptive as to how the work gets done. The words "will have" make it compulsory for the public sector to have significant responsibility for fulfillment. Functionally, it compels a multiple agency/institution collaboration to create the organizational structure and programmatic initiatives that get the job done through down-line agencies, communities, and programs.

The vision states a superordinate ideal, the implicit purpose of which is to motivate and catalyze energy among stakeholders at all levels and in multiple bureaucracies to forge a new path of change and coherence.

Strategic Mission Statements

The translation of the vision into a system must be bold and operational, and take into account current realities (Flamholtz & Randle, 2000). Being practical does not diminish the idealism of the vision; indeed, it speaks to purposefulness and intentionality for achieving it.

The strategic mission statement model of Flamholtz and Randle is useful for its specificity and utility; its content describes *what you will achieve at the end of a designated time period.* Here, the mission statement translates the vision (a long-term goal) into concrete reality that contains four dimensions: what you will do, with what result, as measured by what metric, and who (the "customers") will benefit from these actions. An example of what a comprehensive system could be follows.

> **National Level.** Within 10 years, 95% of states will have formed their early childhood governance/advisory body. Within 5 years, 80% of the states will have completed and published a Ten-Year Master Plan for a comprehensive early childhood system, and 50% will have started to provide coordinated developmental services to 35% of eligible children under the age of 8, meeting federal standards to begin direct services to children within a decade of the passage of legislation.
>
> **State Level.** Within 1 year of system launch, participating agencies will have registered 45% of eligible 4-year-old children in a state-supported preschool program that meets at least Level 3 of 5 on that state's Quality Rating Scale.

With several strategic mission statements for each domain of a system (e.g., workforce, quality, curriculum, health, accountability), the corpus of the new system will be defined. All the timetables for progressive completion of each mission statement, the regulations, manuals, and operational documents are developed based on these statements. Once this level of strategic planning is complete, it will be possible to estimate—politics notwithstanding—to what extent it is possible and/or how long it will take to fulfill the vision.

Embracing Conjoint Incrementalism

If the vision statement states what ought to be, and the strategic mission statements outline how to get there, then the operational plan must embrace something I call conjoint incrementalism. This is a response to the *disjointed incrementalism* (Braybooke & Lindblom, 1970; Lindblom, 1959) that characterizes American social policy formulation. This perspective posits that policymaking rarely emanates from systematic evaluation of alternatives or formulations of long-term plans, but from developing separate partial initiatives (such as categorical programs) independent of one another. The idea proposed in this essay, *conjoint incrementalism,* is to adopt a sustained and purposeful strategy to remedy the disconnectedness of existing policies. Advocates should consistently press for new or proposed policies to conform and track back to the underlying vision for a comprehensive system.

Embracing conjoint incrementalism means that no matter the direction in which the political pendulum swings, the vision is held constant. Even if system build-out across all elements is not conveniently or logically enacted, support among advocates could remain united, because each opportunity will be used to make a conforming fit to prior and future accomplishments. If the timing is right to explore other policies that will advance the vision, advocates and policymakers will be prepared to use that opportunity to repair gaps and smooth out conflicts caused by prior disjointed decision making.

DEVELOPING INFRASTRUCTURE

The plan for a comprehensive system is an expression of multi-agency engagement and resource commitment around a superordinate goal or mission. In the ideal planning process, each agency would weigh in to generate the strategic mission statements (with goals and indicators), design the system flows that apply to achieving those goals, and articulate each nexus or institutional connection so process flows are not disrupted.

Leadership

Within each agency, it takes senior-level leadership to make decisions and internally champion participation in a collaboration of this magnitude. Just as important as having internal system leadership on board, the early childhood system often needs an external champion, usually an elected official or civic leader who will maintain focus and assiduously shepherd the system to its launch. That leadership may be charismatic or simply tenacious and strategic. But there has been no major achievement in early childhood systems development without a champion buttressed by a very strong bench of knowledgeable collaborators from multiple specialties and constituencies.

Today's leaders also need to contemplate succession planning and develop a talent pipeline. Fulfilling the comprehensive systems vision is at least a 10-year process punctuated by significant wins and achievement of milestones along the way. Sustainability is a defining characteristic of a system; it must live beyond the founders and early champions.

Systems Architecture

It would not be unusual for child development content experts to collaborate and agree to work together, assembling their programmatic platforms to formalize a comprehensive system. However, without enterprise architecture—an information technology methodology for capturing the core information flows and functional processes of the diverse contributors into a whole—a comprehensive system will not exist. Developed and first described by John Zachman (1987), enterprise architecture (EA) constitutes the knowledge infrastructure of the system. It provides a sequencing plan for moving from a baseline asset state to the target or end-state system, including capital planning and investment controls. EA is especially functional for multi-agency, multi-organizational systems development.

The Clinger–Cohen Act of 1996 mandated the creation of a Federal EA Framework. Each Executive Agency of the federal government has adopted the EA Framework, which, according to the U.S. Office of Management and Budget (2010), has been responsible for "improving the quality, availability and sharing of data and information government-wide; and increasing the transparency of government operations by increasing the capacity for citizen participation and cross-governmental collaboration"(p. 1). The bottom line is that a multi-organizational system for early childhood development should be recognizable and understood by a consumer, an elected official, and a systems engineer. EA produces multiple views of the same organization so each audience can access the agency database for information.

Organizational Development

Developing a comprehensive system, even in mature organizations such as state bureaucracies, is an entrepreneurial undertaking. Organizing under the rubric of a new vision and agreeing to implement programmatic change is a process, not an act. Creating new processes while implementing the spread of an idea is a steep challenge, and the pace of change (which seems so easy on paper) will take time for absorption of new practices to become routine. Thus, organizational development should be incorporated into EA or run parallel to it. A new comprehensive system will need metrics on the achievement of process goals as well as the achievement of programmatic goals such as enrollment, teacher–student assessments, or children's health status.

IMPLEMENTATION

While some critics contend that the widespread expansion of publicly supported prekindergarten programs will result in a standardized childhood, or the beginnings of a "nanny state," my experience visiting programs and creating systems has been that every community has its own fingerprint. And considering the nature of classroom interactions between adult and child, and among children, it becomes clear that the labels may be standardized, but the expression of the system varies, just like DNA. This is why, at the local level, the most important stakeholders in comprehensive child development systems are parents and their children.

Stakeholders

If there is any single factor that amplifies the dosage effect of an early childhood program, it is the complementary focus of the parent on the child. The boldest recommendation I could make about comprehensive systems is to engage the investor/customer much earlier in the process and continue the flow of exchange from ideation to implementation. There are many ways to achieve this, from opinion polling at the macro level, to social networking and mobile apps for outreach and education, to leveraging traditional peer and family networks in neighborhoods for day-to-day support.

The bottom line is that a comprehensive system will rely on 8 years of a continuous trust relationship with families. Parents' role and responsibility for what happens to children are more than equal to the investment made by any program. The value of parent engagement to their children and to the success of a comprehensive system cannot be ignored.

The Developmental Continuum

What is most different about a comprehensive early childhood system, in contrast to the extensive but still not complete prekindergarten systems across the country, is the coverage of a full developmental continuum, from birth to age 8. This is a model that leverages existing resources to provide family supports throughout the first phase of the child's life cycle. It includes parental leave policies, infant–toddler care, developmental assessments, early intervention, and preschool services for 3- and 4-year-olds that are aligned and articulated with a full-day kindergarten through 3rd grade school experience, including before- and after-school care. If implemented effectively, such a system could just about ensure a high rate of graduation from secondary school in every community. After all, the comprehensive system will have provided what the vision promises: *a secure, healthful, and learning filled childhood that sets the foundation for a productive and successful life.*

REFERENCES

Braybooke, D., & Lindblom, C. E. (1970). *A strategy of decision: Policy evaluation as a social process*. New York: Free Press.

Flamholtz, E. G., & Randle, Y. (2000). *Growing pains: Transitioning from an entrepreneurship to a professionally managed firm* (3rd ed.). San Francisco: Jossey-Bass.

Lindblom, C. E. (1959). The science of "muddling through." *Public Administration Review, 19*, 79–88.

U.S. Census Bureau. (2008). *2008 American community survey 1-year estimates.* Tables: S0201, R2304, R2302, & R1502. Retrieved from http://factfinder.census.gov

U.S. Office of Management and Budget. (2010, January). Enterprise Architecture Assessment Framework, released June 2009. Retrieved from http://www.whitehouse.gov/omb/E-Gov/eaaf/

Zachman, J. A. (1987). A framework for information systems architecture. *IBM Systems Journal, 26*(3), 276–292.

EARLY CHILDHOOD SYSTEMS:
AN IMPORTANT MEANS TO AN ESSENTIAL END

Lisa G. Klein

The time is ripe for taking new steps to narrow the achievement gap and put the most vulnerable children on track for succeeding in school. Many states have developed innovations to promote early childhood learning and development that have resulted in benefits to children, families, and community economic development. States can serve as laboratories to inform federal policies and actions. Under leadership from the Obama Administration, reforms such as the reauthorization of Early Head Start, new home-visiting legislation, and the American Recovery and Reinvestment Act are providing support for essential services to young children and their families.

However, as federal and state budget deficits grow, there will be pressure to pull back from these investments. Despite public support and strong political will, the federal commitment to supporting system-building work, most notable in the recent announcement of the $500 million Early Learning Challenge, is a fraction of its investments in K–12 system reform. In a perfect world, the United States would have a system that effectively and efficiently coordinated early childhood programs, services, and funding streams. Building this system should not be an end in itself. Rather, it should be the means to improve the lives of vulnerable children starting in the earliest years.

A POLICY TAKE ON THE STATE OF EARLY CHILDHOOD SYSTEM BUILDING

Much has been written about early childhood systems, including some of the latest thinking presented in this book. Recent public and private initiatives and proposed federal legislation suggest growing support for early childhood system building. Like all reform efforts, system building requires time and resources.

In 2003 the Early Childhood Comprehensive Systems Initiative (ECCS) was created with funding from the federal Maternal and Child Health Bureau. To date, 49 states have each received annual grants up to $140,000 to design systems. In September 2009 the House passed an appropriation for ECCS of $5.46 million (Satkowski, 2009).

The U.S. Department of Health and Human Services enacted legislation through the Head Start for School Readiness Act of 2007 that requires governors to designate or establish state advisory councils on early childhood care and education. States had until August 2010 to apply for a portion of $100 million to develop plans for improving the quality, availability, and coordination of early childhood services. Early Childhood Advisory Councils (ECACs) are intended to provide a strategy for bringing together top decision makers to discuss and improve service coordination. As of June 2010, four states had been awarded funds to support their ECAC, as many as 16 had submitted applications for funding, and all but four of the remaining 30 had said they would apply (Satkowski, 2009).

And despite the fact that the Early Learning Challenge Fund was taken out of the Student Aid and Fiscal Responsibility Act (H.R. #3221) in 2010, there is still public and political will to recoup some funding for early childhood systems. Indeed, as this volume went to press, the Obama Administration announced the $500 million Early Learning Challenge as part of Race to the Top. Awards from this grant competition are intended to go to states that are leading the way with ambitious plans for implementing comprehensive early learning and education reform.

In addition to public-sector activities, a group of private foundations interested in early childhood came together in 2002 to invest in BUILD, an initiative that supports seven states directly and many more indirectly through learning-community activities aimed at creating a comprehensive, coordinated system of early childhood programs and services (www.buildinitiative.org). The Birth to Five Policy Alliance, a pooled investment with multiple private investors, works to improve state policies that serve as the base for effective early learning systems, programs, and services for vulnerable young children. Their strategies include supporting quality rating and improvement systems; developing integrated, cross-sector early childhood professional development systems; providing technical assistance to state Early Childhood Advisory Councils; and developing comprehensive and coordinated statewide early learning data systems that align with K–12 (www.birthtofivepolicy.org).

BALANCING LONG-TERM CHANGE AND IMMEDIATE NEEDS

System building is a long-term enterprise. As efforts to build an efficient and effective early childhood system are ramping up, it begs questions about what is happening to vulnerable young children today.

In *Leaving Too Many Children Behind,* demographer Harold Hodgkinson (2003) described the kindergarten class of 2000, the children who will be responsible for funding the retirement benefits for more than 70 million baby boomers. Using Census data from 2000, he revealed that the United States had a higher percentage of children living in poverty than any other developed nation. The percentage of young children born into the poorest families was 25% larger than the percentage born into middle- and upper-income families. In 1999, 45% of the nation's nearly 4 million 3-year-olds were in some type of center-based program (child care, preschool, public prekindergarten, or Head Start). And although Head Start celebrated its 35th anniversary in 2000, it served only three of five eligible children at that time.

Flash forward nearly a decade. About the same number of children are born in the United States each year yet, between 2000 and 2008, the number considered low-income increased by 12% and the number considered poor increased by 21%. Children under age 6 are disproportionately poor and have the distinction of being the largest group growing up in, or near, poverty (Wight & Chau, 2009). Unfortunately, estimates are that Head Start reached only about half of all those eligible for the program in 2009.

Why does this matter? The science of early childhood development is clear: Stress in early childhood can lead to lifelong negative consequences in health and development (National Scientific Council on the Developing Child, 2007). Children growing up poor are often under great stress and experience delays in their development (Wight & Chau, 2009).

This should set off alarm bells and an urgent call to action. Today's vulnerable children cannot wait until a coordinated and effective early childhood system is put into place. They need access to quality services and supports now.

MAKING SURE CHILDREN BENEFIT

A more effective early childhood system of supports is certainly needed, especially for the most vulnerable children. The difference between viewing system building as a means or an end may be subtle, but it is important. The position offered here is to make sure the ultimate goal is not to develop a perfectly coordinated and integrated system, but what happens to help vulnerable young children as a result.

There is a case to be made that if all we do is build a system that links together the components that exist in most places today, we risk spending lots of limited resources and having little to show for it. Too many of today's early childhood programs continue to be of moderate or poor quality. Research and evaluation on a variety of interventions show positive impacts for high-quality programs and a lack of impact (and in some cases negative impacts) for low-quality programs. This suggests that knitting together mediocre and poor-quality programs into a comprehensive integrated system will not improve children's trajectories.

As a result of the economic downturn, the market value of the combined assets for all U.S. private foundations declined by 25% from $670 billion in 2007 to just over $500 billion by the end of 2008 (Lawrence & Mukai, 2008). It is not surprising that when resources are more limited, there are increased expectations that investments will yield benefits. The pressure from both private and public sectors to show positive impacts for early childhood investments is clearly on the rise.

Against this backdrop of increased accountability, two key questions should be kept in mind: (1) What is the risk that devoting precious resources to system building will divert funding away from direct services that could help children now? (2) What are the potential negative impacts of spending precious resources on systems if positive outcomes for children do not result?

The first question is best answered by making sure that system-building efforts do not replace funds that address the current needs of vulnerable children. Resources devoted to system building must be married with investments in high-quality programs and services for those that most need and want them. These efforts should identify gaps and redundancies in programs and services. If they are cost-effective, investments can be justified.

Answering the second question may be best accomplished by asking and answering another: To what extent are system-building efforts making a difference in the everyday lives of young children? No one wants to invest a great deal of time, effort, and money to build an early childhood system, only to find that children are no better off than they were before. Not only would that set back the momentum in early childhood, but it also could fan the fire from critics who claim that resources directed toward programs or services for young children yield small results and therefore are not a wise use of public funds.

There is consensus that the early childhood system today is fragmented at best and nonexistent at worst. Creating an effective system that addresses the comprehensive needs of vulnerable young children, ties together high-quality programs and services, and aligns with K–12 education is an important means to achieving an essential end. But it is just that, a means to an end. In the real world that we live in, as well as the better one we are working toward, we are at our best when resources are directed to programs and policies that make a difference before it is too late for the most vulnerable young children to succeed in school and beyond.

REFERENCES

Hodginkson, H. (2003). *Leaving too many children behind*. Washington, DC: Institute for Educational Leadership. Available at www.iel.org

Lawrence, S., & Mukai, R. (2008). *Foundation yearbook, 2008 edition*. New York: Foundation Center.

National Scientific Council on the Developing Child. (2007). *The science of early childhood development*. Available at http://www.developingchild.net

Satkowski, C. (2009, November). The next step in systems building: Early childhood advisory councils and federal efforts to promote policy alignment in early childhood. Washington, DC: New America Foundation. Available at www.earlyedwatch.org

Wight, V. R., & Chau, M. (2009, November). *Basic facts about low-income children: Children under age 18*. Available at http://www.nccp.org/publications/pub_892.html

WHEN ENGLISH IS NOT SPOKEN HERE:
CREATING A SYSTEM THAT SUPPORTS LINGUISTIC
AND CULTURAL DIVERSITY FOR YOUNG CHILDREN

Eugene García

Many of us have seen the sign in shopping establishments, "Spanish (Arabic, Portuguese, Cantonese, etc.) is spoken here." It acknowledges the "new" U.S. reality of linguistic diversity where, in many families, "English is not spoken here." Unfortunately, it may be more common for our business establishments than early learning venues to market to and serve these populations. Why is it that the early learning community of educators has remained relatively unchanged over the past few decades? Why have recent research efforts failed to improve early learning practices for and the performance patterns of children from immigrant families? How can the relative strengths of non-English-speaking students and families be leveraged to buffer the influence of salient risk factors in order to nurture sustained learning success, particularly in the critical early years? While progress and improvements take time, and early learning opportunities alone do not account for variations in learning, some brief reflections on development and early learning research, policy, and practice for this set of linguistically and culturally diverse children and families may aid in answering these questions—and provide a path for new systemic partnerships, collaborations, and relationships among students, parents, early education personnel, and researchers to identify and implement more effective and meaningful practice.

IS DEMOGRAPHY DESTINY?

Demography need not be destiny regarding the present circumstances in early care and education for this population of children that come from linguistically and diverse family circumstances. What we know now regarding the absence of positive services and outcomes for this population need not predict what this population's future holds in store. Two useful reports outlining the demography of the population of students that speak a language other than English are *The Health and Well-Being of Young Children of Immigrants* by Randy Capps and colleagues (2004) at the Urban Institute, and *Young Hispanic Children in the U.S.* by Donald Hernandez (2006) at the University at Albany, State University of New York. These reports draw primarily from the most recent U.S. Census data to describe the ethnic, linguistic, economic, domestic, educational, and geographic (including origins and destinations) characteristics of immigrant and dual language learner (DLL) children and families. This information, summarized below, is useful for projecting the future demographic characteristics of the U.S. student body.

Currently, at least one in five children ages 5 to 17 in the United States has a foreign-born parent and many, although not all, of these children learn English as their second language. The overall child population speaking a non-English native language in the United States nearly tripled from 1979 to 2009, with the number of language minority students in K–12 schools estimated to be over 14 million. Most of these students are in the pre-K–3rd range (García & Jensen, 2009). This is because young children who speak a primary heritage language other than English and attend prekindergarten and kindergarten in the United States tend to develop oral (and in many cases academic) English proficiency by 3rd grade.

While a majority of the pre-K–3rd population comes from Spanish-speaking immigrant families, the children represent many national origins and more than 350 languages, with over half of them coming from Latin American immigrant families. Leading the way, nearly 40% of children from immigrant families are of Mexican heritage. The Caribbean, East Asia, and Europe (combined with Canada and Australia) each account for 10–11% of the overall population of children from immigrant families; Central America, South America, Indochina, and West Asia each account for 5–7% of the total; and the former Soviet Union and Africa account for 2–3% each. It is important to point out that at least four in five children in immigrant families are born in the United States and, among the pre-K–3rd population, nine in ten children from immigrant families are born in the United States.

Therefore, as immigrant families are settling new destinations in response to labor demands, and not returning to their sending countries even in these down economic times, their children increasingly are attending child care centers, preschools, and elementary schools in districts and states that served few of these children prior to the 1980s. In too many cases, they face the "English only is spoken here" reception.

CREATING A SYSTEM FOR YOUNG CHILDREN

To date, researchers have made some satisfactory efforts to provide caregivers, teachers, administrators, and other practitioners with evidence-based practices that enhance the academic engagement and learning of students whose primary language may not be English. We know, for example, that culturally knowledgeable teachers who are proficient in English and the child's native language are a particular asset, and that the strategic inclusion of the child's native language in classroom instruction can increase overall language and academic learning. In addition to speaking the child's native language, it is also beneficial when teachers reflect, in the classroom, a rich cultural knowledge of the children's families and communities. We also know that screening for and closely monitoring learning problems, intensive small-group interventions, extensive and varied vocabulary instruction, and regular peer-assisted learning opportunities improve the effectiveness of literacy instruction for these students.

Yet, despite efforts by researchers and their respective funders to increase knowledge about how to support young DLLs, these students continue to underperform, and evidence-based practice goes unimplemented in many schools or poorly implemented in others. Why is this the case? At least part of the implementation problem lies in the silos in which we—as researchers, practitioners, and policymakers—tend to work. Time and experience show that the demonstrated added value of high-quality programs is weak when implementation potential is not sufficiently considered or evaluated. And it is difficult for researchers to consider implementation potential without collaboration from policymakers and/or practitioners. A far better approach would be to link the work and intentions of researchers, practitioners, and policymakers into an integrated whole.

Examples of the existing nonsystemic approaches are abundant. Notably, the preparation of bilingual and culturally knowledgeable teachers is a clear case of the nonuse of data that could improve policy and practice. Years of data analysis and interpretation indicate that children with fluently bilingual and culturally responsive teachers tend to perform better than those without. Yet, most students do not have access to these resources in classrooms. This is particularly detrimental during the early years of schooling when native language foundations are established in and outside the family. In some cases, this deficiency is due to policy initiatives constraining dual language education programs. In others, however, it is due simply to poor implementation. Any system that serves these children and families must put linkages between research, practice, and policy as priority "numero uno."

VISION FOR A SYSTEM

Fully realizing a system that provides high-quality services for DLL children and families will require better integration of research, policy, and practice. Change is required across multiple dimensions of the system. The following discussion illustrates just three of the possibilities.

Workforce Preparation

Federal, state, and local governments, in collaboration with private foundations, nonprofit organizations, and local agencies should accept the responsibility for producing large increases in the number of culturally knowledgeable preschool and elementary teachers proficient in two languages—particularly Spanish. And their efforts can be magnified as they work collaboratively with researchers and families. These federal, state, local, and philanthropic units should underwrite tests of programs designed to produce large increases in bilingual and culturally knowledgeable teachers; state government should fund and experiment with teacher preparation programs, and provide incentive pay for teachers with these credentials; local government should support state initiatives by proposing specific strategies to develop the workforce needs; and private and nonprofit organizations should serve as liaisons between organizations and provide strategic fiscal support where possible.

Monitoring and Evaluation

All the while, educational researchers should document the sustained effectiveness of implemented practices using validated measurement techniques (across socioeconomic status segments) to determine the relative benefit of dual language curricular and instructional strategies. Of particular significance is the development, implementation, and utilization, at the student, family, instructional, and program levels, of reliable and valid assessment tools that address linguistic and cultural diversity.

Funding and Finance

Funding the augmented resources to properly address the linguistic and cultural diversity of the children and families served must be prioritized. Resources that can assist in the appropriate diagnostics and assessment of children in languages other than English will be required, as will curricula that address the linguistic and cultural assets children bring to the early learning venues. The range of augmented fiscal resources needed to appropriately serve such a population has been estimated at between $800 and $1,400 per student yearly.

Collaborations and strategic partnerships between these groups certainly do not come easily. They are not instinctive. Yet, innovative collaborations and partnerships among knowledge producers (i.e., researchers), consumers (i.e., practitioners), and enactors (i.e., policymakers) are necessary to expedite educational change needed for DLL students. These can diminish the implementation gap by resulting in the application of evidence-based practice at scale, while creating new knowledge of best practices. Other languages and cultures need to be recognized, understood, and addressed in our efforts to support and enhance our diverse children and families. It has to happen here and now.

REFERENCES AND ADDITIONAL READINGS

August, D., & Shanahan, T. (Eds.). (2006). *Developing literacy in second language learners: Report of the National Literacy Panel on Language Minority Youth and Children.* Mahwah, NJ: Erlbaum.

Capps, R., Fix, M., Ost, J., Reardon-Anderson, J., & Passel, J. (2004). *The health and well-being of young children of immigrants.* Washington, DC: Urban Institute.

Darling-Hammond, L., & Bransford, J. (Eds.). (2005). *Preparing teachers for a changing world: What teachers should learn and be able to do.* San Francisco: Jossey-Bass.

García, E. (2005). *Teaching and learning in two languages: Bilingualism and schooling in the United States.* New York: Teachers College Press.

García, E., & Jensen, B. (2009). Early educational opportunities for children of Hispanic origins. *Social Policy Report, 23*(2), 1–20.

Hernandez, D. (2006, June 26). *Young Hispanic children in the U.S.: A demographic portrait based on Census 2000* (Report to the National Task Force on Early Childhood Education for Hispanics). Available at http://ecehispanic.org/work/young_hispanic.pdf

National Task Force on Early Childhood Education for Hispanics. (2007). *Para nuestros niños: Expanding and improving early childhood education for Hispanics—main report.* Tempe, AZ: Author. Available at http://www.ecehispanic.org/work/expand_MainReport.pdf

Slavin, R. E., & Cheung, A. (2005). A synthesis of research on language of reading instruction for English language learners. *Review of Education Research, 75*(2), 247–284.

A Systems Approach to Young Children's Healthy Development and Readiness for School

Charles Bruner

Since the turn of the 21st century, policymakers at the state and federal levels have turned increasing attention to ensuring that all children start school healthy and equipped for success. Brain research has confirmed the critical importance of nurturing in the earliest years as the scaffolding for future growth and development. Fundamental changes in workforce participation have meant that the majority of parents now are working and cannot be at home throughout the day when their children are very young. Shifts in the economy require much higher levels of skills among the adult population for America to remain competitive in the international economy. Profound disparities in child outcomes across education, health, and justice system involvement threaten the fabric of society, with a significant share of these disparities having their roots in the earliest years (Bruner & Schor, 2009; Rouse, Brooks-Gunn, & McLanahan, 2004). Labor economist and Nobel Prize laureate James Heckman (2000), reviewing early childhood research on exemplary programs and their returns on investment, has reduced the policy implications to a five-word conclusion, "Invest in the very young."

The question becomes how best to make such investments. While investing in individual exemplary or evidence-based programs may yield high returns on investments, this does not equate with closing the gap in results experienced by young children or providing all children with equal opportunities for success. Developing public policy to ensure that all children start school healthy and equipped for success requires a systemic focus that responds to the universal needs of children, recognizing that children start from diverse backgrounds, under different conditions, and with different capacities.

These universal young child needs include:

- Consistent and nurturing parenting to guide and support their growth and development within a safe and supportive community, including meeting basic needs for shelter, clothing, food, and other necessities;
- Timely responses to physical and mental growth, including primary and preventive health and nutrition services that support parents in keeping their children healthy and responding to illness and injury;

FIGURE 2.1. State Early Childhood System Components

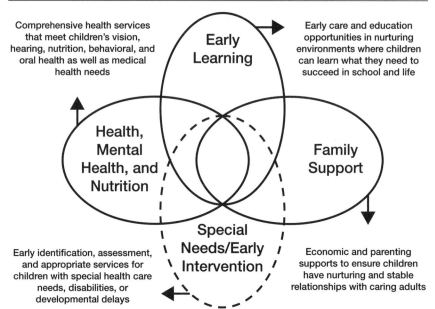

Comprehensive health services that meet children's vision, hearing, nutrition, behavioral, and oral health as well as medical health needs

Early care and education opportunities in nurturing environments where children can learn what they need to succeed in school and life

Early identification, assessment, and appropriate services for children with special health care needs, disabilities, or developmental delays

Economic and parenting supports to ensure children have nurturing and stable relationships with caring adults

Source: Early Childhood Systems Working Group

- Early identification and response to special health, developmental, behavioral, or environmental needs that can jeopardize health and development; and
- Continuous supervision throughout the day in developmentally appropriate environments where young children can safely explore their world and learn, including intentional learning environments where children gain mastery across the domains of early learning.

In 2005, representatives from a variety of leading national organizations working on young children's issues came together as an Early Childhood Systems Working Group[1] to create a common visual framework for describing the public sector's role in ensuring young children's healthy development and readiness for success in school. The Working Group agreed upon a "system of systems" approach, which recognizes that multiple public service systems are needed to ensure young children's needs are met and that these different systems, as elements of the overarching system, must be connected and aligned with one another. The framework is shown in Figure 2.1 as four intersecting ovals. In effect, these correspond with the universal needs of children outlined in the four bullets above.

FIGURE 2.2. State Early Childhood System Elements

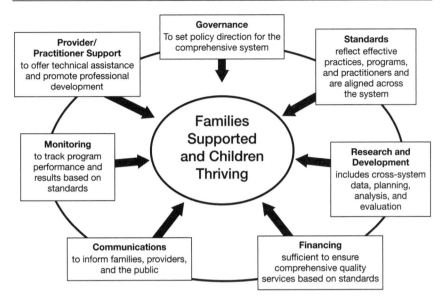

Source: Early Childhood Systems Working Group

The Working Group continued by describing seven elements, applicable to each of the ovals/components, and to the overarching system, necessary for effective system functioning. This framework is shown in Figure 2.2. The value of the two frameworks is not in their originality, but in their ability to offer a common language for depicting the "what" of a comprehensive system. Children's healthy development cannot be secured through a single program or intervention but requires continuing and multiple supports and responses to different developmental issues, stages, challenges, and opportunities. The diagrammatic frameworks enable policymakers, practitioners, and communities to see where they fit into ensuring children's healthy development, where they need to connect with one another, and where there are gaps that need to be filled.

Using the frameworks for policy development and public investment ultimately requires an assessment of the current status of the presence of each of the ovals shown in Figure 2.1, the degree of each oval's connections with the other ovals, and the effectiveness of each oval's overall operation according to the seven different elements. For illustrative purposes, a preliminary assessment is applied to the health, mental health, and nutrition oval, highlighting what is needed for an effective health system in its own right and in the context of an overall early childhood system.

THE FIVE "C'S" OF AN EFFECTIVE EARLY CHILDHOOD HEALTH SYSTEM

In effect, five "C's" are needed to ensure that the health oval operates effectively as part of the overall early childhood system (Bruner, 2009a). The first two C's relate to health as its own system, and the latter three C's relate to health's role as part of the overall early childhood system.

Coverage

Without a financing system and array of pediatric providers (pediatricians, family physicians, nurse practitioners, developmental psychologists, nutritionists, pediatric dentists), there would be no health oval available to young children and their families. At best, health care for young children would be episodic and place financial burdens on families, jeopardizing their ability to meet other basic child needs. Affordable and available health coverage is the first C to addressing fundamental child health needs.

Clinical Care

Advances in medical science have improved clinical health responses to many more childhood diseases, conditions, and injuries. Advances also have enabled health practitioners to provide preventive and developmental health services related to children's social, emotional, and intellectual development. *Bright Futures*, developed with the American Academy of Pediatrics (Hagan, Shaw, & Duncan, 2008), provides evidence-informed guidance on comprehensive well-child care, but much clinical care falls short of this standard. Improvements in the content and quality of clinical care are essential to fulfilling health's role in healthy child development.

Coordination

Nearly 90% of all young children see a primary care practitioner at least annually for a well-child visit, but fewer than one third are in any formal early care and education arrangement (Bruner, 2009b). The primary child health practitioner is the one point of near universal contact with children and their families during the birth-to-school years. Primary care practitioners can identify parental stress or lack of parenting knowledge that can adversely affect child development and screen for developmental concerns that require additional attention. The health oval overlaps with the other three ovals precisely because health must link children and their families to programs and services in other ovals that can address these nonclinical needs.

Consultation

Some children coming into early care and education programs or family support centers have physical or behavioral challenges requiring special health expertise. Some states have employed nurse practitioners and nutritionists to assist child care providers in maintaining healthy environments. Others have established behavioral health consulting systems to enable providers to respond to challenging child behaviors. Health practitioners must be available to train, consult with, and support early childhood educators and family support center staff to address children's health needs and challenges.

Community Health

To be healthy and learn, children must be in safe and supportive environments. This includes the absence of lead and other toxins in the environment and the presence of safe play areas for recreation and learning. The health oval can make particular contributions to improving environmental and community conditions to support healthy child development through collaboration with leaders in each of the other ovals.

Assessing the health oval in this way shows the multiple responsibilities of health and how health must be a strong system in its own right while connecting with and supporting the other components/ovals in the system. With some adaptation, these five C's can be applied to each of the four ovals. In some instances, particularly around family support, parts of the oval may barely exist and need to be developed. In other instances, such as early learning, the quality and effectiveness of early childhood services in the oval may require substantial attention. In the long run, however, ensuring children's healthy development and school readiness requires attention to all four ovals, their interconnections, and the quality and effectiveness of their operations, individually and collectively. This holistic approach also is crucial in working to strengthen the resiliency of families by ensuring that all public services contribute to building protective factors within the family and community (Bruner, 2007; Bruner, 2009c; Horton, 2003).

America's K–12 system of education did not emerge overnight, nor did America's higher education system. System-building work in early childhood will not occur overnight either. Advocates, practitioners, and policymakers all can accelerate the process by promoting needed public investments within a systemic vision that recognizes the many actions that will need to be taken.

NOTE

1. The Early Childhood Systems Working Group includes the following organizations: Alliance for Early Childhood Finance, BUILD Initiative, Center for Law and Social Policy, Children's Project, Council of Chief State School Officers, National Center for Children in Poverty, National Child Care Information Center, National Conference of State Legislatures, National Governors Association Center for Best Practices, Smart Start National Technical Assistance Center, State Early Childhood Technical Assistance Resource Center, United Way of America, and Zero to Three.

REFERENCES

Bruner, C. (2007). *Village building and school readiness: Closing opportunity gaps in a diverse society.* Des Moines, IA: State Early Childhood Policy Technical Assistance Network.

Bruner, C. (2009a). *Issue brief: Connecting child health and school readiness.* Denver, CO: The Colorado Trust.

Bruner, C. (2009b). *Healthy child storybook.* Washington, DC: Voices for America's Children and Child and Family Policy Center.

Bruner, C. (2009c). *Philanthropy, advocacy, vulnerable children, and federal policy: Three essays on a new era of opportunity.* Des Moines, IA: National Center for Service Integration.

Bruner, C., & Schor, E. (2009). *Clinical health care practices and community building: Addressing racial disparities in healthy child development.* Des Moines, IA: National Center for Service Integration.

Hagan, J., Shaw, J., & Duncan, P. (2008). *Bright futures guidelines for health supervision of infants, children, and adolescents* (3rd ed.). Elk Grove, IL: American Academy of Pediatrics.

Heckman, J. (2000). *Invest in the very young.* Chicago: Ounce of Prevention Fund and University of Chicago Harris School of Public Policy Studies.

Horton, C. (2003). *Protective factors literature review: Early care and education programs and the prevention of child abuse and neglect.* Washington, DC: Center for the Study of Social Policy.

Rouse, C., Brooks-Gunn, J., & McLanahan, S. (2004). Introducing the issue: School readiness: Closing racial and ethnic gaps. *The Future of Children, 15*(1), 5–14.

A State Vision for an Early Childhood System:
Meaningful Governance

Karen Ponder

Nationwide, early childhood services are delivered under the auspices of multiple organizations, operate with varying levels and kinds of regulatory oversight, contend with a complex array of different funding mechanisms with varying rules, and respond to competing public and private expectations. The results of these complicating factors are uneven levels of service quality, unequal distribution of services, and a delivery system that is difficult for families to understand.

Given these realities, a comprehensive, well-coordinated, and centralized system of early care and education within a cabinet-level department at the state level provides a clear, solid approach for states to successfully promote positive school readiness outcomes within a context of program and fiscal accountability, ensure equity and quality for all children, and support local decision making on behalf of the needs and interests of children and their families.

Because a strong system relies on strong governance, consideration must be given to the kinds of structures that will advance the effective, equitable, and efficient delivery of quality services. A state cabinet-level department is one clear governance structure to bring together all government-funded programs and services for children from birth to kindergarten. Such a department can raise the visibility of early childhood education programs and promote their importance; combine all relevant funding sources into a children's budget and enhance the oversight of resources; and offer better accountability to those who provide the resources, including the public. The department should be linked to a public/private partnership with both a state-level and county/regional presence, and with the goal of improving the school readiness of all children.

ORGANIZATION AND OUTCOMES OF A CENTRALIZED SYSTEM

The overall goal of a department that centralizes and unifies the early childhood system is to improve the school outcomes and future success of young children from birth until they enter kindergarten as well as facilitate their transition into kindergarten. Potential outcomes are listed below.

- Children who are all healthy and ready for success when they enter kindergarten
- Increased understanding by the public of the needs of young children
- Stronger public and private support and adequate funding
- Efficient, effective, and accountable use of financial and other resources
- An integrated data system that identifies trends and unmet needs
- Timely services for children and families that are culturally compatible with and responsive to their needs and interests
- Higher quality early care and education programs
- More equitable geographic and demographic delivery of services to children and families
- A more effective and accessible professional development system that produces and retains well-educated, professionally compensated early childhood teachers
- Accountability for the outcomes produced and the levels of consumer satisfaction
- Smoother transitions into the public school system

ELEMENTS OF THE DEPARTMENT

The envisioned department will include child care licensing, child care subsidy, professional development, scholarships and compensation, the Federal Child Care and Development block grant, prekindergarten programs, the Head Start Collaboration Office, the Interagency Coordinating Council for Services to Children with Special Needs and other programs and funding streams for children with disabilities from birth to age 5, child preventive health funds, Title I Preschool Funds, the Exceptional Children's Preschool Program, Even Start Literacy, and the Child Care Food Program. Bringing all of these components and funding sources together under a centralized budget authority will maximize resources and effectiveness. There will be a single standard of accountability for all programs, services, and contractors related to the department. This structure will provide the best opportunity to make decisions based on the analysis of population-level indicators, such as the percent of children entering kindergarten with age-appropriate skills in all domains of learning, and the percent of infants born with low birth weight. These kinds of analyses will allow program decisions to be made using more comprehensive information and ensure that vital services are provided to high-risk populations.

A public/private partnership with both a state-level and local presence will be a vital component of the state's system and will function outside of government to support and assess the state system. Functions will include engaging and building coalitions with private citizens and business leaders, creating a strong accountability system for overall results for children, and reporting the status of children to the public on a regular basis.

A state partnership will provide administrative oversight to the local partnerships and have the responsibility to build, support, and monitor their capacity and provide technical assistance and resources from public and private sources. Local (county) or regional partnerships will conduct assessments of local needs; engage in community planning; build a coherent, family-friendly system at the community level; and maximize the community conditions that support positive outcomes for children. When local partnerships achieve a high level of capacity, they can become involved in making program and funding decisions for their communities.

While the delivery of direct services will be done in a variety of programs and settings outside of the department, the department has the responsibility for the results of all services that it funds. Specific functions of the department are listed below.

- Develop statewide goals, policies, and program-specific standards that include curricula, program and facility standards, professional development, and program accreditation
- Establish expectations and accountability mechanisms in collaboration with the state-level nonprofit organization for child-related, programmatic, and community results
- Use population data for decision making
- Allocate funds to direct services as well as service intermediaries and the state-level nonprofit organization, and provide service payments for all programs
- Establish policies for the use of public funds
- Monitor directly funded programs for accountability
- Support families by providing high-quality programs for young children that are affordable and accessible and meet families' needs
- Receive consumer input and implement due-process systems
- License, credential, and certify early education personnel
- Implement regulations for facilities
- Develop and maintain integrated data systems
- Conduct policy research and evaluation
- Support and assist early childhood teachers and programs to achieve a high level of quality

FIGURE 2.3. Structure for a Department of Child Development and School Readiness

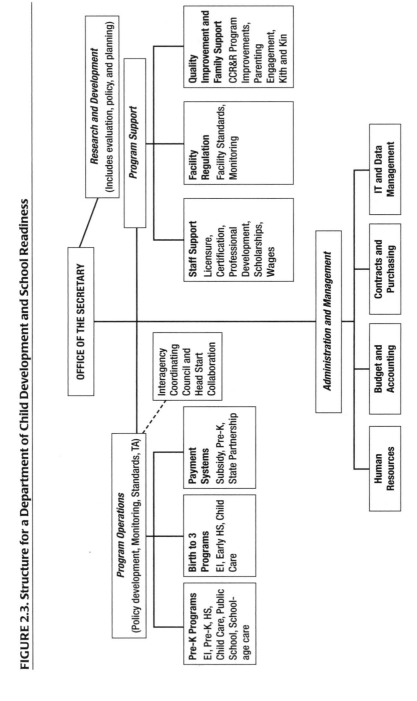

Figure 2.3 suggests possible divisions of labor and technical infrastructure for the department and the programs to be included within each division. Each division should interrelate with other divisions and each should incorporate policy development, monitoring, standards, and technical assistance that are unique to its programs.

LINKAGES TO OTHER SYSTEMS

While the proposed centralized department will integrate all publicly funded programs that are directly related to early learning, it is important to recognize that there is an array of early childhood services that will not be inside the department. These programs should have strong linkages because they are critical to young children and their families. Examples of these programs are public health services, including women, infants, and children (WIC); mental health; child protective services; child health insurance; public education K–12; and institutions of higher education. Coordination and partnerships across departments will ensure optimum outcomes. Bruner (2004) recommended that, in this instance, there would need to be some cross-department governance structure to ensure rules and regulations were aligned across age groups.

GENERALIZING A VISION

This proposed vision combines my experiences in North Carolina in addition to work I have done in other states. While all states differ, they do share the need for common governance and, whatever governance structure is developed, it will need to embrace many of the goals and functions discussed. In advancing this vision, it is important to note that in 2003 and 2004, a key group of early childhood leaders participated in a facilitated study of North Carolina's system of care and education and called for a new structure that would consolidate the state's existing early care and education programs and agencies by promoting increased coordination and effectiveness, maximizing efficient use of government resources, and enhancing public understanding of and access to the state's early care and education programs and services (NC Early Childhood Leaders, 2004). Although the group did not recommend a specific controlling authority for centralized oversight of early childhood services in North Carolina, my vision suggests that such a governance mechanism is the essential ingredient in advancing not only a consolidated vision for early education, but an effective and sustainable system.

REFERENCES

Bruner, C. (2004). *The ABC's of early learning system building: Some rules of thumb in developing, planning, governing, and management strategies.* Des Moines, IA: State Early Childhood Policy Technical Assistance Network (SECPTAN).

NC Early Childhood Leaders. (2004). *Ensuring school readiness for North Carolina's children: Bringing the parts together to create an integrated early care and education system.* Unpublished report.

Bringing Early Childhood into the Education System: Pre-K–3rd

Fasaha Traylor

System building in early childhood must be anchored in the public purpose of educating American children. Buttressed by research evidence that the first decade of life is a critical period for children, there increasingly exists an expectation that early childhood programs be educational as a condition of public financial support.

Education that strengthens our shared society requires a high-performing system that works for all children, especially children from low-income, immigrant, or non-English-speaking families and communities. It also requires public commitment to the primacy of this goal, for which there exists an emerging consensus that a crucial first step is a strong early education system for children from ages 3 to 8.[1]

The early education system must support practices based on the best knowledge available about teaching and learning and must be governed by policies that support and disseminate evidence-based practice. The system must include benchmarks that tell us whether children are meeting expectations and a sophisticated data system that provides not only information about the performance of our education system, but also better information to improve practice and programs.

Early childhood programs for 3- and 4-year-olds should be aligned with the mission and goals of the K–12 education system. One of the most promising approaches to accomplishing this is pre-K–3rd, a term for efforts that link the earliest years of education to the K–12 education system. To meet educational goals, focused attention to teacher practice—based on evidence of student learning—should be central to pre-K–3rd efforts.

WHY PRE-K–3RD?

Transforming the disconnected programs, funding streams, and institutional sites (such as center-based programs and K–12 schools) that offer children's earliest educational experiences into a rational organization of programs, people, and resources (i.e., a system) tied to the mission and goals of K–12 education has been somewhat elusive. Pre-K–3rd aims to eliminate the artificial distinctions between early childhood and early elementary education, and to provide continuity, coherence, and support for children. The

Foundation for Child Development (2008) has been actively promoting the view that pre-K–3rd entails:

- Universal access to voluntary, high-quality prekindergarten programs for all 3- and 4-year-olds;
- Universal full-day kindergarten;
- Quality, developmentally appropriate curriculum and standards aligned from pre-K through 3rd grade;
- Qualified teachers with both a bachelor's degree and specialized training in how young children learn;
- Opportunities for teachers to share data, planning, and professional development within and across grade levels;
- Strong leadership committed to providing children with a seamless educational experience; and
- Opportunities for parent and community engagement.

While the merits and value of system building often are argued from the early childhood perspective, K–12 stakeholders also have compelling reasons to re-engineer the beginning of school. Evidence abounds that the current system is failing large numbers of children and that the failure begins early. By 3rd grade, children are expected to read to get information, to regulate their own learning behaviors, and to understand and manipulate mathematics. If the system fails children by 3rd grade, the failure ripples upward through the rest of the K–12 system.

Most efforts to "fix" American schools more or less ignore the crucial role of the primary years, recently exemplified by the two largest federal education initiatives in decades—Race to the Top and the Investing in Innovation Fund. Both of these multibillion dollar grant programs focus heavily on middle and high school, while incorporating modest early education rhetoric that walls off pre-K from the policies and structures of the K–12 system. Moreover, only 2–3% of Title I funding is directed to pre-K (Ewen & Matthews, 2009), full-day kindergarten remains on the margins (Kauerz, 2010), and neither is required or funded by most states. Most important, the current use of Title I funds for scattered activities for which the evidence of effectiveness is weak indicates the low priority given to the early education years by policymakers and practitioners.

The problems of American education cannot be solved at the middle or high school level while the primary grades continue to supply the ranks of underperforming students. Both the 2005 and 2007 National Assessment of Educational Progress indicate that no more than one third of American students read proficiently by grade 4 or 8 (Foundation for Child Development, 2008; National Center for Education Statistics, 2007a). While there has been improvement in mathematics proficiency, with nearly two fifths of 4th graders scoring proficiently, this is not enough (National Center for Education Statistics, 2009a). The achievement levels of low-income children, English language learners, and children of color are even lower than these shocking national averages (National Center for Education Statistics, 2007b, 2009b).

The implications of widespread inability to "read to learn," or to use mathematics to understand and grasp phenomena, are enormous (National Research Council, 1998, 2009). For the majority of American children, 3rd grade is their Waterloo. But it doesn't have to be. Perhaps the most impressive of recent evidence is from Montgomery County, Maryland, where school district programs are organized to ensure that all students perform at proficient levels across the curriculum by 3rd grade. From 2003–2009, the gap by race and ethnicity in grade 3 reading proficiency scores shrank from 35 points to 15 points, and by grade 5 shrank to ten points (Weast, 2010).

TEACHING AT THE CENTER

Teachers are at the center of pre-K–3rd. Teachers' enactment of curriculum and standards is how alignment occurs within and across settings and impacts student learning. Through assessing student work in relation to curriculum and student performance goals, teachers know and understand what students have already learned, and guide their current performance to create a solid foundation for what they must learn next.

Most teachers from pre-K–3rd grade do not play this role now. The training and qualifications of pre-K teachers are very different across programs, ranging from high school diplomas or less to master's degrees; many have little contact with or knowledge about kindergarten or other early elementary grade teachers, standards, or curriculum. K–3 teachers are also isolated, both from pre-K teachers and one another. It is impossible for teachers to work toward a goal if there are varied perspectives on what the goal is, or if the organizational structure within which they work does not facilitate their joint problem solving and practice.

Some might think this problem will be addressed by the recent move toward adoption of common core standards and other collaborative efforts to develop and improve data on student achievement. But unlike the highly focused efforts in Montgomery County, none of these initiatives has yet emphasized the expected results of this period of students' education. Like middle or high school, pre-K–3rd must be held accountable for specific results: delivering proficient readers and users of mathematics to the next levels of education.

GETTING INTO THE BLACK BOX OF THE CLASSROOM

Two recent streams of work focus on the importance of what teachers do in classrooms during the pre-K–3rd-grade years. The first is based on the CLASS (Classroom Assessment Scoring System), an assessment tool that has been used in research on thousands of classrooms from pre-K to 5th grade. Three of the CLASS instrument's most important attributes are that it correlates with children's achievement, provides a common language for describing and assessing teacher effectiveness from pre-K–3rd grade, and is related to a customized professional development system for teachers.

Standardized observations using the CLASS in more than 3,000 classrooms across the country yield the conclusion that American classrooms provide moderate levels of emotional and social support, but very low levels of instructional support (Center for Advanced Study of Teaching and Learning, 2010). In research on 1st, 3rd, and 5th grades, Pianta and colleagues determined that across all three grades, only 7% of children experienced classrooms high on instructional and emotional climate (Pianta, Belsky, Houts, & Morrison, 2007). Most troubling—and contrary to what many early educators believe about "developmentally appropriate practice"—is that students spend too much time on classroom routines instead of learning, ranging from 42% of the time in preschool classrooms to 30% of the time in 5th-grade classrooms (Pianta & Hamre, 2009). The conclusion is that "there is a high degree of variability in classroom quality . . . [so that] very few of the students who are in greatest need of high-quality classroom experiences receive them, and the few who do are unlikely to receive them consistently, making it unlikely that the positive effects will be sustained" (Pianta & Hamre, 2009, p. 115). These findings suggest that, despite their best intentions, many pre-K–3rd-grade teachers do not know how to create, support, or sustain learning environments that produce learning gains for children.

The second stream of work that focuses on what happens in classrooms stems from work with charter schools in Chicago's South Side neighborhood (Hassrick & Raudenbush, 2009). There, the isolation of traditional teaching is found to be a primary barrier to effectiveness. Once the classroom door is closed, neither teacher performance nor student learning is visible to colleagues, principals, parents, or anyone else. This lack of teachers' group problem solving, shared learning, and team effort on behalf of students is costly.

University of Chicago researchers found that a shared commitment to ensuring that every child meets defined achievement benchmarks can counter this isolation. Beginning with pre-K, teachers assess student progress frequently, share the results with colleagues, and together devise ways to address student needs. In this manner, teachers are accountable for child progress, and classroom practice is no longer an isolated endeavor. In addition, teachers begin working as a team, observing each other and seeking feedback (Hassrick & Raudenbush, 2009).

Not surprisingly, both streams of work come to similar conclusions about American education: What the Chicago team observes as "enormous variation in the educational experience," Pianta and his colleagues describe as a "high degree of variability in classroom quality." Central to both approaches is grounded professional development focused on specific needs of children and teachers in classrooms.

This kind of intentional and collaborative professional development could end wars between alternative and traditional teacher preparation. If classroom quality and teacher effectiveness in supporting student achievement benchmarks become the coin of the realm, then the preparation of teachers offered by community colleges, 4-year colleges and universities, alternative paths into teaching, and Teach for America all will be subject to the same metric: how effective are teachers in the classroom? Are they prepared to work with colleagues to adapt their practices to achieve student learning goals?

Pre-K–3rd is a reform based on the idea that the separation of early childhood and early elementary education is counterproductive for teachers and students. K–12 and early childhood educators have much to gain from aligning, coordinating, and strengthening curriculum, instruction, and assessment of children across the pre-K–3rd-grade years. Teachers and their practice are central to this vision of a stronger foundation for the first years of school.

NOTE

1. Far less of a consensus exists on the purposes and goals of programs for children from birth to age 3.

REFERENCES

Center for Advanced Study of Teaching and Learning (CASTL). (2010). *Research summary: Measuring and improving teacher-student interactions in PK–12 settings to enhance students' learning.* Retrieved from http://www.teachstone.org/wp-content/uploads/2011/05/class-mtp-pk-12-brief.pdf

Ewen, D., & Matthews, H. (2009). *The potential of Title I for high-quality preschool.* Retrieved from http://www.preknow.org/documents/CLASP_on_Title_I_and_prek.pdf

Foundation for Child Development. (2008). *America's vanishing potential*. New York: Author.

Hassrick, E. M., & Raudenbush, S. (2009). *University of Chicago model for urban elementary schooling*. Unpublished book prospectus.

Kauerz, K. (2010). *PreK-3rd: Putting full-day kindergarten in the middle* (PreK-3rd Policy to Action Brief No. 4). New York: Foundation for Child Development. Available at http://fcd-us.org/resources/prek-3rd-putting-full-day-kindergarten-middle

National Center for Education Statistics, National Assessment of Educational Progress. (2007a). *Reading report card*. Washington, DC: U.S. Government Printing Office. Available at http://nationsreportcard.gov/reading_2007/r0003.asp

National Center for Education Statistics, National Assessment of Educational Progress. (2007b). *Reading report card—Achievement levels*. Washington, DC: U.S. Government Printing Office. Available at http://nationsreportcard.gov/reading_2007/r0009.asp?subtab_id=Tab_2&tab_id=tab1#chart

National Center for Education Statistics, National Assessment of Educational Progress. (2009a). *Grade 4 national results*. Washington, DC: U.S. Government Printing Office. Available at http://nationsreportcard.gov/math_2009/gr4_national.asp?tab_id=tab2&subtab_id=Tab_1#chart

National Center for Education Statistics, National Assessment of Educational Progress. (2009b). *Grade 4 national results/achievement levels/race-ethnicity*. Washington, DC: U.S. Government Printing Office. Available at http://nationsreportcard.gov/math_2009/gr4_national.asp?tab_id=tab2&subtab_id=Tab_3#chart

National Research Council. (1998). *Preventing reading difficulties in young children*. Washington, DC: National Academies Press.

National Research Council. (2009). *Mathematics learning in early childhood: Paths toward excellence and equity* (C. T. Cross, T. A. Woods, & H. Schweingruber, Eds.). Washington, DC: National Academies Press.

Pianta, R. C., Belsky, J., Houts, R., & Morrison, F. (2007). Opportunities to learn in America's elementary classrooms. *Science, 315*, 1795–1796.

Pianta, R., & Hamre, B. (2009). Conceptualization, measurement, and improvement of classroom processes: Standardized observation can leverage capacity. *Educational Researcher, 38*(2), 109–119.

Weast, J. (2010, April 27). *Early childhood education and the college-ready trajectory*. Presentation at the Council on Foundations annual conference, Denver, CO.

Part II

ESSENTIAL SUBSYSTEMS

CHAPTER 3

Early Learning and Development Standards

An Elixir for Early Childhood Systems Reform

Sharon Lynn Kagan

A seminal rationale for the existence of this volume is the widespread recognition that early childhood development and education is a polyglot, with little consistency binding the wide array of services and programs that aim to enhance children's early development and learning. Clearly, public commitments to young children are not characterized by the same organization or investment that pertain to children of school age. More fragmented and more inconsistent in its sponsoring agencies and funding streams than K–12, early care and education, structurally, is an enigmatic policy afterthought. Pedagogically, although more coherent than K–12 education, early care and education also is fractured. Argument persists regarding precisely what children should learn as well as who should teach and what their levels of preparation should be; adults, depending on where they will teach, often are trained using different standards, with different pedagogical and content foci. Indeed, on virtually every measurable indicator, early education is plagued by consequential inconsistencies.

Early learning and development standards are one tool gaining currency as a means of transcending some of the above inconsistencies. Defined as statements of what young children should know and be able to do, early learning and development standards can serve as the basis for improved early pedagogy, revised curriculum, teacher preparation curricula, and even national evaluation and monitoring. Indeed, these expectations can be incorporated into and link different policies, programs, and early education settings. Although recognized as a viable way to bring disparate programs and services into harmony, standards also have been remarkably controversial, effecting strident discussions about their content, intentionality, and ultimate utility. This chapter is about those arguments and about the potential (or lack thereof) of early learning and development standards to help bind the fragmented nonsystem of early care and education that exists in the United States. To address standards' role in systems development, this chapter will examine the evolution of standards in general and of early learning and development standards in particular. It will present information on the status of standards domestically and will offer a suggested model for the use of standards as an integrating force in early childhood. The chapter suggests that early learning and development standards can and should be used to create an integrated pedagogical subsystem that forms the basis for a comprehensive, well-articulated early childhood system.

THE UBIQUITY AND UTILITY OF STANDARDS

Paradoxically, standards are as old as humanity itself and as new as this volume. From the observation that standards appear in the Book of Genesis (Ravitch, 1995) to current debates about the viability and content of common K–12 standards, standards are ubiquitous and have seeped into the very fabric of human life. At the most basic level, standards guide civic behaviors: They determine what will be law, who will lead, and who will follow. Standards contour economic interchanges: Who will be paid and how much for a good or a service? Standards drive transactions: Which side of the road do we drive on? Standards ensure the healthfulness and safety of goods: What constitutes clean air or water? Standards provide sanctions and entitlements—who may drive, who may be an architect or doctor, who may go to school, and who may vote. Standards determine adequacy or quality: What is the desired weight of an infant at birth? What constitutes evidence in science or the law? Standards drive economic and social values: What is the value of one's home or mode of transport? Finally, standards drive measures: Will a nation use inches or meters? What are the criteria and measures for assessing student performance?

Pervasive, standards are created because they fulfill multiple purposes. First, standards provide a means of securing agreement on matters of importance. Second, standards help expedite and improve processes. Third, standards provide evidence of quality. Fourth, standards ensure protection and safety. Fifth, they can eliminate uncertainties and the chaos of life and living. Finally, standards provide a means of understanding and expressing commonalities.

Yet despite their pervasiveness and their multiple social utilities, standards are not without controversy. By dint of establishing commonalities, for example, standards may drive down excellence, particularly when everyone must adhere to a single standard. Standards also are criticized because they can reduce liberties and impose constraints. They may inhibit access and limit variation and creativity. Finally, standards are criticized because they contour values and thus impact what is considered acceptable variance—in goods, services, or even lifestyles. Given these criticisms, how have standards come to be regarded as a potential fulcrum for the development of an early care and education system? To address this question, a brief discussion of the emergence of, and regard for, standards in K–12 education is necessary.

K–12 EDUCATIONAL STANDARDS

Perceived as an antidote to low quality and productivity, standards gained currency in fields as diverse as business and industry, marketing, economics, political science, and even the arts in the mid- to late 20th century. Spawned by this trend, a standards industry took hold. Manifest in countless handbooks, benchmarking and behavioral objectives became commonplace as management became both increasingly professionalized and effectiveness driven (Kogut, 1992; Nelson & Wright, 1992). Alongside standards' transformation from a remote construct to one that was both normative and utilitarian, education increasingly came to be seen as integral to economic advancement and global competitiveness—an educated population provided the necessary fodder for workforce competence. With business and industry already accustomed to productivity standards for employee performance and for product outputs, it was not surprising that as an economic patina swept education, a call for standards accompanied it.

Joining the press for standards from business and industry, cognitive learning theorists were concerned about the lack of creativity, invention, higher order thinking skills, and attention to cultural variation that characterized American education. Rejecting time-honored associationist and behaviorist principles that regarded learning as a process of reinforcing chains of associations through repeated practices and behaviors, and evoking one-dimensional responses, they posited new approaches to pedagogy, curricula, and assessment (Glaser, 1981). More specifically, they called for the establishment of a curriculum that focused on creative thinking, and new performance assessments based on standards that would not simply specify expected mastery of content area subjects, but would advance capacities for knowledge gathering, processing, and application (Bruer, 1993; Resnick & Resnick, 1983).

Important as they were, the contributions of the business community and the cognitive scientists would not have met with such receptivity if other factors were not also at play. Abetted by a serious decline in test scores and the highly influential publication of *A Nation at Risk* (National Commission on Excellence in Education, 1983), the American public became concerned that complacency and mediocrity had garnered a foothold in American education. As a result, a focus on equity, which had framed educational policy since the civil rights era, was back-burnered in favor of positions that prioritized quality. Standards, which arguably do support an equity stance, became the cornerstone of new efforts as they clearly embraced a fervent commitment to quality as well (Porter, 1994).

Presidents George H. W. Bush and William J. Clinton, along with the National Governors Association, historically established national education goals for American students and their educating institutions. National professional associations heeded the call and set forth to create model content standards, with the National Council of Teachers of Mathematics (NCTM) leading the way. Given the federalist system of education, states began to create standards and soon, with the high-level visibility accorded educational improvement generally and standards specifically, the movement toward standards became ensconced as a key element of educational reform.

Given this coalescence of forces, that a movement toward educational standards took hold was to be expected. Less expected, however, was the controversy that surrounded standards and the differences that emerged regarding their meaning.

Advantages of Educational Standards

Proponents of educational standards cite many advantages they afford (Ravitch, 1995). Prominent among them is that standards bring clarity regarding what is to be taught and learned (Jennings, 1995). In so doing, they can redirect the content of education from that which promotes the superficial mastery of facts to that which advances higher order thinking skills. Content, then, can be elevated to achieve what the cognitive scientists purport should be the purpose and function of education (Porter, 1994; Resnick & Resnick, 1983).

Standards also have the advantage of creating the platform for more equitable approaches to education. Rather than advancing diverse expectations for students hypothesized to have different learning capacities, standards ensure that all students—not just the privileged—will have access to challenging content. In so doing, standards level the playing field and promote equity.

Disadvantages of Educational Standards

Concerns about educational standards are widespread, beginning with the sentiment that standards, rather than elevating the quality of education, may deplete it and may occasion greater inequity. If standards are set too low, they may be intellectually restrictive and undercut the potential of the education system. On the other hand, the establishment of very high standards may cause underachieving students to drop out, either physically or psychologically, exacerbating the equity divide. Moreover, to the degree that standards are used as the basis for assessments, such assessments, critics argue, will not help reduce the equity gap; they will only confirm it.

A second set of concerns relates to who will set and control standards (Darling-Hammond, 1994). Many conservatives disparage significant governmental involvement in determining standards, contending that such involvement seriously interferes in the private lives of citizens. Others contend that because standards represent the canons of the professions, they should be set by those most familiar with the disciplines, notably professionals or the organizations that represent them. Finally, controversy exists regarding the degree to which standards should be national or should be developed and monitored by localities and/or states.

Far and away the greatest concern about standards relates to their potential misuse by teachers, administrators, schools, districts, and governments (Darling-Hammond, 1994). Burdened by the number and nature of standards, teachers may elect to ignore them totally or to use them selectively, thereby fostering a narrowing of the curriculum (Darling-Hammond, 2004). Coupled with intense accountability demands, standards can propel teachers to teach to the test, thereby trivializing instruction and accelerating what they were designed to eliminate—drill and kill pedagogy. Because standards should invoke a new way of organizing pedagogy, they will need to be accompanied by intense professional development, thereby increasing the standards' price tag.

Other fiscal concerns plague the standards movement. First, funds used to establish, implement, and monitor the standards may take away from the already severely restricted funds for education, thus perhaps depriving children of even basic educational services. Second, if schools perform poorly on the assessments that accompany the standards, sanctions in the form of limited resources may be imposed, thereby penalizing those schools most in need. Fragile programs and schools are put in double jeopardy: They assume the challenge of serving the neediest students with the clear possibility of having reduced resources to do so. Finally, as a result of these limitations, standards could fuel support for enhanced private-sector alternatives.

In short, however pervasive they are in K–12 education, standards are not without criticism.

EARLY CHILDHOOD STANDARDS

Turning from a discussion of the evolution of K–12 standards to the emergence of standards in early childhood education, some similarities exist. In both K–12 and early childhood, external forces precipitated the standards movement. As business played a key role in advancing standards in K–12, it also played a key role in promoting increasing investments in early education. Moreover, as early education sought to link itself with the schools where standards were firmly entrenched, standards became more normative in early education. Given the educational press as well as increased attention from scholars, researchers, economists, and policymakers, early childhood could not escape the standards momentum (Kagan & Scott-Little, 2004). And like the impact of the standards movement in elementary and secondary education, the contemporary standards movement brought dramatic changes to early education.

Despite these similarities, however, the advent of standards in early childhood is a greater anathema than for K–12 education as their very existence defies historic pedagogical and policy traditions. From the pedagogical perspective, early educators have long been taught to take their instructional and curricular cues from young children. The children, not any prescribed documents, were to drive early childhood content, children's interests serving as the basis for eliciting genuine motivation and a natural inclination toward learning. From the policy perspective, an equally persuasive position prevailed. Early education had been regarded essentially as a private affair involving those closest to the children who understood their needs best. Moreover, early childhood programs functioned as semi-, if not totally, autonomous entities. The idea of governments creating, much less imposing, a set of standards on early education directly opposed early childhood principles of localism, autonomy, and privatization.

Pedagogical History

Having noted these stances, it is important to underscore that historically while *explicit* early learning standards did not exist, early childhood is laden with writings that formed *implicit* standards regarding how children should be taught. Young children, given their immaturity and vulnerability, were to be protected from the premature demands of an unrelenting society; in the Rousseauean tradition, the goal of early education was to preserve the natural state of the child through play (Rousseau, 1762/1979). Pestalozzi, a seminal founder of early education and an opponent of memorization, advanced the "standard" that the best learning happened through doing. Building on the work of Rousseau and Pestalozzi, Froebel—the acknowledged father of the kindergarten movement—respected the role of the child in constructing his or her learning. Promoting not standards, but "gifts," a sequenced set of hands-on learning activities for young children, Froebel, like his predecessors and successors Owen and Malaguzzi, held an unswerving commitment to child-initiated play as the means of instruction (Wolfe, 2002). Guiding centuries of early childhood pedagogy, this stance rendered standards not simply something to be tolerated, as they were in K–12 education, but a fundamental attack on the historic canons of early education.

Policy History

The policy history of American early education also confounds the ease with which standards may take hold. Unlike K–12 education, early education has vied for its legitimacy. Long considered the purview of the home, raising young children by public entities has been deemed an inappropriate intrusion into the life and culture of the family. Families had the right to determine whether their children would attend early education programs and to select from an array of options as to where they would send them. Often such choices were made based on the programs' ability to address the culture of the home (Greenfield, 1994; LeVine, 1974). Yet, families and communities differ widely both culturally and in their goals for the development of young children (Hofstede, 1980; Holloway, 2000; Markus & Kitayama, 1991; Tobin, Wu, & Davidson, 1989). Indeed, two policy characteristics, antithetical to standards and standardization, were deemed key to early education—its diversity and the choice it afforded parents who could pay the requisite fees.

Another policy stance that complicates the emergence of early childhood standards is the transcendent fact that American early education has never been regarded, from a policy perspective, as an end in and of itself. When publicly funded, early education has always been a handmaiden to greater social needs, promoted alternately as an answer to political, social, and economic challenges. With these diverse intentions, various programs emerged with differing goals, funding streams, and supports, rendering, from the earliest days of American early education, a two-track system, with one approach for serving the poor and one for middle- and upper-class youngsters (Cahan, 1989; Tank, 1980). The notion of commonality in what needed to be taught and what needed to be learned—the heart of all standards—varied as well. Established early on, this pattern continued as early education served as an antidote to the demands of formalized education, a mechanism for socializing the poor, a means of fostering religious purity and devotion, and a means of supporting the nation in times of crisis. Given the lack of any coherent approach to early education, coupled with the local nature of the programs, standardization of the field, using standards or any other mechanism, seemed not only a pedagogical anathema, but something that the very policy structure of the field prohibited.

THE CONTEMPORARY STATUS OF STANDARDS

Although emanating from somewhat different historical trajectories, K–12 and early childhood standards have come a long way, creating the need to better understand their contemporary contexts.

Kindergarten Through Grade 12

Recently, the use and influence of standards in kindergarten through grade 12 have expanded dramatically. Standards exist in all 50 states and have served as the basis upon which accountability and testing practices are being reformed. Historically the purview of the states, standards are now being discussed as national or common. Globally, they have become ubiquitous, an accepted component of education.

Without doubt, much of this activity was hastened by the 2001 reauthorization of the Elementary and Secondary Education Act (ESEA) and its conversion into the No Child Left Behind (NCLB) Act. Taking the largest funding stream for elementary and secondary education and recontouring it with a clear accountability thrust, federal policymakers called for state testing in grades 3, 8, and 10, predicated on the specification of standards in the tested areas. With controversial effects well documented elsewhere, the next reauthorization of ESEA will likely bring changes. Recommendations for reform are numerous and range from complete abolition to modification (Finn, Julian, & Petrilli, 2006). An ambitious approach advocates that the federal government impose standards on the states and that these standards be used for accountability (Barton, 2009). A less drastic approach would incentivize the use of standards and assessments rather than mandate it; another suggests that subsets of states be incentivized to join together to develop common standards.

Common standards for K–12, once thought impossible to achieve, are surging forward (Klein, 2009). At the time of this writing, draft standards have been released and are out for comment. Debate ensues, however, at a conceptual level, with some questioning the feasibility of creating common

FIGURE 3.1. Many Uses of Early Learning and Development Standards

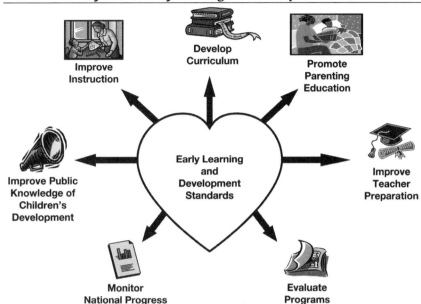

standards given that the content of standards and what constitutes proficiency vary considerably across states (Cronin, Dahlin, Xiang, & McCahon, 2009; Porter, Polikoff, & Smithson, 2008). Establishing common standards that will both support the diversity that exists in this vast country and help drive consistently high performance represents an immense challenge, yet is gaining currency throughout the United States.

Two major issues transcend discussions of both common and individual state standards. The first, fundamentally philosophical, concerns who is responsible for student achievement. Instituting educational standards and testing regimes suggests that the schools are the "responsible" parties. Yet, increasingly, learning takes place well beyond the schoolhouse doors, suggesting that mechanisms for shared accountability among institutions must be devised (e.g., consolidated data systems, discussed in this volume). The second issue, fundamentally practical, addresses the implementation of standards and concerns the accommodation of differing approaches to instruction, the nature and ability of assessments to capture higher order skills, and the development and implementation of incentives that will improve outcomes, not simply punish poor-performing students or schools. With no less controversy than accompanied their introduction into education decades ago, standards continue to both command attention and shape education, including early childhood education.

Early Childhood Standards

Just as dramatic changes characterize the present state of standards in K–12 education, so too do they characterize early childhood. Today, in America, early childhood standards or guidelines exist for preschool-aged children in every state. In over half of the states, such guidelines exist for infants and toddlers (Scott-Little, Kagan, Frelow, & Reid, 2009). Whereas once early learning standards or guidelines existed primarily in one or two domains, notably language and math, today many states have expanded the number of domains addressed by their standards. In addition, rather than covering a single age group (e.g., 36–48 months), today early learning standards are being revised to cover broader ranges of development, usually embracing birth to age 5.

Another trend in the contemporary standards movement is the alignment of preschool standards with other early childhood standards documents (Kagan & Kauerz, 2007; Scott-Little, Kagan, Frelow, & Reid, 2009). States are aligning their standards with those that exist in kindergarten and in grades 1 through 3, thus promoting continuity through the primary years of schooling. Additionally, states are analyzing their standards to ensure linkages between those developed for infants and toddlers and those developed for preschoolers. Finally, some states are working to ensure that multiple sets of standards that may exist for a single age group (e.g., state early learning guidelines and the Head Start Performance Outcomes) are aligned. Standards also are being aligned with curriculum and assessments. Finally, within early childhood, some consideration is being given to the desirability and feasibility of developing common standards.

Although not national in spread, these efforts are sufficiently robust to support the durability of early childhood standards. Moreover, they lay the groundwork for expanding standards' roles and for their use as a centerpiece of reform for early childhood pedagogy and systems development.

A SUGGESTED APPROACH

In the contemporary K–12 and early childhood contexts, multiple efforts are underway to advance the nature, content, and alignment of early childhood standards. The salient debate in the K–12 area seems to be focused on two broad and important questions: should standards become national and how can standards be used most effectively to improve student performance? With searing consequences for the development and implementation of an early childhood system, these conversations are spilling over into early childhood education. This chapter, however, suggests that these preoccupations are somewhat ill-placed generally, and particularly with regard to young children. Rather, a new approach for all standards, including early childhood standards, must consider the multiple dimensions and uses of standards, as well as their potential to bring early childhood pedagogy and early learning systems into alignment.

In work conducted for UNICEF, an integrated approach to standards has been developed and implemented globally with some success (Kagan & Britto, 2009). The approach suggests that standards sit at the heart of early childhood education. Once consensually developed and scientifically validated—the latter a step often neglected in the United States—standards can serve multiple utilities. Conceptually, the work advances the understanding that what children should know and be able to do (and in some countries, be) is at the core of the early childhood enterprise. Based on clear definitions or standards: (a) teachers can be taught what and how to teach, thereby forming the basis of teacher education and, consequently, certification; (b) parents can be guided in what to expect from their children at particular ages, thereby guiding the development of parenting support and education efforts; (c) the public can be made aware of appropriate expectations for children, forming the basis for public information efforts; (d) curricula that are age and content appropriate can be developed, thereby guiding content developers and textbook publishers, along with local curriculum design efforts; (e) checklists that chronicle children's progress can be developed, thereby improving the individualization of teacher practice; (f) items from the standards, once subjected to item analysis, can be selected for state or national monitoring; and (g) data can be used for program evaluation and for the planning of inservice technical support for teachers.

In this way, standards may be used to align disparate elements of early care and education and other systems (Kagan & Kauerz, 2007; O'Day & Smith, 1993). Used not simply as the basis for discerning what students should know and be able to do, standards for students can drive what teachers should know and be able to teach, thereby influencing the content of teacher preparation and potentially even teacher certification (Kagan, Kauerz, & Tarrant, 2008). In so doing, standards have the potential to align what is expected of students and what is taught by their teachers. Standards also can serve as the basis for assessment, aligning what is expected, what is taught, and what is assessed (Egertson, 2008; Kagan & Britto, 2009; Schultz, 2008). In short, standards can serve as the pivot around which early childhood pedagogy—in all its related forms—rotates. By using standards for these multiple purposes, an integrated approach to early education and development, one that unites what children are expected to know and be able to do, and what their parents and teachers can and should do to support their development—is achieved. Such an integrated approach also links what children are taught to the content of the assessment and to the national reports that give evidence of progress.

Graphically, as depicted in Figure 3.1, this approach to standards places early learning and development standards at the core of the early education pedagogy and hence at the core of the system (Kagan & Britto, 2009).

The obvious advantage of using early learning and development standards as the core is that they promote an integrated approach to early education. No longer are state-level committees developing standards, teachers in local programs developing curriculum, test developers creating assessments, and evaluations looking at decades-old instruments to gauge program performance. On the contrary, using the consensually developed standards as the base, all these elements are integrated so that, far more honestly and equitably than ever before, what children are taught comports with what they are tested on, how their teachers are trained, and how their programs and policies are evaluated and monitored. The process puts children and their needs squarely at the center of policy efforts. By impacting teacher training, parenting education, instruction, curriculum, and even national monitoring and evaluation, early learning standards can be the glue that integrates diverse activities and aspects of the field.

The Utility of the Approach

Used in countries throughout the world, this approach highlights the potential of standards to enhance multiple components of early childhood development, and thereby shifts the conversation regarding standards. Rather than being regarded as the precursor to heavy-handed, high-stakes testing and assessment, standards are regarded as useful, if not central, to creating an integrated approach to early childhood pedagogy. The climate for standards in early education is transformed, correctly placing the focus and the angst not in arguing against standards, but in making them as comprehensive and culturally sensitive as possible. The multiple-use approach to standards is grounded in the mores of those who create them, so that they reflect the goals, values, and desires that adults hold for their children.

Throughout the world, countries have adopted the approach, with many seeing powerful results. In Ghana, for example, standards have been used as the basis for curriculum development as well as teacher training and credentialing. In Fiji and Mongolia, they have supplied a foundation for the development of parenting education curricula, and in Romania, the basis for a public information campaign. These are just some of the diverse ways in which countries have applied new standards.

This is not to say that the approach is not without challenges. In some countries, the word "standards" connotes government imposition of rules, and where this is the case, some have re-termed their standards as guidelines. Concerns emerge about the reliability and validity of standards, especially since they will be used for so many purposes. For this reason, a validation method has been developed and implemented in all the countries using the approach. Moreover, there are concerns regarding the use of standards with highly diverse—in the form of variability in ethnicity, religion, geography, tribe, language, and ability—populations within a given country. Accommodations for such diversities have been made, although in each country the standards are developed with the goal of embracing all children. Finally, in many countries where resources are severely constrained, there is concern about the broad-scale implementation of all the uses simultaneously. In these cases, countries prioritize the uses within a temporal plan for near-term and more long-term implementation.

Implications of the Approach for System Building

There is no single approach that can be used to develop the early childhood system, regardless of how it is defined. If, however, the field were to consider that the early childhood system has several subsystems, as this book does, one of them surely concerns pedagogy. As this chapter has tried to suggest, early childhood is well positioned to model the development of an integrated approach to pedagogy, one that is built on the existence of a set of standards that are culturally salient and age appropriate, and that have been statistically validated.

The premise for this stance suggests that no matter how well governed, funded, credentialed, and assessed the early childhood system and its participants are, advancements will remain haphazard and unrealized unless there is some intellectual core holding the field together. Stated differently, subsystems that support the early childhood infrastructure are necessary and work to render a system whole. While attention has been accorded pedagogy, less has been accorded the development of a pedagogical subsystem. This chapter calls for such a subsystem to be developed with early learning and development standards at its core. Thus, early learning and development standards must be the intellectual foundation for curriculum, teacher professional development (in- and preservice), program standards, parenting education, and monitoring and evaluation. This stance says that in order for the field to have integrity regarding what and how it teaches and how it fosters early learning and development, standards must be directly, clearly, and unequivocally linked not only to curriculum and checklists—to what happens inside the classroom—but to the system's efforts that prepare teachers, evaluate programs, and monitor progress.

How to go about this is not unknown; the technology and the models are readily available. Most fundamentally, standards need to be conceptualized within the context of a fully integrated approach to early education.

They must be seen to have multiple applications; and a plan for developing these multiple applications must be developed. It is no longer sufficient to create early learning standards and let them sit on the shelf, or to limit their use to one or two purposes. As the engines for integrating early childhood education, today their potential is underestimated. In countries with far lower GDPs and in settings with far less technical and technological sophistication than that of the United States, standards are the acknowledged centerpiece of early childhood system building. In short, American early education is missing the boat in terms of how we use standards. Pedagogically integrated systems are not only within our reach but must sit at the core of all systems development efforts. Implemented well and widely, they are the essential systems elixir.

ACKNOWLEDGMENTS

The author acknowledges the exemplary research and editorial work done for this chapter by Jocelyn Friedlander. She also acknowledges UNICEF for providing the opportunity to convert the visions presented herein to reality and for the role of Pia Rebello Britto in so doing.

REFERENCES

Barton, P. (2009). *National education standards: Getting beneath the surface.* Princeton, NJ: Educational Testing Service.

Bruer, J. T. (1993). *Schools for thought: A science of learning in the classroom.* Cambridge, MA: MIT Press.

Cahan, E. D. (1989). *Past caring: A history of U.S. preschool and education for the poor, 1820–1965.* New York: National Center for Children in Poverty.

Cronin, J., Dahlin, M., Xiang, Y., & McCahon, D. (2009, February). *The accountability illusion.* Retrieved from the Thomas B. Fordham Institute website: http://www.edexcellence.net/index.cfm/news_the-accountability-illusion

Darling-Hammond, L. (1994). National standards and assessments: Will they improve education? *American Journal of Education, 102*(4), 478–510.

Darling-Hammond, L. (2004). Standards, accountability, and school reform. *Teachers College Record, 106*(6), 1047–1085.

Egertson, H. (2008). Assessment in early childhood—A primer for policy and program leaders. *The State Education Standard,* (June), 28–34.

Finn, C. E., Julian, L., & Petrilli, M. J. (2006). *To dream the impossible dream: Four approaches to national standards and tests for America's schools.* Retrieved from the Thomas B. Fordham Institute website: http://www.edexcellence.net/doc/National%20Standards%20Final%20PDF.pdf

Glaser, R. (1981). The future of testing: A research agenda for cognitive psychology and psychometrics. *American Psychologist, 36*(9), 923–936.

Greenfield, P. M. (1994). Independence and interdependence as developmental scripts: Implications for theory, research, and practice. In P. M. Greenfield & R. R. Cocking (Eds.), *Crosscultural roots of minority child development* (pp. 1–37). Hillsdale, NJ: Erlbaum.

Hofstede, G. (1980). *Culture's consequences.* Beverly Hills, CA: Sage.

Holloway, S. D. (2000). *Contested childhood: Diversity and change in Japanese preschools.* New York: Routledge.

Jennings, J. F. (1995). School reform based on what is taught and learned. *Phi Delta Kappan, 76*(10), 765–769.

Kagan, S. L., & Britto, P. (2009). *Concept paper regarding early learning and development standards.* New York: UNICEF.

Kagan, S. L., & Kauerz, K. (2007). Reaching for the whole: Integration and alignment in early education policy. In R. C. Pianta, M. J. Cox, & K. Snow (Eds.), *School readiness and the transition to kindergarten in the era of accountability* (pp. 11–30). Baltimore: Brookes.

Kagan, S. L., Kauerz, K., & Tarrant, K. (2008). *The early care and education teaching workforce at the fulcrum: An agenda for reform.* New York: Teachers College Press.

Kagan, S. L., & Scott-Little, C. (2004). Early learning standards: Changing the parlance and practice of early childhood education. *Phi Delta Kappan, 85*(5), 388–396.

Klein, A. (2009). "Race to Top" viewed as template for a new ESEA. *Education Week, 29*(16), 17–20.

Kogut, B. J. (1992). National organizing principles of work and the erstwhile dominance of the American multinational corporation. *Industrial and Corporate Change, 1*(2), 285–317.

LeVine, R. A. (1974). Parental goals: A cross-cultural view. *Teachers College Record, 76,* 226–239.

Markus, H. R., & Kitayama, S. (1991). Culture and the self: Implications for cognition, emotion, and motivation. *Psychological Review, 98*(2), 224–253.

National Commission on Excellence in Education. (1983). *A nation at risk: The imperative for educational reform.* Washington, DC: Author.

Nelson, R. R., & Wright, G. (1992). The rise and fall of American technological leadership: The postwar era in historical perspective. *Journal of Economic Literature, 30*(4), 1931–1964.

O'Day, J. A., & Smith, M. S. (1993). Systemic reform and educational opportunity. In S. Fuhrman (Ed.), *Designing coherent education policy: Improving the system* (pp. 250–312). San Francisco: Jossey-Bass.

Porter, A. C. (1994). National standards and school improvement in the 1990s: Issues and promise. *American Journal of Education, 102*(4), 421–449.

Porter, A. C., Polikoff, M. S., & Smithson, J. (2008). Is there a de facto national curriculum? Evidence from state content standards. *Educational Evaluation and Policy Analysis, 31*(3), 238–268.

Ravitch, D. (1995). *National standards in American education: A citizen's guide.* Washington, DC: Brookings Institution.

Resnick, D. P., & Resnick, L. B. (1983). Improving standards in American schools. *Phi Delta Kappan, 65*(3), 178–180.

Rousseau, J. J. (1979). *Emile* (A. Bloom, Trans.). New York: Basic Books. (Original work published 1762)

Schultz, T. (2008). Tackling PK-3 assessment and accountability challenges: Guidance from the National Early Childhood Accountability Task Force. *The State Education Standard*, (June), 4–11.

Scott-Little, C., Kagan, S. L., Frelow, V. S., & Reid, J. (2009). Infant–toddler early learning guidelines: The content that states have addressed and implications for programs serving children with disabilities. *Infants and Young Children, 22*(2), 87–99.

Tank, R. M. (1980). *Young children, families, and society in America since the 1800s: The evolution of health, education, and child care programs for preschool children* (Doctoral dissertation, University of Michigan, Ann Arbor). University Microfilms. (International No. 8106233)

Tobin, J. J., Wu, D. Y. H., & Davidson, D. H. (1989). *Preschool in three cultures.* New Haven, CT: Yale University Press.

Wolfe, J. (2002). *Learning from the past: Historical voices in early childhood education.* Alberta, Canada: Piney Branch Press.

CHAPTER 4

Quality Rating and Improvement Systems

Frameworks for Early Care and Education Systems Change

Diana Schaack, Kate Tarrant,

Kimberly Boller, and Kathryn Tout

Quality rating and improvement systems (QRIS) emerged in the late 1990s as a method to assess, communicate, and improve the availability of high-quality child care in an effort to enhance children's school readiness skills (Mitchell, 2005). Operating in 26 states as of 2009 (Tout, Starr, Soli, et al., 2010), QRIS increasingly are being seen not simply as a stand-alone quality initiative for child care, but as a mechanism for aligning and strengthening a state's early care and education (ECE) system[1] (Mitchell, 2009). This chapter explores several conceptual frameworks that can be used to explain how QRIS invoke ECE systems change and discusses how these frameworks can inform the implementation and evaluation of QRIS. To provide context, the chapter opens with a brief historical account of how QRIS developed, followed by a description of QRIS.

AN HISTORICAL PERSPECTIVE

QRIS grew out of several strands of highly publicized research. The first strand focused on model early intervention preschool programs for children living in poverty. Studies originating from this tradition consistently found that carefully crafted, high-quality preschool had positive and enduring effects on children's development (Campbell & Ramey, 1994; McCarton et al., 1997; Schweinhart, Barnes, Weikart, Barnett, & Epstein, 1993). This research also produced cost–benefit analyses that revealed that investments in high-quality early education yielded savings to society: Children who had participated in these programs were less likely to repeat grades, require special education, and engage in criminal behavior—all costly social conditions (Currie, 2000; Karoly, Kilburn, & Cannon, 2005).

The second strand of research focused on more typical community-based child care programs. The most notable, the Cost, Quality and Outcomes Study, demonstrated that higher structural and process quality indicators[2] in child care centers predicted gains in children's academic and social skills, with some gains lasting through 2nd grade (Peisner-Feinberg et al., 2001). This study, along with others, exposed the generally low quality of child care in the United States, particularly for very young children (Helburn, 1995; Kontos, Howes, Shinn, & Galinsky, 1995).

The third strand of research examined families' selection of child care and noted that families tended to prioritize cost and convenience, not quality, when making decisions about child care. Several studies attributed families' child care preferences to a lack of information about the quality of their children's child care arrangements (Helburn, 1995).

These findings, combined with public attention to the national decline in children's academic performance (National Commission on Excellence in Education, 1983), fueled calls to improve child care quality and children's school readiness skills (Zellman & Perlman, 2008). It was widely recognized, however, that state licensing standards for child care provided only a baseline of quality to protect children's health and safety, and that national accreditation standards that likely would enhance children's development were unattainable for most programs (Westervelt, Sibley, & Schaack, 2008). With program quality standards already in place for Head Start and under development for the burgeoning state prekindergarten movement, the need was identified to create a progressive set of child care program standards linked to financial incentives and supports to improve quality (Mitchell, 2005); thus QRIS were born.

QUALITY RATING AND IMPROVEMENT SYSTEMS

QRIS establish program quality standards that are organized into levels and utilize a multidimensional program assessment to assign star ratings to programs based on their compliance with these standards. Ratings often assess classroom learning environment, staff training and education, parent involvement, classroom ratios, director leadership and business practices, and the use of child assessments and developmentally appropriate curricula.

The overall ratings often are made public and used to direct financial and technical assistance to improve program quality. According to the National Early Childhood Accountability Task Force (2007), these interconnected parts—standards, assessment, and use of assessment data to improve services—are essential to an effective ECE accountability system.

As an accountability framework, QRIS originally were developed to address a major factor underlying poor program quality in the child care sector of the ECE industry: market failure. Helburn and Bergmann (2002) have suggested that within most consumer markets, including child care, purchasers act in their own interests to select the products or services that best meet their needs. In efficient markets, price is typically an indicator of quality. Furthermore, consumers have access to information to evaluate product quality, which fuels demand for high-quality, affordable products. Demand for high-quality child care, however, is suppressed by a number of factors. First, price is typically a poor indicator of quality; second, families lack adequate information to differentiate the quality of services; and third, families often are unable to pay the high price for quality care. As a result, families may not demand care that will promote their children's development (Helburn & Bergmann, 2002).

Weak consumer demand creates a ripple effect on the supply side of the child care market, limiting the availability of quality care. Because families are unwilling or unable to pay for quality care, the cost of improved program quality typically falls largely on the shoulders of an underpaid workforce, fueling high teacher turnover rates, which further suppress quality (Whitebook, Howes, & Phillips, 1989). Within a context of scarce resources, programs either compromise quality or increase parent tuition, which often funnels children into unregulated, and, perhaps, lower quality, care (Helburn & Bergmann, 2002). Theoretically, QRIS can intervene on both the supply and demand sides of the child care market to solve these inefficiencies, resulting in higher quality programs (Mitchell, 2005; Stoney, 2004).

To address the demand-side problem in the child care market, quality ratings are intended to serve as an education tool so consumers (i.e., families and governments) can make informed decisions about where to invest their ECE dollars (Mitchell, 2009; Stoney, 2004). Policymakers may further enhance demand by using ratings to direct funding, for example in the form of tax credits or differential tuition support, toward families who select higher quality programs (Stoney, 2004).

QRIS also are intended to intervene on the market's supply side by giving policymakers and private funders a rationale for investing in ECE (Stoney, 2004). That is, QRIS provide a coherent accountability system that includes program standards, a method of assessing how well programs meet standards, and a way to track the effectiveness of spending that lends legitimacy to increased investment. Additional investments from both public and private sectors can be used to offer grants, scholarships, coaching, and bonuses for staff to improve their services (Mitchell, 2005).

According to this argument, QRIS hold the potential to minimize inefficiencies within the child care market, by increasing demand for and availability of high-quality services. As a relatively new strategy, however, a comprehensive research base describing the effectiveness of QRIS in reaching these aims has yet to be developed. The research that does exist instead approaches QRIS primarily as a program-level quality improvement intervention and concentrates on helping states address implementation concerns, assess changes in the quality of participating programs, and, to a minimal extent, consider its impact on outcomes for young children and families (Tout, Zaslow, Halle, & Forry, 2009).

Recently however, a shift in thinking about the systemic impact of QRIS has occurred. QRIS are now seen not merely as a program-level quality improvement intervention, but as a mechanism for strengthening a state's overall ECE system that reaches beyond child care to include the Head Start and prekindergarten sectors as well. Consequently, frameworks are needed to explain how QRIS may invoke systems change, and research is needed that considers system-level QRIS outcomes and how systems change may influence programs, children, and families (Tout & Maxwell, 2010). The following discussion—guided by theory and observation—lays the groundwork for a research agenda that views QRIS as a policy tool for system reform.

QRIS AS A SYSTEM BUILDER

The vision of QRIS as a policy mechanism for system alignment and building has been attractive to stakeholders not only because of the potential for positively impacting children and families but also because of the expectation that an aligned ECE system will function more effectively and efficiently. While it seems straightforward among QRIS stakeholders to envision the results of an effective system, it is far more challenging to articulate the processes that are necessary to create these essential system connectors. In the remainder of this chapter, three models are explored that can be used to explain how QRIS may strengthen the ECE system. These models, taken alone or in combination, provide specific examples of activities and indicators that may provide evidence of QRIS as a system-building mechanism.

Model 1: Functional Analysis

To produce an ECE system that results in positive changes for system beneficiaries—children and families—Coffman (2007 and Chapter 12, this volume) argues that it is essential to focus on changes in five interconnected areas of the system: (1) context, (2) components, (3) connections, (4) infrastructure, and (5) scale. The analysis presented below examines the ways in which QRIS are hypothesized to affect each area.

The first area, context, suggests that in order to build a high-functioning ECE system, public and political support for such a system is needed. According to frame theory (Bales, 1998), public perception of an issue often is based on scripts individuals use to organize their views on a topic. In some sectors of the ECE industry, such as pre-K and Head Start, the public and policymakers *may* be inclined to draw from scripts that include educational benefits to children and society. Because the public often frames community-based child care not as an educational benefit but as a babysitting service (Bostrom, 2002), policymakers and families have been concerned almost exclusively with ensuring that child care policies keep children safe and enable families to work (Brauner, Gordic, & Zigler, 2004).

QRIS may alter these frames by providing a new language for the ECE industry. QRIS attempt to communicate that higher quality programs across sectors can influence children's school readiness skills and benefit society; they also provide an easy-to-understand symbol of quality (e.g., star rating) that indicates that quality can be both measured and achieved. Star ratings then may trump other descriptive labels attached to a program, such as preschool or Head Start. Moreover, ratings may tilt the dominant frames surrounding child care, in particular, toward quality, thereby cultivating new advocates and galvanizing public support for increased investment in the system. Thus, QRIS designers may consider directing resources to communicating the importance of quality and the potential benefits of QRIS to decision makers. Changes in decision-maker attitudes about the purposes of child care in particular, the presence of new advocates, and additional dollars invested in the ECE system are then important indicators of improving the context for system building.

The second focal area, components, is concerned with the development of high-quality ECE programs that positively affect children and families; it is the essence of QRIS implementation. As states move forward with QRIS design, many are creating systems of technical assistance designed to support program quality improvement. Technical assistance frequently includes in-classroom coaching, facilitated guidance to create and implement program-level improvement plans, and the distribution of materials, grants, scholarships, and staff bonuses to meet higher quality levels. Important indicators of system building may be the degree to which local communities have the capacity and infrastructure to support program improvement, and the alignment of technical assistance content with early learning and QRIS program standards.

Importantly, as states build their technical assistance systems, further research is needed to better understand types and amounts of coaching and financial investments that improve quality. More information also is needed regarding the competencies, skills, and content knowledge of the workforce providing the technical assistance.

Connections, the third focal area, suggests that linkages across components of the system bring coherence to it, promote consistency across ECE programs that may reduce developmental inequities (Kagan, 2006), and decrease system redundancies, thereby funneling more resources directly to programs and families. The inclusion of all ECE sectors is a key consideration when evaluating the degree to which QRIS foster connections within the system. While many states include a full array of ECE programs in their QRIS, some states simply have added another set of program standards, monitoring procedures, and technical assistance efforts to ECE programs with existing accountability structures (Tout, Starr, Soli, et al., 2010). QRIS with a focus on system building align quality standards across the industry, create multiple pathways to achieve quality ratings,[3] and coordinate technical assistance efforts across sectors of the industry to eliminate redundancies and contradictions (Mitchell, 2009). Evaluation efforts may help to inform effective linkages across the system by examining the comparability of different program standards and validating them with early learning outcomes. This type of information could lead to the adoption of a common set of program, professional development, and early learning standards for the full array of ECE programs (Howes et al., 2008).

The fourth focal area, infrastructure, addresses the supports necessary to enable high-quality programs for children and families. In theory, well-developed QRIS simultaneously link to and strengthen other system infrastructure. In many states, the most prevalent system infrastructure building has occurred between QRIS and professional development systems. Some states have created staff training registries or credentialing systems that are linked to their QRIS and provide scholarships and training opportunities connected to practitioner standards articulated across these system components.

QRIS also may serve to build the infrastructure for a state's data system by collecting comprehensive information on program quality and holding that information in one unified repository. In addition, QRIS may serve as an important mechanism for developing state and local ECE governance structures. When QRIS include the full array of programs and collect data on ECE program quality across a state, local councils comprising stakeholders can use this information to make decisions about ECE investments and to coordinate their efforts. Thus, coordination agreements across agencies that support ECE, shared definitions of quality, and the alignment of agencies' work around the standards in the QRIS may serve as indicators of system building.

Coffman's (2007) fifth and final focal area, scale, suggests that a high-functioning ECE system provides high-quality programs to all system beneficiaries. QRIS may achieve scale in several ways. When QRIS are embedded within states' regulatory systems, they directly aim to assess and improve quality statewide. QRIS also can affect the availability of quality care at scale by indirectly affecting the entire child care market. That is, if a critical mass of programs participate in QRIS and a growing number of families begin to demand high quality, nonparticipating programs may be forced to improve their quality to remain competitive, helping to ensure widespread availability of quality programs. To the degree that QRIS embrace all ECE programs, families using ratings and increasing numbers of programs participating in a state's QRIS would signal successful system building.

While it may be unrealistic to fully address each focal area outlined above, it may make practical sense for states to begin the work of developing system-focused QRIS by aligning standards across ECE sectors, mapping existing resources, and reducing monitoring and technical assistance redundancies. Making the critical linkages between children's early learning standards, articulated practitioner competencies, practitioner registries and standards, QRIS program standards, and technical assistance supports may bring additional coherence to the system.

Model 2: Institutional Analysis

New institutional theory offers another framework for exploring the mechanisms through which QRIS may invoke ECE systems change. Based on the premise that organizations need legitimacy in order to garner resources and succeed, this model approaches QRIS as a multidimensional strategy to raise the status of ECE programs or to "institutionalize" the ECE system.

New institutional theory suggests that human service providers rely on norms to signal their competence to consumers and the public because the technical aspect of their work is so complex that it is difficult to define, measure, and monitor (Scott, 1995). This is certainly the case in ECE, where effectively teaching young children depends on unique interactions between teachers and children, and the idiosyncratic nature of quality care is difficult to communicate to consumers. A strong institutional environment, characterized by well-developed rules and norms, is one way to overcome this communication breakdown so that ECE programs may attract adequate investments (Fuller, 2007). However, competing ideas over the purpose of ECE—whether it is intended to facilitate parental employment or to support children's development—undermine the strength of ECE's institutional environment. As noted by Goffin (Chapter 20, this volume), pervasive definitional ambiguity regarding the core purpose of ECE serves as a roadblock to system-building efforts.

QRIS may address these prevailing conditions in several ways. The first is by establishing a common purpose and definition of quality for all ECE programs. According to new institutional theory, a strong system depends on "mutual awareness among participants in a set of organizations that they are involved in a common enterprise" (DiMaggio & Powell, 1983, p. 148). In setting standards for all ECE programs around quality service provision, QRIS define programs' common enterprise. The establishment of such a definition strengthens the ECE system by guiding the interactions among the many organizations in the ECE system: centers, family child care homes, Head Start and state prekindergarten programs, as well as government agencies, higher education institutions, and technical assistance providers that support ECE. For instance, in many states, QRIS channel government funding and technical assistance toward programs that participate in the QRIS. Within this perspective, a common definition of ECE quality serves as a fundamental binding element for a well-functioning system.

In designing QRIS, then, it is important to solicit wide-ranging perspectives (e.g., across child care, Head Start, and state-funded prekindergarten) on quality and to set standards that all programs and allied agencies within the "system" buy into. For evaluation purposes, the systemic impact of QRIS can be measured by the degree to which these organizations embrace a common definition of quality.

The second mechanism for building the ECE system, according to new institutional theory, involves organizations' adherence to institutionalized norms set by QRIS. Because the craft of successful teaching is complex and context-dependent, structural quality norms such as teacher qualifications, class size, and ratios set by QRIS play an important role in signaling quality service. Indeed, consumers, government agencies, and funders typically rely on structural indicators when assessing program quality (Meyer, Scott, & Deal, 1983). When the full range of ECE programs raise their performance on similar structural dimensions of quality that comport with the research base on quality service provision, the ECE system gains legitimacy that theoretically translates into greater investments in ECE. When these norms are technically driven, that is, they reflect a valid and reliable assessment of quality practice, legitimacy also may be gained through demonstrable improvements in children's school readiness. QRIS may provide a framework for communicating and spreading these norms across the system.

Thus, QRIS must be designed with careful attention to raising public awareness about the importance of structural quality indicators. Informed by this perspective, an evaluation of QRIS system building may assess organizations' compliance with quality norms, such as technical assistance providers focusing on these norms in their work with teachers. Another indicator that QRIS are building the ECE system would include parents and government basing ECE choices on programs' adherence to these norms. Finally, a positive change in public perception of the legitimacy of ECE also would signal the systemic impact of QRIS.

A third mechanism that assists in creating a coherent ECE system involves isomorphism: the degree to which organizations within the same field, but with disparate origins, come to resemble one another (DiMaggio & Powell, 1983). DiMaggio and Powell note that "once a field becomes well established . . . there is an inexorable push toward homogenization" (p. 148) and that this may occur through coercive processes. For instance, government agencies and funders may promote homogeneity by basing funding for ECE programs and allied agencies responsible for technical assistance and professional development on their adherence to QRIS standards. Normative processes also may contribute to isomorphism Through the pursuit of formal education, teachers may begin to adopt norms regarding developmentally appropriate practice and, in turn, teachers' instructional techniques may begin to resemble one another. Uniformity across program types indicates that system building has occurred.

By invoking new institutional theory to understand how fields become systematized, insights also can be gained regarding important issues for QRIS developers to consider and potential consequences of institutionalization. For example, within this framework, since a system is underscored by a field gaining legitimacy through adherence to rules and norms (e.g., structural quality standards) and through potentially coercive mechanisms that lead to program homogeneity, it is crucial that program and teacher standards reflect meaningful indicators of quality that enhance the development of the diverse population of children. The insistence on a common definition of quality also holds the potential of reflecting a dominant cultural construction that may accommodate only particular approaches to ECE service provision (Dahlberg, Moss, & Pence, 1999; Lubeck, 1998). In turn, programs that reject this definition may be driven out of the field. In light of these potential consequences, the institutionalization of ECE should be pursued carefully and incorporate diverse and meaningful perspectives on quality.

Model 3: Complex Adaptive Systems Analysis

While the functional and institutional perspectives provide insight into the mechanisms through which QRIS invoke systems changes, the final perspective offers an evaluative framework to understand dynamic factors that may influence the systemic impact of QRIS. Indeed, previous research has viewed QRIS primarily as a program-level quality improvement intervention, considering outcomes typically related to classroom quality (Tout et al., 2009) and has used analytic methods appropriate for such a focus. When considering the degree to which QRIS assist in building ECE systems, new evaluative frameworks are necessary—frameworks that account for the messy nature of public policymaking and consider the interdependent agents that interact through QRIS to build ECE systems. Complex adaptive system analysis (Leischow et al., 2008) may be a particularly useful framework because it acknowledges the complex and unpredictable nature of policymaking and the dynamic nature of system-building efforts. It also creates feedback loops that help to identify next steps to achieve desired systems change (Foster-Fishman, Nowell, & Yang, 2007).

Drawing on the work of systems theorists, Hargreaves and Paulsell (2009) define three key characteristics of complex adaptive systems. First, they comprise agents and agencies that are nested and networked (Barabasi, 2002). In ECE, an underlying cause of inequitable access to high-quality programs is the fragmented nature of the current system; that is, ECE system components function relatively independently from one another. Accordingly, one systemic goal of QRIS is to create an organizing framework to align the work of other system components. Thus, QRIS function in an environment of nested and networked system agents.

Second, Hargreaves and Paulsell (2009) suggest that, within complex adaptive systems, the interactions among the nested and networked agents and agencies are nonlinear in nature; that is, the actions of different system agents are dynamic and can affect one another in unpredictable ways (Patton, 2008). To create system linkages and build infrastructure, QRIS agents must interact within and across system components, and the interactions that QRIS agents have with other system agents can change over time. These dynamic interactions can affect the degree to which QRIS invoke systems change in both positive and negative ways. As an illustration, the economic crisis has put some states' QRIS goals and implicit logic models into question by reducing the amount of public funding available for quality improvement grants. These conditions may result in lower program participation, requiring states to revisit expectations of QRIS systems change. Recognizing these nonlinear conditions serves to strengthen evaluations of the systemic impact of QRIS.

Finally, Hargreaves and Paulsell (2009) note that a complex adaptive system comprises individual system parts that are distinct from one another but, as a whole, function in ways that are qualitatively different from the individual parts (Eoyang, 2007). This key concept lies at the heart of a QRIS theory of systems change. For example, QRIS with a focus on system building contain multiple system elements: accountability and monitoring systems, data systems, professional development systems, consumer education, and financing mechanisms. The system elements work in distinct ways but, in theory, they function more efficiently and effectively when they work together under the umbrella of QRIS. For example, when QRIS align teacher competencies with professional development systems, technical assistance and financial supports, and program quality standards, the coordination of individual system parts into a cohesive whole is likely to result in greater teaching effectiveness than if each system component functioned independently (Howes et al., 2008).

Because QRIS system-building efforts are predicated on interactions across system agents, three core complex adaptive system concepts can lend precision to evaluating the systemic impact of QRIS. These concepts include: (1) boundaries, (2) relationships, and (3) perspectives (Parsons, 2007; Williams & Imam, 2007).

Defining the boundaries of a specific QRIS initiative involves delineating the players and activities that are included within QRIS. A logic model may help to identify boundaries by outlining the inputs that may lead to ECE systems change outcomes. If a state's theory of change suggests that stable ECE financing depends on families' access to information about the importance of quality care, the boundaries of system-focused QRIS may be extended to include agencies focused on consumer education and family supports (e.g., Child Care Resource and Referral or CCR&R networks, welcome baby programs). Therefore, a systems-oriented evaluation of QRIS must account for the actions of these agents.

Relationships refers to interactions among the agents contained within the boundaries of QRIS. The relationships among individuals, groups, and institutions are important to understand because they influence the flow of information, funding, and the capacity of QRIS to effectively invoke systems change. For example, developing QRIS standards that transcend program type requires collaboration among key QRIS stakeholders, the state's department of education, Head Start State Collaboration office, credentialing systems, community colleges, and 4-year universities. Relationships among these stakeholders may change as key staff come and go. Systems theory acknowledges the importance of these dynamic circumstances and quantifies them to understand how they may affect QRIS system-building progress.

The final concept, perspectives, captures the views, motivations, and goals each stakeholder brings to the table. For example, with regard to the development of data systems, each stakeholder group may have different interests. Policymakers may be interested in data systems that address accountability requirements (e.g., linking quality ratings to kindergarten readiness assessments); QRIS administrators may be motivated to connect QRIS and licensing data to avoid giving a center with an open child abuse investigation a high rating; and technical assistance agencies may be interested in tracking the effectiveness of quality improvement efforts. The perspectives of each stakeholder are complex and important for QRIS developers to understand.

Applying these three concepts to QRIS can provide decision makers with a deeper understanding of how stakeholders interact to influence the capacity and effectiveness of QRIS for building the ECE system. Guided by feedback loops that exist throughout the system, data collection and evaluation approaches can account for changing circumstances. This more "developmental," nonlinear approach to evaluation allows policymakers, program operators, and evaluators to continuously track and improve the progress of QRIS in building an ECE system.

QRIS AS LEVERS FOR SYSTEMS CHANGE

The three frameworks described in this chapter provide complementary perspectives on how QRIS may produce a more integrated and effective ECE system. The functional analysis outlines five key areas (context, components, connections, infrastructure, and scale) that potentially are affected by a QRIS initiative and the ways in which changes in each area could be indicative of QRIS as a system-building endeavor. Institutional theory suggests that system building occurs because of shifts in the perceptions and norms among system stakeholders that occur through the promotion by QRIS of a common vision of quality, subsequent adherence to the new standards, and greater legitimacy. The complex adaptive system lens provides a perspective for considering the dynamic nature of a multifaceted initiative like QRIS and how recognition of relationships and boundaries among system participants, as well as change in goals and context over time, can assist system participants in managing systems change and reaching realistic goals. As QRIS stakeholders begin to embrace the broad potential of their initiatives to create high-quality, seamless, efficient services that promote positive outcomes for children and families, a variety of tools and evidence will be needed to bring system building from theory to practice.

To begin, QRIS stakeholders need concrete planning tools and expert guidance to help them develop a blueprint for identifying and strengthening system connection points. Ideally, tools would recognize the reality of QRIS and incorporate them into the planning process. For example, although changes in perception of norms among institutions (in institutional analysis) and the focus on scale (in functional analysis) imply that broad participation and buy-in to QRIS are central requirements for system building, the reality in most states is that fewer than half of all ECE programs actually are participating in QRIS (Tout, Starr, Soli, et al., 2010). Many QRIS have a limited budget for marketing and outreach efforts, increasing the challenge of achieving buy-in by programs and parents or increasing levels of participation (Tout, Starr, Soli, et al., 2010). Additionally, some states report reluctance about involvement with QRIS among family child care providers (because of the perception that the standards are more appropriate for center-based programs) and difficulties of QRIS to adequately address the needs of culturally diverse providers (Tout, Starr, Knerr, et al., 2010). These and other realities of QRIS in practice must be acknowledged to help QRIS stakeholders plan for system building.

New evidence on QRIS is also necessary to bolster their system-building potential. In particular, QRIS stakeholders need evidence about the intensity of technical services required to achieve maximum impact on the overall goal of an early learning system (e.g., school readiness). Quality improvement activities are a critical component of QRIS, yet the evidence base on how to support programs is limited. Similarly, while the provision of financial incentives to encourage participation and support quality improvement may drive the impact of QRIS, little research documents the types and amount of incentives needed for optimal functioning. Investment in evaluation efforts is needed to identify these and other QRIS parameters that can promote progress toward positive outcomes.

QRIS are now well into their second decade and the promise of QRIS as a system builder is clear. Also clear, however, are the multiple challenges of making the vision of a system into the reality on the ground. The models proposed in this chapter offer direction for identifying the underlying engines of systems development, the development of concrete tools for promoting system linkages, and the opportunities for evaluating the dimensions of QRIS that can inform decision making. These activities will offer vital information to the field for shaping the next decade of QRIS and ECE system building.

NOTES

1. In this chapter, we define the ECE system as comprising the following interconnected elements: an accountability system that includes early learning, program, and practitioner standards and a way to assess how well programs meet those

standards; a professional development system that enables the workforce to meet the aforementioned standards; financing strategies to support high-functioning programs; and a governance structure to oversee the system (Early Childhood System Working Group, 2007, as cited in Mitchell, 2009). The ECE system includes child care, prekindergarten, and Head Start program sectors.

2. Structural quality includes the documentable features of a program, such as group size and staff qualifications. Process indicators are related to children's experience, including teacher–child interactions.

3. For example, cross-walking Head Start performance standards with QRIS quality standards and including the use of the Office of Head Start Monitoring System in QRIS rating tools for Head Start programs.

REFERENCES

Bales, S. N. (1998). *Early childhood education and the framing wars: Effective language for discussing early childhood education and policy*. Washington, DC: Benton Foundation.

Barabasi, A. (2002). *Linked: The new science of networks*. Cambridge, MA: Perseus.

Bostrom, M. (2002). *The whole child—Parents and policy: A meta-analysis of public opinion concerning school readiness, early childhood, and related issues*. Washington, DC: Frameworks Institute.

Brauner, J., Gordic, B., & Zigler, E. (2004). *Putting the child back in child care: Combining care and education for children ages 3–5* (Social Policy Report XVIII (III)). Ann Arbor, MI: Society for Research in Child Development.

Campbell, F. A., & Ramey, C. T. (1994). Effects of early intervention on intellectual and academic achievement: A follow-up study of children from low-income families. *Child Development, 65*, 684–698.

Coffman, J. (2007). *A framework for evaluating systems initiatives*. Retrieved from the BUILD Initiative website: http://www.buildinitiative.org/content/evaluation-systems-change

Currie, J. (2000). *Early childhood intervention programs: What do we know?* Northwestern University/University of Chicago Joint Center for Poverty Research.

Dahlberg, G., Moss, P., & Pence, A. (1999). *Beyond quality in early childhood education and care: Postmodern perspectives*. Philadelphia: Falmer Press.

DiMaggio, P. J., & Powell, W. W. (1983). The iron cage revisited: Institutional isomorphism and collective rationality in organizational fields. *American Sociological Review, 48*, 147–160.

Eoyang, G. (2007). Human systems dynamics: Complexity-based approach to a complex evaluation. In B. Williams & I. Imam (Eds.), *Systems concepts in evaluation: An expert anthology*. Point Reyes Station, CA: EdgePress/American Evaluation Association.

Foster-Fishman, P., Nowell, B., & Yang, H. (2007). Putting the system back into systems change: A framework for understanding and changing organizational and community systems. *American Journal of Community Psychology, 39*, 197–215.

Fuller, B. (2007). *Standardized childhood: The political and cultural struggle over early education.* Palo Alto, CA: Stanford University Press.

Hargreaves, M., & Paulsell, D. (2009). *Evaluating systems change efforts to support evidence-based home visiting: Concepts and methods.* Children's Bureau, Administration for Children and Families, U.S. Department of Health and Human Services. Contract No. GS-10F-0050L/HHSP233200800065W. Available from Mathematica Policy Research, Princeton, NJ.

Helburn, S. W. (1995). *Cost, quality and child outcomes in child care centers: Technical report.* Denver: University of Colorado, Department of Economics, Center for Research in Economic and Social Policy.

Helburn, S. W., & Bergmann, B. (2002). *America's child care problem: The way out.* New York: Palgrave.

Howes, C., Pianta, R., Bryant, D., Hamre, V., Downer, J., & Soliday-Hong, S. (2008). *Ensuring effective teaching in early childhood education through linked professional development systems, quality rating systems and state competencies: The role of research in an evidence-driven system.* Charlottesville, VA: National Center for Research in Early Childhood Education.

Kagan, S. L. (2006). *American early childhood education: Preventing or perpetuating inequity?* (Research Review No. 1). New York: Campaign for Educational Equity.

Karoly, L., Kilburn, M. R., & Cannon, J. (2005). *Early childhood interventions: Proven results, future promise.* Santa Monica, CA: RAND Corporation.

Kontos, S., Howes, C., Shinn, M., & Galinsky, E. (1995). *Quality in family child care and relative care.* New York: Teachers College Press.

Leischow, S. J., Best, A., Trochim, W. M., Clark, P., Gallagher, R. S., Marcus, S. E., & Matthews, E. (2008). Systems thinking to improve the public's health. *American Journal of Preventive Medicine, 35*(2, Supplement), 196–203.

Lubeck, S. (1998). Is developmentally appropriate practice for everyone? *Childhood Education, 74*(5), 283–293.

McCarton, C. M., Brooks-Gunn, J., Wallace, I. F., Bauer, C. R., Bennett, F. C., Bernbaum, J. C., & Meinert, C. L. (1997). Results at age 8 years of early intervention for low-birth-weight premature infants. *Journal of the American Medical Association, 277*, 126–132.

Meyer, J. W., Scott, W. R., & Deal, T. E. (1983). Institutional and technical sources of organizational structure: Explaining the structure of educational organizations. In J. W. Meyer & W. R. Scott (Eds.), *Organizational environments* (pp. 45–70). Newbury Park, CA: Sage.

Mitchell, A. (2005). *Stair steps to quality: A guide for states and communities developing quality rating systems for early care and education.* Alexandria, VA: United Way Success by 6.

Mitchell, A. (2009). *Quality rating and improvement systems as a framework for early care and education system reform.* Boston, MA: BUILD Initiative.

National Commission on Excellence in Education. (1983). *A nation at risk: The imperative for educational reform.* Washington, DC: U.S. Department of Education.

National Early Childhood Accountability Task Force. (2007). *Taking stock: Assessing and improving early childhood learning and program quality.* Washington, DC: Pew Center on the States.

Parsons, B. (2007). *Designing initiative evaluation: A systems-oriented framework for evaluating social change efforts.* Kalamazoo, MI: W.K. Kellogg Foundation.

Patton, M. Q. (2008). *Utilization-focused evaluation* (4th ed.). Thousand Oaks, CA: Sage.

Peisner-Feinberg, E. S., Burchinal, M., Clifford, R. M., Culkin, M., Howes, C., Kagan, S. L., & Yazejian, N. (2001). The relation of preschool child care quality to children's cognitive and social developmental trajectories through second grade. *Child Development, 72*(5), 1534–1553.

Schweinhart, L. J., Barnes, H. V., Weikart, D. P., Barnett, W. S., & Epstein, A. S. (1993). *Significant benefits: The High/Scope Perry Preschool study through age 27.* Ypsilanti, MI: High/Scope Press.

Scott, W. R. (1995). *Institutions and organizations.* Thousand Oaks, CA: Sage.

Stoney, L. (2004). *Financing quality rating systems: Lessons learned.* Alexandria, VA: United Way of America, Success by 6.

Tout, K., & Maxwell, K. M. (2010). Quality rating and improvement systems: Achieving the promise for programs, parents, children and early childhood systems. In V. Buysse & P. Wesley (Eds.), *The quest for quality* (pp. 91–111). Baltimore: Brookes.

Tout, K., Starr, R., Knerr, T., Cleveland, J., Soli, M., & Quinn, K. (2010). *Evaluation of Parent Aware: Minnesota's quality rating system pilot: Year 2 evaluation report.* Minneapolis, MN: Child Trends.

Tout, K., Starr, R., Soli, M., Moodie, S., Kirby, G., & Boller, K. (2010). *Compendium of quality rating systems and evaluations.* Produced for the Office of Planning, Research and Evaluation, Administration for Children and Families, U.S. Department of Health and Human Services.

Tout, K., Zaslow, M., Halle, T., & Forry, N. (2009). *Issues for the next decade of quality rating and improvement systems.* Washington, DC: Child Trends.

Westervelt, G., Sibley, A., & Schaack, D. (2008). Quality in programs for young children. In S. Feeney, A. Galper, & C. Seefeldt (Eds.), *Continuing issues in early childhood education* (3rd ed., pp. 83–98). Upper Saddle River, NJ: Pearson.

Whitebook, M., Howes, C., & Phillips, D. (1989). *Who cares? Child care teachers and the quality of care in America* (Final report of the National Child Care Staffing Study). Oakland, CA: Child Care Employee Project.

Williams, B., & Imam, I. (2007). *Systems concepts in evaluation: An expert anthology.* Point Reyes, CA: American Evaluation Association.

Zellman, G. L., & Perlman, M. (2008). *Child care quality rating and improvement systems in five pioneer states: Implementation issues and lessons learned.* Santa Monica, CA: RAND Corporation.

CHAPTER 5

Governance and Early Childhood Systems
Different Forms, Similar Goals

Kristie Kauerz and Sharon Lynn Kagan

Early childhood systems work is proliferating in different ways in states across the country, and a barrage of frameworks, graphics, and diagrams have been created that depict how various programs and sectors should align. Nearly every system-building initiative has described what a system should look like from a family's, child's, or provider's perspective, using words like "seamless" delivery and "blended funding" to describe the end goal. Nearly every initiative also has identified governance as a crucial aspect of the infrastructure needed to make early childhood systems a reality.

Under the label of governance, all 50 states have been offered various forms of federal funding to increase linkages and alignment across early childhood programs and services; many, if not all, states have commissions, task forces, or work groups that address issues related to early childhood systems; and a few states have developed entirely new government agencies. Some of these efforts center on the early care and education (ECE) domain and strive to better align learning-related programs and services (e.g., child care, prekindergarten, Head Start, early intervention) for children from birth to age 5. Other efforts attempt to address multiple domains that impact early childhood—health, mental health, family support, among others—and involve a comprehensive array of programs and services for children from birth through age 8.

While there is no dearth of systems work, there is a lack of a comprehensive review of governance and the role it plays in early childhood system building. Based on the diverse conceptual and practical approaches that exist, this chapter provides an analytic, albeit fresh, look at the role of governance in early childhood system building. We address the structures, functions, and instruments of governance. From our review of the literature, current practice, and evolving policy innovations, we suggest that two kinds of governance structures—within-government and cross-sector—are necessary if we are to fully realize comprehensive early childhood systems. Moreover, we suggest that these two types of governance structures must both use similar governing tools and be characterized by authority and accountability in order to drive meaningful systems reform.

To illustrate our stance, we take as our starting point the diagram of the four interconnected ovals (see Figure 2.1), which portrays an overlapping set of domains. While the schematic provides a helpful conceptualization of an early childhood system, we believe there are important governance issues to consider within each independent oval, as well as governance issues related to the intersection of the ovals. Our intent is to examine the ways in which governance has been and is being addressed in one of the ovals, early care and education, as well as in the cross-sector work that is being carried out at the intersection of the multiple ovals.

Before elaborating our suggested taxonomy for this work, we describe the broad context for governance work, addressing definitional challenges within the early childhood field and summarizing some major trends in governance scholarship around the world. We then review briefly early childhood governance trends in the United States, those initiated both by the federal government and at the state level. Next, we explicate our delineation of two types of governance effort needed in early childhood and posit that both must rely on the core governance principles of authority and accountability.

THE BROAD CONTEXT FOR GOVERNANCE IN EARLY CHILDHOOD

Several factors provide important background to this chapter. First, throughout both policy and practice, many different definitions of "system" are used, as are many different definitions of "governance." Even more confusing, often definitions are used interchangeably. This is not unique to the early childhood field. Scholars in other disciplines note that "the concept of governance is notoriously slippery; it is frequently used among both social scientists and practitioners without a definition all agree on" (Kohler-Koch & Rittberger, 2006, p. 28). To minimize this challenge here, we offer our own definitions of system, system building, and governance. For us, a system is an orderly and comprehensive assemblage of interrelated elements that creates equitable, accessible, comprehensive, and quality services for young children. System building is the cadre of efforts that are undertaken to create such a system. Governance includes the structures, processes, and policies that enable a system to function consistently, effectively, and efficiently.

Second, policy often addresses specific issues, programs, or funding streams and distinguishes clean lines of authority. In contrast, system building often works in the opposite direction; it attempts to span boundaries and build bridges among agencies, sectors, organizations, and even disciplines. As such, "seamless," "blended," and blurred boundaries are not natural states for the policies and governance entities that guide early childhood. By definition, attempts to create distinct governance structures counter the natural flow of comprehensive systems work.

Third, there is much to be learned about governance from other disciplines. We draw many of our ideas from theoretical work on systems development and governance reform taking place in other social sectors, including environmental protection, health, social welfare, and physical planning. In those literatures, scholars distinguish between two forms of governance. In the first, they discuss traditional governance that focuses on the hierarchical design and (re)structuring of entities that establish and enforce efficient rules and regulations to both standardize and raise the quality of public services. Reforms emerge as government agencies shrink, expand, or reorganize to meet current needs. In the second, scholars discuss "modern" (Kooiman, 1993), "new" (Salamon, 2002), or "informal" (Hajer, 2006) governance wherein there is intentional effort to establish nontraditional mixtures of the public and private sectors. With cross-sector governing mechanisms, both public and private actors engage in the intentional regulation of complex societal and programmatic relationships, thereby creating a conceptual coordination of social systems (Kohler-Koch & Rittberger, 2006). While we adapt some of our thinking from other disciplines, for purposes of clarity we do not adopt their terms. Because "new" or "modern" might connote that "traditional" is outdated and no longer relevant, and because we deem both new and traditional forms to be essential in early childhood work, we instead use the terms "within-government" and "cross-sector" to distinguish these two approaches to governance.

A LOOK BACK AT GOVERNANCE IN EARLY CHILDHOOD

Attention to governance is not new to early childhood education in America. As public early childhood programs grew throughout the 1960s, 1970s, and 1980s, each had its own governance structure. Head Start, for example, had its Policy Councils and Committees, private nonprofit programs had their boards, and for-profit programs were governed by their owners or stockholders.

As the patchwork of programs and services began to be seen as ineffective, scholars, practitioners, and governments called for service integration, systems development, and allied services (Kagan, 1993; Steiner, 1976; Sugarman, 1989). Efforts to define effective governance approaches to consolidate and align programs and services date at least to the 1970s, with the development of the Allied Services Act. Since then, there have been a number of federal and state efforts to foster cross-agency and cross-sector coordination and alignment of early childhood programs and services. The most notable of these efforts are reviewed below.

Federal Efforts to Coordinate and Align

The federal government has provided legislation, vision, and funding to create more cohesion for the early childhood field and to link and align programs in a more systematic way.

Legislation Related to Children with Disabilities. In 1975, the Education for All Handicapped Children's Act (P.L. 94-142) mandated that free appropriate public education and related services be made available to all handicapped children between the ages of 3 and 21. Revolutionary for its time, this legislation altered the way children with disabilities were served and the ways in which agencies were asked to come together. Never directly mandated, collaboration was necessary because state education departments, while the recipients of the funds, did not provide the requisite diagnostic, social, or rehabilitative services. With a history detailed elsewhere (Harbin & McNulty, 1990; Kagan, 1991), subsequent legislation (P.L. 99-457) mandated interagency coordinating councils that were to collaborate in the planning and administration of services across agencies, programs, and levels of government. With the advent of Individuals with Disabilities Education Act (IDEA) Section 619 and IDEA Part C Early Intervention, coordination for children with disabilities grew in importance, setting into motion an array of other federal efforts designed to avoid duplication of effort and promote more equitable service distribution.

Head Start State Collaboration Grants. In 1990, the federal government began funding Head Start State Collaboration offices; today, grants are provided to each of the 50 states, the District of Columbia, the Commonwealth of Puerto Rico, and each national administrative office serving American Indian Head Start programs and migrant and seasonal Head Start programs. These grants are intended to support the development of multi-agency and public/private partnerships at the state level and to encourage collaboration among Head Start, Early Head Start, and other agencies and entities that benefit low-income children from birth to school entry and their families. While Head Start State Collaboration offices have no authority to mandate partnerships, they represent another important federal effort to align disparate but complementary programs and services.

Early Childhood Comprehensive Systems Grants. In 2002, the Maternal and Child Health Bureau launched the Early Childhood Comprehensive Systems Initiative (ECCS) to help states develop systems that more effectively meet the needs of children birth to age 5 and their families. Since then, 49 states and the District of Columbia have used the annual grants to build and integrate comprehensive early childhood systems that increase access to health services and medical homes, support the social-emotional development and mental health of young children, and improve access to and quality of early care and education, parenting education, and family support services. ECCS efforts involve a broad range of public and private agencies and organizations, parents, and communities. Together, these stakeholders plan, develop, and implement collaborations and partnerships to support families and communities to raise children who are healthy and ready to learn at school entry.

State Advisory Councils on Early Childhood Education and Care. Most recently, the Improving Head Start for School Readiness Act of 2007 requires governors to create or designate an entity dedicated to improving the coordination and quality of programs and services for children from birth to school entry. Although authorized by Head Start legislation, the councils are intended to focus broadly on the comprehensive needs of young children, and must include representatives from health, education, child care, Head Start, and early intervention (IDEA, Part C) programs or agencies. One of their responsibilities is to identify opportunities for, and barriers to, collaboration and coordination among federally funded and state-funded programs and agencies responsible for child-related programs and services. Council responsibilities also include providing advice on components of an early childhood system, such as professional development systems, standards, and data for accountability.

These federal efforts to promote collaboration and systems work co-exist in most states today and each is part of a larger network of coordination efforts and councils (Satkowski, 2009). What is notable about these federal efforts is that they often straddle multiple domains of a comprehensive early childhood system—striving to incorporate not just early care and education services, but also services and programs in the health, mental health, and family support domains.

State Efforts to Support Coordination and Alignment

States, too, have been innovative and bold in their efforts to support linkages among agencies, programs, and organizations. Described more fully elsewhere (Kagan & Kauerz, 2009), we provide a brief summary here.

Coordination and Collaboration Efforts. In the mid-1980s, many states established efforts to bring together providers of different programs to discuss and plan how to achieve common goals. These coordinative efforts took several forms: (1) within-government cabinets, often called Children's Cabinets; (2) within-government management teams, comprising primarily mid-level bureaucrats from state agencies and often established to support and complement the higher profile Children's Cabinets; (3) state-level collaboratives, often labeled as Task Forces or Councils and established to meet a single need such as to create a strategic plan or address a legislative issue; (4) managing partnerships, created to oversee new large-scale and long-term programs; and (5) state–local partnerships, wherein local entities had specific responsibilities that were coordinated with a state-level entity.

A substantive part of early childhood's history, these efforts continue to guide many states' alignment work and provide useful and, in many cases, highly visible venues for collaborative processes and decision making. Many of these entities, however, lack the legal authority or accountability to enforce their processes or decisions. In response to this, some states have taken bold steps to restructure the organization of government itself.

Structural Changes to State Government. Since the turn of the 21st century, a small number of states have made structural changes to state government. To better coordinate and align programs, services, and funding streams, states have combined and integrated administrative responsibilities within a single agency or entity. Three states—Georgia, Massachusetts, and Washington—have each created an entirely new state agency dedicated to early care and education. Labeled as *stand-alone administrative integration* (Kagan & Kauerz, 2009), these newly established executive branch agencies have powers similar to other state departments, namely, a secretary or commissioner with responsibilities equivalent or similar to those of gubernatorial cabinet members, their own staff, and their own monitoring, regulatory, fiscal, and enforcement duties. Chapter 16 provides a perspective on Massachusetts's efforts.

Pennsylvania took a similar approach and created a new entity, albeit not a new department, to oversee the administration of the state's child development and early learning efforts. Jointly overseen by the Department of Public Welfare and the Department of Education, the Office of Child Development and Early Learning (OCDEL) was established in 2004. Discussed in Chapter 17, OCDEL provides a framework of supports and services that help ensure that all families have access to high-quality services. OCDEL executes administrative, fiscal, and monitoring functions without creating an independent state agency.

Another approach to creating structural change inside government is *subsumed administrative integration* wherein a subunit (e.g., a division or department) of an existing agency is given authority for ECE. In this model, programs and funding are consolidated in a unit within an existing state agency that has a broader scope. For example, Maryland, North Carolina, Ohio, and Tennessee have consolidated ECE programs within a unit in their state Departments of Education; and Arkansas did so in a unit within the Department of Human Services.

Notable about these structural changes to state government is that they focus on one domain of the early childhood system—they all strive to better align programs, services, standards, and funding streams within the early care and education domain. None of them incorporate the full complement of comprehensive systems work that includes health, mental health, and family support, instead focusing on the integration and administrative consolidation *within* ECE. Moreover, these approaches focus primarily on the realignment of within-government offices, services, and funding streams.

TWO NECESSARY GOVERNANCE MODELS

Based on the scope, variety, and impact of these federal and state efforts, as well as our analysis of what the field needs to bring more coherence and stability to system building, we contend that governance must be at the core of early childhood systems work, but that *two* different forms of governance are needed.

First, the early care and education domain, one of the independent ovals in the widely popularized diagram, does not currently function as a system in and of itself. As a result, linking and aligning ECE to other systems (e.g., health, mental health, family support) is messy, idiosyncratic, and often unduly complicated. To establish ECE as a functioning system that can be aligned with other systems that, together, form a comprehensive early childhood system, there must be intentional and intensive efforts to establish within-government governance for early care and education. Second, in order to establish comprehensive early childhood systems, cross-sector governance efforts must be undertaken that formalize the relationships between ECE and other domains. Graphically, the within-government form is directed exclusively to the early care and education oval itself (see Figure 2.1). The cross-sector form is directed to the area where the ECE domain overlaps with health, mental health, family support, and other service sectors.

Both of these governance efforts—within-government and cross-sector— bring greater alignment and coherence to early childhood programs and services and to systems themselves. The forms of governance and the systems they link, however, are quite distinct. One must address the agencies and entities that exist within government. Termed in this chapter *within-government* governance, this form primarily restructures existing government agencies, merging administrative authorities, or creates new entities within government. The second form, termed in this chapter *cross-sector* governance, structurally transcends government and brings together programs and services from both public and private sectors and across multiple extant systems (e.g., health, mental health, child welfare, ECE). Rather than creating new government agencies, this form of governance links and aligns, although it does not necessarily merge, separate administrative authorities.

While the *form* of these two governance types differs, they should share common *functions* and use similar governing *tools*. Both should derive their legitimacy from the democratic process and be publicly sanctioned. Both should be imbued with the authority to act in the public good and be accountable for those actions. In order to coordinate disparate services, to increase access to and improve the quality of services, and to streamline administrative and management functions, both types of governance should rely on the development and implementation of common standards (for children, programs, and practitioners), common budgets, and shared data systems.

For the field to move forward most effectively, we believe there needs to be greater conceptual clarity about the differences between the two types of governance efforts, as well as greater intentionality to infuse both types with authority and accountability. To this end, we explicate the differences between within-government and cross-sector governance approaches and discern how each should embody what we consider to be the essential functions of meaningful governance: authority and accountability.

Within-Government Governance

A 2008 review of governance efforts (National Child Care Information and Technical Assistance Center, 2008) highlights the compelling need for within-government coordination and governance. The within-government entity responsible for key early care and education functions—including child care subsidy, licensing, quality initiatives, Head Start State Collaboration, and state-funded prekindergarten—was chronicled in each of the

50 states and the District of Columbia. The distribution of these essential functions occurred in just one agency in only three places (Maryland, Pennsylvania, and the District of Columbia). Of the remaining 48 states, 16 had functions distributed between two state agencies; 24 had functions distributed among three agencies; 5 among four agencies; and 3 among five agencies. Clearly, mechanisms to bridge these key functions across multiple departments within a single state are necessary. Within-government governance, functioning primarily as an arm of government and deriving legitimacy from the rule of law, permits early care and education to function as a unified domain.

Efforts to establish within-government entities to organize and manage a social sector are not new; the current trends in ECE mirror what happened in higher education decades ago. As postsecondary enrollment grew dramatically between 1950 and 1980, states created new organizational structures to govern higher education; by 1979, every state had such an entity (Venezia, Callan, Finney, Kirst, & Usdan, 2005). The impetus behind these efforts was to guide, steer, control, and manage a sector of society that previously had been scattered and regulated by different (at best) or conflicting (at worst) policies.

Any time such consolidation takes place within government, the process is slow and what may be seen by some as streamlining governance functions may be regarded by others as fragmentation. In ECE, for example, where a new entity has been established, there has been some fear that its existence might fragment effective relationships with state departments of education. It is for this reason that some states have elected to place their within-government governance efforts inside departments of education (e.g., Maryland, North Carolina, Ohio, and Tennessee), while others have sought to establish linkage mechanisms between the new department and the existing department of education (e.g., Georgia, Massachusetts, Pennsylvania, and Washington).

With only a few states having undertaken meaningful governance reform of this type and with the varying organization of the within-government entity, no one approach has been rigorously evaluated and deemed to be preferable to any other. Where such within-government entities exist, however, they demonstrate clarity of authority and accountability. Across all of the ECE approaches, within-government governance works to ensure that all publicly supported programs are expected to attain quality standards, and assisted in doing so, for themselves and for their teachers, to be affordable and meet the needs and demands of the local community, to be cost-effective, and to provide children with meaningful experiences that prepare them to be successful lifelong learners.

Cross-Sector Governance

The fragmentation of ECE-related services is not the only governance challenge facing early childhood system building. As noted in chapters throughout this volume, most states recognize that crucial services for young children extend beyond the conventional boundaries of ECE. Many have established cross-sector councils that guide comprehensive planning efforts and focus on the intersection of multiple systems, including ECE, health, mental health, family engagement, child welfare, K–12 education, and other community supports. Typically, these cross-sector entities include multiple state agencies and private-sector organizations that agree to engage in collaborative work that often leads to joint commitments regarding cross-agency/program standards and eligibility requirements.

Efforts to establish cross-sector forms of governance are similar to those in other fields where shifts toward decentralization and the ever-increasing complexity of public problems—problems that cross-cut multiple areas of policy and their policy subsystems—require the leadership and influence of multiple government agencies (often at multiple levels) *and* a range of private actors. In this form of governance, the overarching system is less hierarchical and less centralized, and has fewer defined boundaries than those addressed by within-government governance. Some scholars have labeled these efforts as "boundary-spanning policy regimes [that] are usefully characterized as governing arrangements that foster integrative actions across elements of multiple subsystems" (Jochim & May, 2010, p. 304). Accordingly, there is no clear-cut organizational chart because the multitude of programs and funding streams that comprise the system criss-cross not just government departments and government levels, but also nongovernment entities. Here, governance must transcend any single agency or program and establish interdependencies between public and private entities at multiple levels. To do so and to achieve coherence, cross-sector governance approaches often establish a rich set of contractual arrangements, relationships, and agreements.

FUNCTIONS OF GOVERNANCE

Whether talking about within-government or cross-sector approaches, the essential functions of governance—authority and accountability—should remain the same. A meaningful governance structure or mechanism relies on both functions to define, maintain, and, where necessary, enforce an efficient, equitable, and high-quality framework for programs and services. In the next pages, we articulate how authority and accountability can be established and achieved within both forms of governance.

Authority

At its core, the authority function is what makes governance entities more than symbolic in nature. Authority empowers governance entities to make, prioritize, and take action on decisions related to regulations, finance, and data. Authority guides action and enforces decisions.

Authority, especially in the context of systems work, has two valences: negative and positive (Kohler-Koch & Rittberger, 2006). When a governance entity removes barriers or obstacles to integration, this is negative authority; barrier busting is a prevalent and legitimate activity in early childhood systems work. In contrast, when decisions are made that construct (or reconstruct) a regulatory system that encompasses previously smaller or fragmented programs, this is positive authority. Examples include the development and enforcement of regulations that (a) entitle and govern facilities' operation; (b) establish criteria for the necessary competencies and qualifications that enable individuals to practice in a field; (c) influence the distribution of services (e.g., eligibility levels, co-payments, or fees); and (d) establish aligned standards and assessment (Kagan & Kauerz, 2009).

Authority in Within-Government Approaches. Authority in within-government governance structures is achieved through a highly visible and centralized decision-making entity. For example, a new state agency—with a presence on the governor's cabinet and a fiscal allocation from the state legislature—becomes the center of power, imbued with the authority of similar public agencies. Here, clear lines of authority exist for establishing and enforcing aligned and shared standards across programs, for budgeting and managing fiscal resources, and for collecting and analyzing data. In within-government governance, authority is linear and often rests on clear, unambiguous "ownership" of programs, services, and funding streams (e.g., all programs that provide learning environments for children prior to school entry are under the administrative leadership of a single agency).

Authority in Cross-Sector Approaches. In cross-sector governance, consolidation of authority is not always feasible and rarely desirable. For example, consolidating the authority for children's health insurance, medical homes, social-emotional screenings and follow-up care, early care and education programs, early elementary school (kindergarten through grade 3), and family support services for children from birth through age 8 would create a large, unwieldy, unfocused state agency. Such a behemoth would be unnecessarily fragmented from the health care system for older children and adults, from the public education systems serving children in grades 4 through 12 and beyond, and from the social service systems in place for at-risk families.

In cross-sector governance, multiple authorities exist. *Decision-making* authority is centralized in a cross-agency or cross-sector council or commission, but *implementation and management* authority is diffused to different agencies and different players. Despite their independent structures, the multiple authorities are coordinated, striving toward similar goals and enforcing similar decisions.

Within comprehensive systems work, authority often is derived from and built upon interaction and mutual relations around common standards. For example, a cross-sector governing entity may lead the development of a common set of early learning standards. These standards can be adopted by, and enforced in, multiple independent agencies across both public and private sectors. The early learning agency may adopt the standards to define what children should know and be able to do. The health agency may adopt the standards to define appropriate physical, motor, and communicative developmental pathways. The K–12 education agency may adopt the standards to define "school readiness." Agencies and organizations retain considerable implementation control and autonomy, yet the common standards fundamentally transform the ways in which the agencies and organizations go about their business.

In many ways, authority in the cross-sector approach depends on whether a cross-agency or cross-sector council or commission becomes both institutionalized and legitimized to the extent that it becomes respected as *the* place where consensual, common decisions are made and where expectations for enactment are created across a mix of state and nonstate actors. In other words, authority can be exerted when a council or coordinating entity gains both importance and influence within the overall power structure of the field and the organizational ecology (Mitchell & Shortell, 2000). Authority also rests on the legitimacy of the contractual relations between the members of the council (e.g., the strength of memoranda of understanding that clearly delineate expectations for the implementation of shared standards). These variables of institutionalization, legitimacy, and influence are what separate councils and commissions that have *governing authority* from those that are simply collaborative venues for discussion and recommendation making. Cross-sector governing, firmly imbued with authority, is still in its embryonic stages in the early childhood field. Examples of highly authoritative cross-sector governance entities exist in other fields, though. The European Union is perhaps the largest and most prominent example. It is a "system of governance characterized by a unique set of multi-level, non-hierarchical and regulatory institutions, and a hybrid mix of state and non-state actors" (Kohler-Koch and Rittberger, 2006, p. 33).

Accountability

Governance includes accountability *to* someone or some entity and accountability *for* something (Posner, 2002). Taking the "to" first, a governance entity has accountability to those who have a stake in the performance of the governed endeavor. For example, governance can involve accountability to elected officials, interest groups, clients of the direct services provided, the media, and others. The range of people to whom accountability is accorded largely determines which interests frame the debate and the ultimate objectives of the effort(s). In early childhood, governance "for" something typically translates into four kinds of accountability that are highly related: (1) fiscal accountability, or whether money is spent efficiently and for the purposes for which it was intended; (2) program accountability, or whether programs meet specified levels of quality and are accessible to appropriate populations; (3) workforce accountability, or whether the adults who provide professional services meet specified levels of qualifications and are effective in their job roles; and (4) performance accountability, or the effectiveness or achievement of desired outcomes for children and families. Just like authority, accountability can be achieved in both forms of governance, primarily through the governing tools of common standards (for children, programs, and practitioners), common budgets, and shared data systems.

Accountability in Within-Government Approaches. With clear, hierarchical lines of authority—like those found in within-government forms of governance—accountability can be fairly straightforward, although few states have established full-fledged accountability systems for early care and education. Most states have mechanisms for some types of accountability. For example, all states collect data on programs via licensing and enforcement systems, and increasingly, as Chapter 4 indicates, quality rating and improvement systems are being developed to enhance these data and to collect data on the early childhood workforce. As states establish within-government governance for ECE, common budgets will lend themselves to greater fiscal accountability and the capacity to provide information on system-wide investments, costs, and returns on investment. Similarly, unified data systems will lend themselves to greater program, workforce, and performance accountability. As detailed in Chapter 7, the collection and analysis of data that can serve as reliable barometers of effectiveness, and therefore as marks of accountability, are increasingly accepted functions of within-government governance.

Accountability in Cross-Sector Approaches. Within cross-sector governance models, accountability is shared and the partnering organizations must find standard and institutionalized measures of effectiveness (Mitchell & Shortell, 2000). Shared accountability relies on a clear and common vision or framework for the purpose and goals of the mutual work (see, for example, Chapter 13); shared standards (see Chapter 3); common, longitudinal data systems (see Chapter 7); and comprehensive budgets (see Chapter 19).

In cross-sector governance, *what* the system is held accountable for remains the same as for within-government forms (i.e., fiscal, program, workforce, and performance accountability); it is the process of *how* that accountability is established that differs. Accountability gets built into the culture of cross-sector work by investing in collective responsibility. Accountability in cross-sector governance has been called intelligent, meaning it is established through a process that involves building cumulative capacity and responsibility that is both internally held and externally reinforced (Fullan, 2010). In other words, accountability is almost a kind of system-level peer pressure. "It is not, then, whether to have standards and assessments that is the question, but rather the crucial variable is *how they are used*. You get more authentic and powerful accountability paradoxically by getting at it indirectly through collective capacity building" (Fullan, 2010, p. 70, emphasis in original).

We conclude that while two different forms of governance need to be addressed and integrated into early childhood system efforts, both forms must be infused with authority and accountability and both must strive to establish common standards (for children, programs, and practitioners), common budgets, and shared data systems. Lacking authority and accountability, efforts to coordinate and align programs and services in early childhood will lack the meaningful properties of true governance.

LOOKING FORWARD:
GOVERNANCE AND EARLY CHILDHOOD SYSTEMS

Our analysis of governance focuses less on the nuts and bolts of how to build effective early childhood governance structures and far more on how to strategically think about what capacities they should have. Given that we strongly endorse both within-government and cross-sector governance as essential to fulfilling the long-term vision of an early childhood system, we close the chapter with reflections and recommendations.

Governance Doesn't Solve Everything

While it is tempting to endorse governance as the essential strategy, and we do consider it absolutely fundamental, governance is not the silver bullet to early childhood system building. Governance structures by themselves do not ensure meaningful processes of change or implementation of good practices. Governance must be constructed and enacted along with other elements of a system, many of which are discussed in this volume. Governance may stand as a centerpiece of early childhood system-building efforts, but it cannot stand as the only piece.

Furthermore, we have discussed governance as a mechanism to coordinate and align programs and policies at the agency or organization level. What we do not discuss, but what also have a profound impact on early childhood systems, are the structures and forms that the legislative branch of government takes. For example, a new within-government state agency may serve as the coordinating management structure for child care, prekindergarten, Head Start State Collaboration, and early intervention services, but the committee structure of the state legislature may have child care issues addressed by a human services committee, prekindergarten issues addressed by an education committee, and workforce issues addressed by a labor committee. Governance reform at the administrative level is not the same as governance at the legislative level.

Governance Should Simplify, Not Complicate

Achieving an integrated governance system is neither automatic nor easy. It is made complex by the nature of the disciplines, by the number of the players and jurisdictions represented in the early childhood enterprise, and by the sheer force of politics. Before tackling such a Herculean effort, it is important to be aware that, if we are not careful, creating governance entities can be similar to a shell game. Indeed, "centralizing efforts can just add administrative complexity and new layers of accountability" (Clune, 1993, p. 244). As Klein points out in her vision piece (Chapter 2, this volume), much time and money can be spent creating fancy governance that ultimately has no impact on children's outcomes. When considering governance, we need to be certain that our efforts contribute to streamlining linkages, not to creating more complexity.

Governance Should Be Durable, Yet Dynamic

Governance must walk the tightrope between being durable and being dynamic. Meaningful governance does not come and go, but is lasting. To that end, it must transcend political administrations. But to have durable impact, governance entities also must have dynamism and flexibility to change and adapt with shifting administrations and policy priorities. Such balance is best achieved when the creation and dissolution of governance entities require stakeholder input, bipartisan agreement, and official action by a political institution.

One Solution Doesn't Fit All

As this chapter clearly suggests, there is no single form of governance that fits all situations. Within-government governance approaches will vary, as will cross-sector approaches. Such variation needs to be framed by state and local context, existing patterns of governance, strengths of the governorship and the legislature, and the history of collaboration that has characterized early childhood and human service delivery. Having noted the necessity of such variation, it is also worth repeating yet again that the two forms of governance discussed herein (within-government and cross-sector) are needed.

In closing, governance is essential to early childhood systems. We believe, though, that many discussions of and efforts to establish governance often confound and confuse two distinctly different forms of governance. Establishing within-government governance entities for early care and education is a necessity for ultimately realizing a fully comprehensive early childhood system; efforts to build and strengthen cross-sector governance entities that span multiple systems and both public and private sectors are also a necessity. Both forms of governance must have authority and accountability, functions that many extant "governance" efforts lack. We do not pretend that this work is easy or clear-cut. We do know, however, that states around the country are taking bold and creative steps to re-imagine what will best support young children and their families. Governance should remain a clear priority for this work.

REFERENCES

Clune, W. H. (1993). The best path to systemic educational policy: Standard/centralized or differentiated/decentralized? *Educational Evaluation and Policy Analysis, 15*(3), 233–254.

Fullan, M. (2010). *All systems go: The change imperative for whole system reform.* Thousand Oaks, CA: Corwin.

Hajer, M. (2006). The living institutions of the EU: Analysing governance as performance. *Perspectives on European Politics and Society, 7*(1), 41–55.

Harbin, G., & McNulty, B. (1990). Policy implementation: Perspectives on service coordination and interagency cooperation. In S. J. Meisels & J. P. Shonkoff (Eds.), *Handbook of early childhood intervention* (pp. 700–721). New York: Cambridge University Press.

Jochim, A. E., & May, P. J. (2010). Beyond subsystems: Policy regimes and governance. *Policy Studies Journal, 38*(2), 303–327.

Kagan, S. L. (1991). *United we stand: Collaboration for child care and early education services.* New York: Teachers College Press.

Kagan, S. L. (1993). *Integrating services for children and families: Understanding the past to shape the future.* New Haven, CT: Yale University Press.

Kagan, S. L., & Kauerz, K. (2009). Governing American early care and education: Shifting from government to governance and from form to function. In S. Feeney, A. Galper, & C. Seefeldt (Eds.), *Continuing issues in early childhood education* (3rd ed., pp. 12–32). Upper Saddle River, NJ: Pearson.

Kohler-Koch, B., & Rittberger, B. (2006). Review article: The "governance turn" in EU studies. *Journal of Common Market Studies, 44*, 27–49.

Kooiman, J. (1993). *Modern governance: New government–society interactions.* London: Sage.

Mitchell, S. M., & Shortell, S. M. (2000). The governance and management of effective community health partnerships: A typology for research, policy, and practice. *The Milbank Quarterly, 78*(2), 241–289.

National Child Care Information and Technical Assistance Center. (2008). *Early child care and education: State governance structures.* Retrieved from http://nccic.acf.hhs.gov/poptopics/ece_structure.html?&printfriendly=true

Posner, P. L. (2002). Accountability challenges of third-party government. In L. M. Salamon (Ed.), *The tools of government: A guide to the new governance* (pp. 523–551). New York: Oxford University Press.

Salamon, L. M. (2002). The new governance and the tools of public action: An introduction. In L. M. Salamon (Ed.), *The tools of government: A guide to the new governance* (pp. 1–47). New York: Oxford University Press.

Satkowski, C. (2009). *The next step in systems-building: Early childhood advisory councils and federal efforts to promote policy alignment in early childhood.* Washington, DC: New America Foundation.

Steiner, G. Y. (1976). *The children's cause.* Washington, DC: Brookings Institution.

Sugarman, J. (1989). Federal support revisited. In F. J. Macchiarola & A. Gartner (Eds.), *Caring for America's children* (pp. 99–109). New York: Academy of Political Science.

Venezia, A., Callan, P. M., Finney, J. E., Kirst, M., & Usdan, M. D. (2005). *The governance divide: A report on a four-state study on improving college readiness and success.* San Jose, CA: National Center for Public Policy and Higher Education.

CHAPTER 6

Professional Development in Early Childhood Systems

Marilou Hyson and Jessica Vick Whittaker

The evidence is clear: Quality early care and education promotes success in school and in life, especially for the poorest and most vulnerable children (e.g., Peisner-Feinberg et al., 2001). Yet low-quality teaching remains the norm in many programs (LoCasale-Crouch et al., 2007), and we still know too little about the kinds of education and training needed to affect positive child outcomes (Sheridan, Pope Edwards, Marvin, & Knoche, 2009; Zaslow, Tout, Halle, Vick Whittaker, & Lavelle, in press). Despite these challenges or perhaps stimulated by them, professional development has become a central feature of national- and state-level early childhood system-building initiatives.

Yet the desire to move quickly needs to be tempered with an equal measure of reflection and stock-taking if the benefits of early childhood professional development (ECPD) are to be widespread and sustainable. This chapter aims to contribute to that process. We begin by outlining the key components of ECPD systems. Then, after briefly tracing the origins of today's focus on ECPD systems from the late 1980s onward, we offer a current picture of early childhood professional development, describing its status within national and state-level systems. That picture includes close-up snapshots of three states (Delaware, New Mexico, and Pennsylvania) that illustrate diverse ways in which ECPD systems are being strengthened. The chapter will conclude by identifying persistent gaps and new opportunities to improve ECPD as an essential component of early care and education systems.

ELEMENTS AND EVOLVING CONTEXTS OF ECPD SYSTEMS

Conceptualizations of ECPD systems typically identify a set of key features, components, or elements needed in those systems. A good deal of consistency may be seen in various descriptions of ECPD system elements, although each description differs in organization, level of detail, and emphasis (e.g., Kagan, Kauerz, & Tarrant, 2008; National Association for the Education of Young Children, 2009; National Child Care Information and Technical Assistance Center, 2009). As seen in Table 6.1, we propose that these descriptions may be consolidated around six elements. Each element, in our view, corresponds with an important question about ECPD, can be linked to specific indicators, and at least potentially connects with aspects of the broader system of early care and education. Although there is a risk that attention to these elements can become a mechanical end in itself rather than a means to the end of program improvement and better child outcomes, this chapter offers many examples of how thoughtful consideration and implementation of these elements have served as meaningful guides.

With these elements in mind, a look back at the evolution of the "ECPD system" concept from the late 1980s onward may help place today's system-building efforts in context.

The first wave of results from the National Child Care Staffing Study (Whitebook, Howes, & Phillips, 1989) documented the generally low quality of U.S. child care and highlighted the need for much greater attention to caregiver education and training. Yet harsh realities intruded: Those seeking professional development had only limited access and even more limited pathways leading from community-based training toward higher education credentials.

Delaware's experiences illustrate some of the influences on the evolution of ECPD in those early years. By 1990, Delaware's Office of Child Care Licensing and other ECE leaders saw that simply investing state dollars in more of the same kind of training was yielding only marginal improvements in child care quality. A more systemic approach was needed. With technical assistance from Wheelock College, Delaware fleshed out its ideas about potential elements of an ECPD framework. Parts of this framework, including core competencies with aligned training content, training calendars, training approval mechanisms, evaluation of prior learning, higher education articulation plans, and other features, persist today and can be found in our description of ECPD elements (see Table 6.1).

Although Delaware was first (National Child Care Information and Technical Assistance Center, 2009), ECPD system building quickly took hold in other states, notably through "Partners in Change" (PIC) projects with the newly established Wheelock Center for Career Development in Early Care and Education. During the same period the National Association for the Education of Young Children (NAEYC) also played a significant role. With initial support from the Carnegie Foundation, in 1992 NAEYC began annual meetings of its National Institute on Early Childhood Pro-

TABLE 6.1. Elements of an Early Childhood Professional Development System

Overall Goal/Desired Outcome: To positively influence outcomes for young children and families through the development of skilled, knowledgeable, and committed ECE personnel within a system that decreases duplication of effort and increases sustainability and accountability.

Guiding Question	ECPD System Component	Indicators	Potential links to overall ECE system
1. What should ECE personnel know and be able to do?	Core knowledge/ standards	• An evidence-based core body of knowledge, skills, and dispositions is agreed upon • Differentiation is made according to ECE personnel roles and levels • Core knowledge base is widely known and shared • Core knowledge base (with differentiations) is regularly reviewed and revised in light of new evidence and needs in field	Core knowledge/standards for ECE personnel are aligned with early learning standards and ECE program standards
2. How do future and current ECE personnel gain necessary knowledge and skills?	Access	• Future and current ECE personnel are well informed about PD opportunities • All ECE personnel have access to PD • Professional development includes multiple entry points, articulation between PD settings, and pathways to multiple roles across sectors • Multiple delivery systems ensure access and meet diverse needs	Professional development reaches out to ECE personnel across multiple sectors and ECE program auspices, responding to emerging needs in the broad ECE field
3. How is professional development recognized and rewarded?	Recognition	• Specific professional roles are linked with required qualifications • Credentials linked to progressive ECPD levels are clearly established and publicly recognized • Incentives and compensation are in place to encourage participation and progress	Credentials should be consistent across ECE program types and sectors
4. What ensures that ECPD is of high quality?	Quality assurance	• Standards describe expectations for quality ECPD • Credible research guides the establishment of quality criteria • ECPD is monitored to review and approve quality of content and delivery	Standards should align with other relevant ECE standards (e.g., program quality and child outcomes); assessment of ECE program quality should address provision of high-quality PD
5. How is the overall ECPD system governed and supported?	Governance and financing	• Structures are in place to oversee the ECPD system and its implementation • Stable financial support for the ECPD system is ensured	Governance and financial support, including funds for ECPD incentives and system development, should be integrated into the overall ECE system
6. How are overall ECPD effectiveness and impact evaluated?	Evaluation	• Evidence-based criteria for judging the effectiveness and impact of ECPD have been established • High-quality processes for collecting, analyzing, and using data on ECPD effectiveness are implemented	ECPD evaluation should be embedded in and inform overall evaluation of the ECE system

fessional Development, aiming to address "the barriers to achieving an articulated, coordinated professional development system for early childhood educators" (Bredekamp, 1992). During these early years NAEYC also disseminated several influential concept papers (e.g., Bredekamp & Willer, 1992), which offered a rationale for a coordinated, high-quality ECPD systems approach that, in hindsight, had features of today's focus on working across "sectors."[1]

NEW POLICIES, NEW CONTEXTS, NEW RESEARCH

No one event marks a transition from these early beginnings to more recent ECPD work. Federal and state initiatives and new research findings together led to expansion and some rethinking of ECPD issues.

Federal Policies

The 1998 Head Start reauthorization, with its college degree mandates, stimulated efforts to increase higher education access for Head Start staff. At the same time, the mandate prompted debates about the value of college degrees in general. The 1997 reauthorization of the Individuals with Disabilities Education Act (IDEA) created incentives for states to plan comprehensive, high-quality personnel preparation systems in early intervention and early childhood special education, with implications for—but not always connected to—general ECPD. Starting in 2002, the federal "Good Start/Grow Smart" initiative (No Child Left Behind's early education reform component) called on states to create professional development plans aligned with states' early learning guidelines, and to help ECPD delivery systems work in concert across sectors. Taken together, these federal initiatives raised the bar for personnel qualifications and credentials, created incentives for state ECPD system planning, and yet maintained some of the sector divisions that had characterized previous ECPD work.

State Initiatives

State-funded prekindergarten programs and state quality rating and improvement systems (QRIS) have both affected aspects of ECPD. State-funded pre-K programs often mandate bachelor's degrees and certification consistent with public school staff requirements (Barnett, Epstein, Friedman, Stevenson Boyd, & Hustedt, 2008). The growth in the number of states with QRIS also has significant implications for ECPD systems, as many QRIS link levels of staff education and training to ratings of program quality (Child Care Bureau, 2007).

Research

Just as 1990s ECPD system building was influenced by child care quality research, more recent research has stimulated new thinking about ECPD modalities and methods. First, there is now ample evidence that "one-shot" workshops are generally ineffective, but that job-embedded professional development, especially individual technical assistance such as coaching and mentoring, may predict improved teaching practices and child outcomes (Pianta, 2006; Sheridan et al., 2009; Zaslow et al., in press). More controversial but potentially beneficial are research findings that raise questions about the belief that "degrees make a difference" in program quality and ultimately in children's development and learning (Early et al., 2007). For ECPD systems, the often-contentious degree debate may yield greater emphasis on ECPD content and quality, rather than just on the degree itself (Hyson, Tomlinson, & Morris, 2008). State profiles will offer examples of how these and other research findings have influenced ECPD systems decisions.

STATE PROFILES:
DIVERSE PATHWAYS TOWARD COMMON GOALS

In this section of the chapter, we profile ECPD systems in three states (Delaware, New Mexico, and Pennsylvania). Despite their distinctive histories and characteristics, these states—and many others—consistently have incorporated into their ECPD systems the elements summarized in Table 6.1. Yet our interviews with state leaders and review of their ECPD documents suggest that in different ways each has critically analyzed these elements, shifted priorities over time, responded to new demands and knowledge, and created new linkages across ECE sectors.

We introduce each profile with some background and selected highlights of that state's past ECPD work.[2] With that context in mind, we offer examples of states' recent strategic decisions and plans to strengthen one or more of their ECPD system elements.

Delaware

As described earlier, Delaware was the first state to implement a statewide "career development system." Like many others, it focused on the child care sector and the training requirements of its Office of Child Care Licensing. Influenced by Quality 2000/*Not by Chance* (Kagan & Cohen,

1997), the state soon took a wider view, in the mid-1990s developing a comprehensive ECE system plan (Early Success) that incorporated and expanded elements of the earlier ECPD system. The establishment of an early care and education office within the Department of Education widened the scope of ECE and ECPD, positioning it favorably for cross-sector work. Additionally, ECPD, including technical assistance, was a central feature of the state's QRIS, established in 2005.

Recent Strategic Decisions. With this foundation, Delaware's recent establishment of a statewide early childhood institute is being used to strengthen and integrate ECPD into other components of its ECE system. Special attention appears to be given to ECPD quality assurance, governance, and evaluation.

In 2008, the Delaware Department of Education awarded a contract to a partnership led by the University of Delaware to establish the Delaware Institute for Excellence in Early Childhood (DIEEC). Housed within the University and with blended funding from federal child care and education agencies, the state Department of Education, and private foundations, the DIEEC is responsible for coordinating two key aspects of the state's ECE system: (1) Delaware Stars (the state QRIS), and (2) the state's ECPD efforts, now encompassing public schools as well as center- and home-based child care. The DIEEC's dual focus was designed to ensure that ECPD would align with and directly support ECE program improvement and improved child outcomes.

Besides tapping into higher education's strengths in research and evaluation, the decision to house the DIEEC in an institution of higher education was strategically important for another reason. A high priority for the state has been to increase and institutionalize higher education's involvement in all aspects of Delaware's ECE quality improvement efforts, including ECPD.

Evaluation, Quality Assurance, and Governance. Delaware's future priorities flow logically from its current activities. Evaluation of ECPD, with a key role for the DIEEC and linked to evaluation in the overall ECE system, will be a special focus in the next decade. One feature of this emphasis on evaluation is Delaware's plan for an integrated data system that will incorporate data from the child care/ECE Personnel Registry and the K–12 public school data system, again linking the ECPD and ECE systems efforts. Ultimately the vision is for these data to contribute to a large-scale, ongoing evaluation of ECE program quality and impact on child/family outcomes.

New Mexico

Like Delaware, another PIC state, New Mexico was one of the first to develop an ECPD system, with core competencies and other key features. The 1990 creation of a state Office of Child Development and Child Development Board has provided consistent governance and leadership.

Distinctive in New Mexico was the early, consistent engagement of higher education institutions in its system-building work. Among other accomplishments, the state's Higher Education Task Force (representing all public colleges) agreed upon a "universal catalog of courses" for associate and baccalaureate degree programs, with cross-institution articulation agreements. Collaboration between ECE and early childhood special education faculty resulted in the development of an inclusive (blended) ECE birth–grade 3 bachelor's degree. Collaboration and coordination also marked an agreement among multiple state agencies to use the Department of Education's teacher licensure system for those with bachelor's degrees and above, and to use Children, Youth, and Family's certification system for those with associate's degrees and below.

Recent Strategic Decisions. Until recently, New Mexico's career lattice and higher education coursework focused on one career path—early childhood classroom teacher. However, in New Mexico and elsewhere, professional roles have grown and diversified as the field has evolved and as new needs have emerged.

In response to this evolution and to feedback from providers and community partners, New Mexico recently has made significant changes to the scope of its ECPD system. While still beginning with a common core, personnel can then select one of three "professional pathways": early childhood teacher (now further differentiated into two licenses: birth–age 4 and age 3–grade 3); early childhood program administrator; and family infant toddler studies (including early intervention and home visiting). These new directions have implications for New Mexico's previously established competencies, professional recognition, and ECPD access. A specific challenge will be to rework New Mexico's teacher competencies and coursework to align with, and ensure quality within, each of these new pathways.

Creating a Unified, Community-Based Training and Technical Assistance System. In contrast to higher education's well-coordinated ECPD presence, the Office of Child Development has had concern about the continuing fragmentation and "silos" in the delivery of community-based training, where sectors continue to operate in relative isolation from one another.

Such isolation has created obstacles to training access and quality assurance. Now that funding streams for different sectors are becoming increasingly braided together, and as more programs are combining services, New Mexico sees opportunities to create greater unity, easier access, and more consistent quality in its training and technical assistance system.

Pennsylvania

Pennsylvania's ECPD systems work began later than in some other states but quickly gained momentum as a vision and collective will to succeed emerged. In 2000, using the PIC framework, Pennsylvania created its initial ECPD system plan, now called Pennsylvania Pathways. This and other components that were put into place through 2005 laid a foundation for later implementation of a fully cross-sector system with strong professional development components. For example, participants in Keystone Stars, Pennsylvania's QRIS, include family providers, school-age programs, Head Start, school districts, and accrediting bodies. Similarly, PA Pre-K Counts, a public/private initiative to create high-quality prekindergarten programs, funds teams across multiple ECE sectors.

Recent Strategic Decisions. As part of the governor's commitment to prioritize early learning, Pennsylvania unified its early childhood programs across the Departments of Public Welfare and Education in the Office of Child Development and Early Learning (OCDEL). The work of OCDEL focuses on ensuring that all programs sponsored with public resources meet high standards for programs, practitioners, and children. This focus has spurred extensive reform and forward momentum for professional development in the entire early childhood system. System components include and integrate Keystone Stars (QRIS), PA Pre-K Counts (quality preschool), early intervention (birth to age 5), Child Care Works (subsidized child care), and family support programs.

Targeting Higher Education. Several specific steps aim to strengthen higher education's role in expanding ECPD access and quality assurance. Pennsylvania will continue to support program-to-program articulation projects between 2- and 4-year institutions. Nine articulation agreements recently have been signed. Pennsylvania has significantly increased financial support for the T.E.A.C.H. Early Childhood Project ® and a voucher reimbursement program to help ECE teachers earn degrees and credentials and move up the career lattice. There will be continued efforts to work with higher education to address barriers to full-time ECE staff accessing courses and continuing education. With more demand for ECE courses, Pennsylvania is working on developing a doctorate in ECE at a state university, to ensure a supply of faculty to meet the growing demand for ECE degrees.

Themes of Progress

The above profiles reflect diverse approaches to states' past, present, and future ECPD work. Despite this diversity, the profiles, along with interviews and reviews of state ECPD resources, also reveal common themes.

- *Leadership.* Consistent leadership, characterized by a clearly articulated vision of ECPD within the state's ECE system and by transparent communications, is essential in developing a successful ECPD system.
- *Meaningful Stakeholder Participation.* Early, meaningful, and continuous involvement of higher education, community programs, public schools, state government, and others promotes shared knowledge and ownership of the ECPD system.
- *Core Principles.* A clearly stated, agreed-upon set of foundational principles (e.g., a commitment that all ECPD decisions—such as articulation—must have statewide implementation), formed through a shared history and periodically reaffirmed, appears to keep ECPD systems development work on track.
- *Flexibility.* While staying true to core principles, successful ECPD systems must be flexible enough to respond to changing needs and new research evidence.
- *Location, Location, Location.* Positioning an office, a program, or an institute in the right institutional location often results in greater ECPD visibility and influence.
- *Seizing the Moment.* Knowing the right time to take action, capitalizing on windows of opportunity, often makes the difference between wasted time and a productive outcome.

CHALLENGES FOR THE FUTURE

The profiled states and many others have made substantial progress toward closing ECPD gaps with the goal of improving outcomes for children and families. Nevertheless, gaps persist and must be frankly identified.

ECPD Structure/Content Gaps

Although potentially valuable, the energy devoted to the *structure* of ECPD—building the system—can swamp the essential work of ensuring that the *standards, content, and pedagogy* used in ECPD are high quality and sufficiently evidence-based. Even the best-constructed, best-aligned, most fully "cross-sector" systems will not yield positive results unless the ECE curricula, specific teaching practices, and ECPD methods embedded in these systems are sound. For example, although in many states great effort has been invested in the structure, governance, and components of QRIS, less attention has been directed to the predictive validity of the systems' ECPD-related quality criteria. As others have noted (Satkowski, 2009b), the "second generation" of state QRIS may be in a good position to go beyond the limited criteria of training hours and years of education.

Sector Gaps

Despite notable progress in bringing together ECPD elements across sectors, in most states significant gaps remain (LeMoine, 2008), with professional development still targeted primarily at center-based preschool programs. With exceptions, ECPD efforts are not yet fully meeting the needs of the family child care and center-based infant–toddler sectors, nor do they encompass professional development within the public schools (including the primary grades) or out-of-school-time programs. Head Start's professional development often remains a separate enterprise, as does professional development within early intervention and early childhood special education. Finally, providers of unregulated care often lack access to appropriate resources and supports.

Higher Education Gaps

States have tried in many ways to involve the higher education system in ECPD. However, a divide often separates the "higher ed folks" (especially those in research-intensive universities) and those who work on ECPD outside of the higher education system. Even states that have made progress in narrowing this gap may struggle to sustain higher education's engagement in tasks such as developing evidence-based standards, crafting articulation agreements, contributing to the ECPD research base, or guiding delivery of ECPD outside their own degree programs. Yet without enhanced leadership from higher education institutions and without changes in institutional reward structures for faculty, ECPD systems will be less effective and less well-integrated than they should be.

Leadership Development Gaps

Across states, considerable progress has been made in leadership development and credentialing for child care directors. Beyond the child care sector, however, little has been done to address the needs of pre-K through grade 3 principals and other public school leaders. Additionally, targeted leadership development is needed for current or potential ECE leaders within higher education, state government, and other influential roles (Kagan et al., 2008). Early childhood academic leadership has a serious pipeline problem, with doctoral programs that are too few in number, have uneven quality, and have limited access for working ECE professionals. A related issue is the gap in continuing professional development for college and university faculty, made worse recently because of budget cuts and increased teaching loads. Without a continuously updated knowledge base, faculty are constrained in their ability to prepare knowledgeable, skilled ECE practitioners (Hyson et al., 2008).

Data Gaps

The state profiles include examples of how data are being used to inform ECPD plans, and many other states also are working to improve their data-gathering systems. However, gaps remain in the quality and extent of these efforts and in coordinating such efforts across sectors (such as linking personnel data from child care registries and public school databases). Federal and state program reporting requirements continue to differ, which makes it difficult to develop a unified early childhood data system (National Governors Association Center for Best Practices, 2010). Without coordination across sectors within states and across state and federal requirements, it will continue to be difficult to obtain an accurate picture of either the ECE workforce or the scope, nature, and effectiveness of professional development. Tools and support for coordination are likely to emerge from the new early childhood emphasis within the Data Quality Campaign, a national collaborative effort aimed at helping state policymakers use education data to improve student achievement.

A serious data gap also exists in ECPD research (Zaslow et al., in press). A high priority is to generate new research about the impact of various kinds and dosages of professional development on practitioners' behavior and related child outcomes, if states and others are to make good decisions about where to invest limited resources. Other priorities include research on teachers' openness to changing their practices and on the responsiveness of ECPD to linguistic and cultural diversity.

USING AVAILABLE RESOURCES TO CLOSE ECPD GAPS

Since the late 1980s, substantial progress has been made in (a) developing ECPD policies and systems to promote sustainability and accountability, and (b) generating more robust evidence about ECPD approaches that are likely to promote quality early learning and improved outcomes. Although a sound foundation has been established, much more needs to be done in both of these areas, and neither is well-enough coordinated with the other. To maintain momentum, it will be important to make the most of available resources and levers for ECPD improvement—federal and state policies as well as new or continuing funding opportunities. For example, the 2007 Improving Head Start for School Readiness law includes both additional ECPD requirements and a significant mandate for states to establish Early Childhood Advisory Councils (ECACs), which are intended to have state professional development planning as one of their core functions. A 2009 report (Satkowski, 2009a) documented that 30 states were in the process of developing their ECACs; in August 2010 states were able to apply for federal funding specifically to support their ECAC work. Because higher education representation is mandated, ECACs afford another opportunity to strengthen links across ECPD research, policy, and practice.

With help from a number of sources such as NAEYC's (2009) Workforce Systems Initiative, NCCIC's (2009) Early Childhood Professional Development Systems Toolkit, and the National Governors Association Center for Best Practices (2010), a critical mass of states has made significant progress in creating integrated ECPD systems with increased attention to ECPD content and supportive state policies.

Other resources can be targeted toward improving ECPD standards, content, and pedagogy. Child Care and Development Block Grants continue to have quality set-aside funds; Title I funds can be used to support cross-sector ECPD, such as joint professional development for staff in public schools and community-based ECE programs. Federal investments in ECPD research are beginning to produce results that can be directly applied to this work.

Our examination of past and present ECPD work suggests some priorities to keep in mind as decisions are made about how best to use these and other resources. Decision makers should direct substantial resources to where the rubber meets the road: improving practitioners' ability to implement effective practices. In this process, decision makers must rely on evidence as much as possible in selecting which ECPD content and methods are most likely to be effective. To this end, resources and policy levers can be used to strategically integrate the knowledge and passion of both content experts and systems experts in the service of common goals.

From their early beginnings as a limited part of a child care workforce improvement effort, professional development systems have evolved toward far more comprehensive supports aimed at improving outcomes for all children in all settings. Today that goal is far from a reality, but with a powerful vision, strategic use of resources, evidence-based implementation, and rigorous evaluation of the results, the full potential of ECPD can be realized.

NOTES

Many thanks go to the leaders with whom we have discussed the issues in this chapter: Janet Carter, Pauline Koch, and Kathy Wilson (DE); Harriet Dichter and Gail Nourse (PA); Dan Haggard (NM); Beth Rous (KY); and Alison Lutton, Sarah LeMoine, and Adele Robinson (NAEYC). We also benefited greatly from the continuing work of the National Child Care Information Center (NCCIC) and the National Association for the Education of Young Children in tracking states' professional development system-building efforts.

1. "Sectors" refer to ECE program settings or subsystems—child care, Head Start, nursery schools, prekindergarten/preschool, public school kindergarten and early primary grades, nonpublic school kindergarten and early primary grades, early intervention, and preschool special education (Mitchell & LeMoine, 2005).

2. A full description of each system may be found in documents cited in this chapter's references.

REFERENCES

Barnett, W. S., Epstein, D. J., Friedman, A. H., Stevenson Boyd, J., & Hustedt, J. T. (2008). *The state of preschool 2008: State preschool yearbook.* New Brunswick, NJ: The National Institute for Early Education Research, Rutgers University.

Bredekamp, S. (1992, June). *Introduction to program for NAEYC's First National Institute for Early Childhood Professional Development.* Washington, DC: National Association for the Education of Young Children.

Bredekamp, S., & Willer, B. (1992). Of ladders and lattices, cores and cones: Conceptualizing an early childhood professional development system. *Young Children, 47*(3), 47–51.

Child Care Bureau. (2007, Winter/Spring). *Child care bulletin* (Issue Brief No. 32). Retrieved January 29, 2010, from http://www.nccic.acf.hhs.gov/ccb/issue32.pdf

Early, D. M., Maxwell, K. L., Burchinal, M., Alva, S., Bender, R. H., Bryant, D., et al. (2007). Teachers' education, classroom quality, and young children's academic skills: Results from seven studies of preschool programs. *Child Development, 78*(2), 558–580.

Hyson, M., Tomlinson, H. B., & Morris, C. (2008). Quality improvement in early childhood teacher education: Faculty perspectives and recommendations for the future. *Early Childhood Research and Practice, 11*(1). Retrieved from http://ecrp.uiuc.edu/v11n1/hyson.html

Improving Head Start for School Readiness Act of 2007, 42 U.S.C. § 9801 *et seq.* (2007).

Kagan, S. L., & Cohen, N. E. (1997). *Not by chance: Creating an early care and education system for America's children.* New Haven, CT: Yale University, Bush Center in Child Development and Social Policy.

Kagan, S. L., Kauerz, K., & Tarrant, K. (2008). *The early care and education teaching workforce at the fulcrum: An agenda for reform.* New York: Teachers College Press.

LeMoine, S. (2008). *Workforce designs: A policy blueprint for state early childhood professional development systems.* Washington, DC: National Association for the Education of Young Children.

LoCasale-Crouch, J., Konold, T., Pianta, R., Howes, C., Burchinal, M., Bryant, D., et al. (2007). Observed classroom quality profiles in state-funded pre-kindergarten programs and associations with teacher, program, and classroom characteristics. *Early Childhood Research Quarterly, 22*(1), 3–17.

Mitchell, A., & LeMoine, S. (2005). *Cross-sector early childhood professional development: A technical assistance paper.* Washington, DC: NCCIC. Retrieved from http://nccic.acf.hhs.gov/pubs/goodstart/cross-sector.html

National Association for the Education of Young Children. (2009). *Workforce systems initiative.* Retrieved from http://www.naeyc.org/policy/ecwsi

National Child Care Information and Technical Assistance Center. (2009). *Early childhood professional development systems toolkit with a focus on school-age professional development.* Retrieved from http://nccic.acf.hhs.gov/pubs/pd_toolkit/index.html

National Governors Association Center for Best Practices. (2010). *Building an early childhood professional development system.* Washington, DC: Author.

Peisner-Feinberg, E. S., Burchinal, M. R., Clifford, R. M., Culkin, M. L., Howes, C., Kagan, S. L., & Yazejian, N. (2001). The relation of preschool child-care quality to children's cognitive and social developmental trajectories through second grade. *Child Development, 72,* 1534–1553.

Pianta, R. C. (2006). Standardized observation and professional development: A focus on individualized implementation and practices. In M. Zaslow & I. Martinez-Beck (Eds.), *Critical issues in early childhood professional development* (pp. 231–254). Baltimore: Brookes.

Satkowski, C. (2009a). *The next step in systems-building: Early childhood advisory councils and federal efforts to promote policy alignment in early childhood.* Washington, DC: New America Foundation.

Satkowski, C. (2009b). *A stimulus for second-generation QRIS.* Retrieved from the New America Foundation website: http://www.newamerica.net/files/042609qris.pdf

Sheridan, S. M., Pope Edwards, C., Marvin, C. A., & Knoche, L. L. (2009). Professional development in early childhood programs: Process issues and research needs. *Early Education and Development, 20*(3), 377–401.

Whitebook, M., Howes, C., & Phillips, D. (1989). *Who cares? Child care teachers and the quality of care in America* (Final report of the National Child Care Staffing Study). Oakland, CA: Child Care Employee Project.

Zaslow, M., Tout, K., Halle, T., Vick Whittaker, J., & Lavelle, B. (in press). Towards the identification of features of effective professional development for early childhood educators. In S. B. Neuman & M. L. Kamil (Eds.), *Professional development for early childhood educators*. Baltimore: Brookes.

CHAPTER 7

Early Childhood Data Systems

A Platform for Better Outcomes for Children *and* Programs

Janice Gruendel and Jennifer M. Stedron

Since the turn of the 21st century, states and the nation increasingly have invested time and intellectual and fiscal capital to build, manage, and sustain coordinated systems of service for young children and their families. Notable among these are the federally funded Early Childhood Comprehensive Systems Grant Program, Project THRIVE at the National Center for Children in Poverty, and the BUILD Initiative, which supports state action around four domains fundamental to child growth and development: health, including oral and mental health; early care and education; family supports and services; and early intervention programs for young children.

While states have begun to connect services *within* each domain (e.g., linking infant and toddler child care to preschool programs), they generally have not been able to connect services *across* domains to create a comprehensive, coordinated early childhood "system." A contributing factor to this lack of progress is often the inability of agencies to connect data sources and share information. Often, as will be seen later in this chapter, the absence of an interoperable data system limits agencies' abilities to connect programs for the betterment of clients, share infrastructure resources such as professional development, identify cost-efficiencies at the management level, or report out on program results and child outcomes. In this chapter, we assert that an early childhood data system is one of the essential core infrastructure components of a coordinated, durable early childhood system and that its design and functionality deserve significant attention and ongoing investment.

Why accord data development and use such a central role in the creation of comprehensive early childhood service systems? From birth, all young children come into contact with many adults: most important, parents, but also caregivers, doctors and nurses, and family support and early intervention professionals. Children who experience challenging circumstances—for example, living in poverty or in families where an adult has a physical or mental health problem—or children who have developmental challenges will interact with many adults across multiple domains in a relatively short period of time. All of these important exchanges generate valuable information necessary for a family to support the child's optimal development. Yet this information frequently resides in isolated agency databases or sometimes—still—on paper, with data records that are generally inaccessible to other programs. Without an information system capable of connecting these bits of data, it is very difficult to create a full picture of the child and her experiences, and both time and opportunities for engagement, support, or intervention are lost.

At a policy level, until data systems *within* each domain can be linked to one another (e.g., infant child care linked to Head Start and preschool) as well as to data *across* domains (e.g., health care, parent literacy, and birth to 3 early intervention programs), policymakers will continue to lack even basic information about children and the services they need and receive. Communities will not know where service gaps exist or whether high-need children have access to effective, high-quality services, and providers will not have the feedback necessary to improve their services or even to document the effectiveness of interventions over time. Just as early childhood data systems are vital to successfully addressing the complex needs of young children and their families, these systems also provide critical information for strategic planning, program improvement, resource management, and public accountability.

THE ROLE OF THE FEDERAL GOVERNMENT IN EARLY CHILDHOOD DATA DEVELOPMENT

The federal government has long required states to collect and report data on specific early childhood services. Program-specific data systems include, for example, those that support Head Start, child care, and child and family nutrition services. Generally these data collection systems were designed to support program compliance and thus cannot readily provide information to states (or other federal agencies) for service coordination, system building across programs and sectors, or program improvement.

However, more recent federally supported efforts have prioritized the development of data systems capable of providing useful information back to states and localities about children, the adults who serve them, and the programs in which they are served. For example, in education, federally mandated state longitudinal data systems track students' academic growth and link those data to information about students' educational experiences (e.g., schools, teachers). Funded largely by U.S. Department of Education Statewide Longitudinal Data System (SLDS) grants, all states now assign unique student identifiers to K–12 public school attendees and collect data on student demographics, enrollment, assessments, and program participation. The majority of states also assign a unique teacher identifier that enables practitioner data to be matched with student data (Data Quality Campaign, 2010a). This allows state and local education agencies to follow students' academic growth over time and see how this progress correlates with individual teachers and schools as well as with family and community circumstances.

New federal initiatives indicate a similar approach to systems development for the early education domain. The $4.3 billion Race to the Top grant program for comprehensive school reform requires K–12 data systems to reach *down* into the early childhood years and *up* into the young adult years of postsecondary education and work. This requirement for state "preschool to postsecondary" data systems is also a key component in the Department of Education's proposal for reauthorization of the federal Elementary and Secondary Education Act (ESEA) in 2011. But federal support is not limited to the Department of Education alone. The Improving Head Start for School Readiness Act of 2007 requires state Early Childhood Advisory Councils to make recommendations for a "unified data system" within the early childhood education domain (e.g., Head Start, prekindergarten, and child care) in order to improve early education and child development services, birth to age 5, at the state and local levels. Initial funding to support state advisory councils in this important infrastructure work has been provided through the federal American Recovery and Reinvestment Act. Perhaps the largest boost in early childhood infrastructure development will come as the Race to the Top—Early Learning Challenge funds are awarded to some states, beginning in December 2011.

Of note, federal support has increased state momentum for early childhood data systems development at the same time that federal privacy protections have stymied progress toward such unified systems both within early education and across other domains. Data sharing across agencies generates legitimate concerns over the privacy rights of individuals about whom data are held in health, child welfare, human services, and other databases. The Family Educational Rights and Privacy Act (FERPA) and the Health Insurance Portability and Accountability Act (HIPAA) (enacted in 1974 and 1996, respectively) define the conditions within which information can and cannot be shared, with the goal of protecting individually identifiable information from inappropriate and unauthorized release and use. However, with advances in information technology and new investments in technology innovation and use, attention has been directed at ensuring that laws protect client privacy but do not unreasonably restrict access to data sharing for legitimate (and necessary) purposes, including improving the health, safety, and educational success of young children and students (National Forum on Education Statistics, 2010). Notable among efforts to re-examine the role and impact of these legal protections are the Interagency Data Working Group of the U.S. Departments of Education and Health and Human Services and the Data Quality Campaign's Privacy Advisory Group (Data Quality Campaign, 2011).

EARLY CHILDHOOD DATA DEVELOPMENT AT THE STATE LEVEL

States have not waited for federal funding to begin the important work of building data systems within and across service sectors. Support for state-level work comes from several national organizations, including the National Governors Association Center for Best Practices (NGA). Staff at the NGA monitor and support the development of state Early Childhood Advisory Councils and, with the help of other national organizations (e.g., the National Conference of State Legislatures), provide technical assistance around data systems development and implementation through the Ready States Policy Academy initiative. In 2009, a significant multi-organization national initiative, the Early Childhood Data Collaborative, was launched. This consortium of seven national organizations was convened to help state policymakers build, link, and use early childhood data systems beginning with the early care and education domain.[1] With input from all major stakeholders, the group has documented data efforts in leading states, outlined key policy questions to be addressed by data systems, and identified ten fundamentals of exemplary state early childhood data systems (Early Childhood Data Collaborative, 2010).

In addition to privacy issues, significant challenges remain for state early childhood system building, including the diffuse array of programs and agencies collecting data, lack of coordinating governance efforts, inadequacy of data for purposes of addressing key policy questions, inefficient methods of data communication, and poor quality of data. To illustrate, we review the experience of one state, Connecticut, where these challenges recently were documented by the state's Early Childhood Education Cabinet in its 2009 Accountability Report to the Connecticut General Assembly. In January 2008, the governor asked the Cabinet to assemble data to answer the following four questions about the state's infants and toddlers: (1) For very young children receiving state services, how many are served by more than one program? (2)

TABLE 7.1. Connecticut Departments and Programs Serving Young Children

Social Services	Education	Public Health	Children and Families
S-CHIP Health	State-Funded Preschool	WIC	Child Welfare
TANF		Birth Registry	Children's Mental Health
CCDBG	Preschool Special Ed	Vital Records	
Child Care Subsidies	Family Resource Centers	Special Health Care Needs	Parent Programs
Child Care Centers	Child Nutrition		Home Visiting
Head Start	K–3 Curriculum & Instruction	Child Care Licensing	Foster Care
ECE Professional Development and Accreditation	Head Start	School-Based Health Centers	
	Family Literacy		
	Even Start		
	Early Reading		
	GED Programs		

What is the total unduplicated count of children served at any given point in time? (3) What is the total cost of serving these children? (4) Which programs result in the best child outcomes for the dollars spent?

To answer these questions, the Cabinet worked for 6 months with five state agencies serving young children and learned that cross-agency data were simply not available and that, even *within* these individual agencies, data often were collected and maintained separately by individual programs, as shown in Table 7.1.

Subsequent "data flow analyses" across Connecticut agencies serving young children illustrated the complexities of data collection, sharing, and reporting common to all states. Challenges identified include: (a) the lack of data dictionaries, common data definitions, and shared terminology; (b) inability to disaggregate and report data at the child, program, or community level for case coordination and/or program improvement; (c) inconsistent communication between data development experts and client and program personnel, both within and across agencies; and (d) multiple databases, even within the same agency, maintained on hardware and software platforms with limited interoperability. When available, data-sharing agreements across programs or departments were applied and communicated inconsistently. Finally, funds allocated to support data quality and staff training were generally very limited and among the first to be reduced in times of budget austerity.

Other authors also have documented data challenges among human service agencies and departments serving children and youth (Nelson, 2009), noting that—until they can be resolved—the development of coherent, effective systems of care will remain elusive, and vulnerable children will continue to lack the support they need for health, safety, and both academic and personal success. Similarly, until these challenges are resolved, states will be unable to perform even basic accountability functions, such as providing unduplicated counts of children enrolled in child care and preschool programs, and information about the skills and training of the child care workforce across various settings, and linking vital information from the child welfare sector to the early care and education sector for purposes of coordinated care and intervention. Finally, in the absence of well-functioning interoperable early childhood data systems, there is scarce capability to link child development outcomes with data on programs and workforce in order to understand what program characteristics work best with what children to ensure their age-appropriate development before kindergarten entry and beyond.

The Early Childhood Data Collaborative has described an early childhood data system as one that collects and links high-quality data on children, programs, and the workforce for use in decision making both within a birth to 5 system of services and beyond, by linking with the state's K–12 data system. Ideally, the tracking and linking of data would occur across the four main early childhood domains: early care and education, health, family support, and early intervention. However, because many states have focused their developing systems on early care and education programs and these programs have a natural link to K–12 data, many states consider this domain a primary starting point for such systems development.

In 2010, the Data Collaborative issued a white paper, *Building and Using Coordinated State Early Care and Education Data Systems: A Framework for State Policymakers*, identifying ten fundamentals of a state early childhood data system. These include child, workforce, and program identifiers, the ability to link these to K–12 SLDS, and a state governance body to manage data collection and use. Below are the ten fundamentals of coordinated state early childhood data systems:

1. Unique statewide child identifier
2. Child-level demographic and program participation information
3. Child-level data on development
4. Ability to link child-level data with K–12 and other key programs
5. Unique program site identifier with the ability to link with children and the ECE workforce

6. Program site data on structure, quality, and work environment
7. Unique ECE workforce identifier with ability to link with program sites and children
8. Individual ECE workforce demographics, education, and professional development information
9. State governance body to manage data collection and use
10. Transparent privacy protection and security practices and policies (Early Childhood Data Collaborative, 2010)

When fully implemented, these essential features will enable states and communities to answer the following questions:

- Defining success: Are children, birth to age 5, on track to succeed at school entry and beyond? How can we minimize or prevent a "preparation gap" in the birth to 5 years? What are the relationships among program quality, program effectiveness, and child (or family) outcomes?

- Determining quality: What are the characteristics of effective programs? How do we track and evaluate areas needing quality improvement? What policies and investments lead to a skilled, stable, and effective workforce?

- Determining effectiveness: Which programs and what characteristics contribute to age-appropriate development through age 5 and readiness for kindergarten among at-risk children?

- Ensuring equitable access: How many and which children are served by high-quality, effective programs and agencies? Are these programs reaching all of the children they are intended to reach?

Early Childhood Data Management Structure

From the outset, an early childhood data system must have a data management structure that includes a process for ensuring data accuracy, privacy, and security. Optimally, the system will provide real-time access to data, including relevant reporting capabilities and presentation tools useful for all stakeholders—from agency heads to teachers and parents. And, in order to answer questions about children and their development and support the continuous improvement of programs and the workforce, an early childhood data system must have the capability to track *and link* data on characteristics of the *child* (and the family), characteristics of *programs* in which the child is served, and characteristics of the *workforce* providing the service.

Unique Child Identifiers

A unique child identifier allows one to answer questions about not only a child's access to programs, but also his or her development, school readiness, and longitudinal academic progress. As noted earlier, unique student identifiers are now assigned to all public K–12 students, and in some states legislation requires the assignment of unique identifiers to children enrolled in publicly funded preschool and child care center programs. Assignment of the unique student identifier when a child enters the "school system" actually may afford the easiest method for providing unique identifiers within the early childhood data system, but there are alternative approaches. Rhode Island, for example, is now working through its Department of Public Health to assign a unique child identifier at birth. To be maximally useful, the unique child identifier should be carried as a data field for all publicly funded agencies and programs (and linked to the K–12 data system). This will obviate or greatly reduce the need to conduct repetitive matching operations on data for individual children provided across agencies.

Unique Workforce Identifiers

A unique workforce identifier allows one to answer questions about workforce training, experience, and competencies, as well as recruitment, retention, and compensation. The workforce identifier should include not only teachers but also assistant teachers (or paraprofessionals), directors and administrators, and early childhood consultants, as all adults may impact the quality of services received. In their state education data systems, 15 states use the social security number of teachers as the K–12 unique workforce identifier, which is encrypted within the data system. In the early childhood education and care domain, 30 states currently are developing "professional and training registries" that generally include individual-level data on workforce education, professional development, and compensation and wage incentives. As in the K–12 system, many of these registries assign a unique workforce identifier based on the social security number, which is deeply encrypted within the registry system. Registries are one component of a state's early education and school-age professional development system, but not all registries include data on the early education (pre-K) workforce employed within the public school system. Determining how to link workforce data will be imperative as states begin to better align their preschool programs with early elementary education using a pre-K–3rd framework (Foundation for Child Development, n.d.).

Unique Program Identifiers

Because of the rich array of programs serving young children within an early care and education context, assignment of unique program identifiers for use across funding agencies is imperative. Unique program identifiers can help answer questions about program quality and improvement, as well as program effectiveness over time. Programs receiving federal funding may have a unique vendor number that could serve as a program identifier. States also assign program identifiers based on their early childhood licensing systems, although some programs, for example, those within public school systems, could be excluded from these systems. However the unique program identifier is constructed, it ideally would be carried as a data field by all agencies that have a referral, regulatory, funding, or accountability relationship with a program, and be specific to the classroom level for center-based programs.

To help clarify how these elements support and promote optimal child development, all of the above—unique child, workforce, and program identifiers—should link to relevant characteristics such as demographic and development information (for children), training and compensation information (for workforce), and services and funding sources (for programs).

Data Audit Process

Fundamental to any data system is a process to ensure that information entered is valid and reliable. Data systems should include both data entry safeguards for quality (e.g., limiting children's birthdates to those that would qualify for early childhood services) and data-auditing measures. At present, no cross-state information exists on the extent to which early childhood data systems incorporate an audit process. However, one leading state, Pennsylvania, has safeguards for and data-audit procedures, including checks and controls of many data fields through the use of drop-down menus limiting selections, and range controls on items such as birthdates (Office of Child Development and Early Learning, 2010). For more information on this state's data system, see Stedron (2010).

Many of the data audit processes developed for use by state K–12 data systems can be incorporated as part of the design of early childhood data systems. All 50 state K–12 systems report the use of statistical checks on school district data and the use of "validation rules" (e.g., ensuring birthdates are within appropriate ranges) before formally accepting data into the system. In addition, nearly all states flag and investigate potentially inaccurate data and provide professional development for staff responsible for data entry (Data Quality Campaign, 2010a).

Governance Agreements

When a single agency (e.g., the state department of education) controls data intake and reporting, issues related to "governance" are less of a challenge. In contrast, early childhood data systems (whether within or across sectors) necessarily draw from a variety of provider services and data sources that span multiple agencies, making essential the development of formal agreements related to data definitions, data collection, privacy and security, data access, and reporting. The form of governance for early childhood data systems development will necessarily be specific to each state and to its partners in the work.

Several states have formally consolidated governance of early care and education, which enables unified early childhood data systems. For example, in Pennsylvania, governance rests with the Office of Child Development and Early Learning, a separate agency established by combining staff from the Department of Public Welfare and the Department of Education (see Chapter 17). Regardless of the form or format of governance determinations, several core functions must be addressed: (a) development of data elements, including common measures and standard data definitions; (b) methods for assigning unique identifiers or conducting data matches; (c) privacy, security, and confidentiality rules; (d) data entry and audit procedures to ensure data quality; (e) data-reporting rules and processes to ensure appropriate data access; and (f) professional development opportunities for all stakeholders to maximize appropriate data use and interpretation.

BUILDING THE EARLY CHILDHOOD INFORMATION SYSTEM: A FEDERATED SOLUTION

When governance arrangements or cost issues do not allow the development of a single system, another solution to coordinating data from the multiple state agencies serving young children is the adoption of a structure or process that "sits above" the various extant data systems. This arrangement, often called a "federated data architecture," provides authorization to extract data from various agencies, analyze these data, and create—from multiple data points—sets of reports to answer a wide variety of important policy, practice, and program questions.

One model of federated data architecture is the Connecticut Health Information Network (CHIN), hosted by the University of Connecticut's Center for Public Health and Health Policy. CHIN was authorized in 2007 by the Connecticut General Assembly as a "federated computer network" linking diverse databases across agencies, including the Office of Health

Care Access and the Departments of Developmental Services (housing Connecticut's Birth to Three System), Children and Families (the state child welfare agency), Public Health, Information Technology, and Education. The system enables individual data to be collected and analyzed across state agencies, while at the same time complying with federal and state confidentiality and security standards (Connecticut Health Information Network, 2009). The Connecticut General Assembly has signaled its strong support of the approach with the passage of legislation (PA 09-05) authorizing CHIN member agencies to transmit personally identifiable information "for network development and analyses in response to network inquiries."

This type of federated information system model will be of interest to those building interoperable early childhood data systems, for several reasons. First, the programming architecture sits outside existing agency databases and thus does not interfere with daily operations; this increases the likelihood of cross-agency participation. Second, the model was built on the health side of the service system, a natural first contact point for babies, families, and services such as prenatal care, nutritional supports, and hospital delivery services. In addition, all births are recorded immediately as part of the vital records process in each state, and most states also employ a variety of newborn screening processes at birth. Thus, a robust set of data is already collected by the health/public health system that could springboard the development of an early childhood information system, including comprehensive services beyond early care and education. Third, substantial federal funds have been committed to build state and regional health information exchanges as a key component in the federal Patient Protection and Affordable Care Act of 2010 (eHealth Initiative, 2010), which, in conjunction with a federated information system such as CHIN, can support an early childhood information system across agencies (since its architecture is non-agency-specific).

MOVING FROM DATA STRUCTURE TO DATA USE

A recent shift in emphasis at the federal level from data architecture to data use can be seen in the federal Race to the Top grant program (and other comprehensive school reform grants). States submitting Race to the Top applications were required to articulate a "high-quality plan" to ensure that data from the state's statewide longitudinal data system were:

- Accessible and used to inform and engage key stakeholders (e.g., parents, students, teachers, principals, local education agency leaders, community members, unions, and policymakers);

- Used to support decision makers in continuous improvement
  in such areas as policy, instruction, operations, management,
  resource allocation, and overall effectiveness;
- Used to support local school districts' professional development
  related to improving instructional systems; and
- Available to researchers to support studies of effective programs
  for groups of vulnerable learners.

It is anticipated that these same data-use requirements will be included in ESEA's reauthorization and will translate into permanent improvement in access to P-20 data across the nation. Importantly, this work is highly relevant to early childhood system building in general and to early childhood data systems in particular. To ensure that curricula are aligned across educational settings from preschool through 3rd grade (pre-K–3rd), joint professional development opportunities are maximized, and data are shared about children's accomplishments and needs in the transition from preschool to kindergarten, effective early childhood data systems linked to the K–12 system are as essential as those at the K–12 level alone.

In January 2010, the Data Quality Campaign released the *Inaugural Overview of States' Actions to Leverage Data to Improve Student Success*, evaluating ten actions to promote data use organized within three main categories: (1) expanding K–12 systems to link from preschool through postsecondary education and work (P-20); (2) ensuring that data can be accessed, analyzed, and used; and (3) building stakeholder capacity to use longitudinal data (Data Quality Campaign, 2010b). A summary of the findings is relevant for *early childhood* information systems development and use. While 33 states have education data warehouses capable of hosting P-20 data, only eight states actually have linked preschool and postsecondary data to K–12, and just four states have implemented strategies to promote stakeholder use of longitudinal data.

Data access and use across sectors is a widespread goal in early childhood; here, we highlight a few examples. One of the more exciting data initiatives focused on informing public policy and research, the Open Indicators Consortium (www.openindicators.org), is underway at the University of Massachusetts at Lowell and the Boston Foundation's Boston Indicators Project. The consortium is developing a set of sophisticated but easy-to-use data analysis and presentation tools that allow different sources of data— from child-level to neighborhood, regional, or national-level—to be quickly manipulated and effectively reported to a broad range of audiences. Because these are "open source" tools, when completed they will be available at no or low cost to nonprofit groups, which in turn can share report templates and other enhancements for use across areas of interest (from early childhood to health). Individuals and organizations interested in a demonstration may access the website, secure a log-in, and test-drive the tools across a variety of data indicators.

In Illinois, the Early Learning Advisory Council created an interactive web-based tool, called the Early Childhood Asset Map, which visually represents state-funded early care and education programs (including Head Start, licensed family-based child care, state-funded prekindergarten, and private-sector services), as well as demographic information such as population distribution and language spoken at home. The combination of information informs community-level gaps in services and quality programming.

Pennsylvania's Reach and County Risk Assessment was designed to help policymakers understand community-level needs and guide decisions on early childhood program investments. The mapping project consists of two components: risk and reach. The "risk" component utilizes population-level indicators predictive of school failure (e.g., poverty level, mother's education level) to calculate a county-wide risk level. The "reach" component compiles county-level information on early childhood program funding and, where applicable, child enrollment information. Together, the data allow for detailed analysis of program accessibility at both the state and county level, in relationship to the risk of the early childhood population for poor outcomes. The data are used for community awareness and engagement and also to drive state funding decisions.

THE BOTTOM LINE

Data are critical to the management and performance of coordinated systems of service for young children and their families, and the stage is set for states to build robust early childhood data systems. Early childhood leaders can leverage the work and lessons learned from K–12 data system building while capitalizing on the unique resources of their field. Within early childhood education and care, emerging data components focused on program improvement—from professional development registries to quality rating and improvement systems—can provide existing platforms to expand information on program and workforce effectiveness. And child-level data, across domains, can spur the expansion of essential child development and demographic information within an "appropriate use" context.

Finally, rapidly advancing technology improvements allow for more elegant and cost-effective approaches to federated systems, real-time information, reports, and displays. We expect that continued incorporation of these advances in building robust early childhood information systems will result in improved child outcomes for all of this nation's youngest learners and for the programs that serve them.

NOTE

1. The Early Childhood Data Collaborative is a partnership of the Center for the Study of Child Care Employment at University of California–Berkeley, Council of Chief State School Officers, Data Quality Campaign, National Center for Children in Poverty at Columbia University, National Conference of State Legislatures, National Governors Association Center for Best Practices, and Pre-K Now, a campaign of the Pew Center on the States. The Collaborative is funded by the Birth to Five Policy Alliance, Pew Charitable Trusts, and David and Lucile Packard Foundation.

REFERENCES

Connecticut Health Information Network. (2009). *Connecticut health information plan.* Retrieved from http://publichealth.uconn.edu/images/pdfs/CHIN_Report_05_21_09.pdf

Data Quality Campaign. (2010a). *DQC 2009-10 annual survey results—10 elements.* Retrieved from www.dataqualitycampaign.org/resources/857

Data Quality Campaign. (2010b). *Inaugural overview of states' actions to leverage data to improve student success.* Retrieved from www.dataqualitycampaign.org/resources/846

Data Quality Campaign. (2011). *Supporting data use while protecting the privacy, security and confidentiality of student information: A primer for state policymakers.* Retrieved from http://dataqualitycampaign.org/files/DQC-Privacy-primer%20Aug24%20low%20res.pdf

Early Childhood Data Collaborative. (2010). *Building and using coordinated state early care and education data systems: A framework for state policymakers.* Retrieved from www.dataqualitycampaign.org/resources/1007

eHealth Initiative. (2010). *2010 survey on health information exchange.* Retrieved from http://www.ehealthinitiative.org/2010-survey-health-information-exchange.htm

Foundation for Child Development. (n.d.) *PreK–3rd education.* Retrieved from http://www.fcd-us.org/our-work/prek-3rd-education.

National Forum on Education Statistics, U.S. Department of Education. (2010). *Forum guide to data ethics* (NFES 2010-801). Washington, DC: National Center for Education Statistics. Retrieved from //nces.ed.gov/pubsearch/pubsinfo.asp?pubid=2010801

Nelson, D. (2009). Counting what counts: Taking results seriously for vulnerable children and families. In the Annie E. Casey Foundation's *2009 KIDS COUNT data book* (pp. 6–29). Retrieved from //datacenter.kidscount.org/Databook/2009/OnlineBooks/AEC186_essay_FINAL.pdf

Office of Child Development and Early Learning. (2010). *Pennsylvania early learning network data repository user guide.* Retrieved from http://admin.pattan.net/Publications.aspx?rnd=3114837772&ContentLocation=/teachlead/Early-Intervention.aspx&pageNumber=1

Stedron, J. (2010). *A look at Pennsylvania's early childhood data system.* Denver, CO: National Conference of State Legislatures in partnership with the Early Childhood Data Collaborative. Retrieved from http://www.ncsl.org/portals/1/documents/Educ/PAEarlyChild-Stedron.pdf

Part III

TRANSCENDENT SYSTEM-BUILDING PROCESSES

CHAPTER 8

Planning an
Early Childhood System
Policies and Principles Matter

Sharon Lynn Kagan, Kate Tarrant, and Kristie Kauerz

Despite the absence of a universally accepted definition of what constitutes an early childhood system, scholars, policymakers, and practitioners have acknowledged its importance, with many taking concrete steps to design and implement such a system. System building does not happen by chance or, we contend, as a natural evolution of program expansion or policy development. System building requires intentional, strategic, and systematic planning.

This chapter focuses on the planning that is necessary to build systems. Whereas other chapters in this volume (see Brodsky; Nagle) address systemic planning efforts from a fiscal or budgetary perspective, we take a perspective that looks at both the state-level policies and principles that must guide systemic planning. To illustrate our stance, we present a systematic approach to planning—one that is inclusive, practical, and comprehensive—that we have used in eight states.

THE NEED FOR SYSTEMIC PLANNING

As at no time before in our social history, the need for systemic planning is clear. Four rationales substantiate this urgency: (1) historically fragmented policies; (2) increasing services/increasing accountability; (3) quality crisis/equity crisis; and (4) the emerging role of the states.

Historically Fragmented Policies

Characterized by low funding, episodic "here-today-gone-tomorrow" policies, disparate administrative entities, and diverse constituencies, early childhood might be regarded as one of the most, if not the most, fragmented of the human service fields. Owing in part to early conceptualizations of the field, with services for young children divided between (a) child care programs for the poor and working poor, (b) nursery school or preschool programs designed to provide educational enrichment for middle- and upper-class children prior to their entry into school, and (c) "compensatory" programs for poor and at-risk children, siloed services are the norm. Affirming this view, a U.S. General Accounting Office (1994) report noted that "90 early childhood programs in 11 federal agencies and 20 offices were funded by the federal government alone" (p. 2). The report also notes that "a patchwork of programs may not provide the most efficient use of resources or provide individuals with needed services" (p. 1). Understanding this reality, countless practitioners and scholars have called for the development of a comprehensive system as an antidote to severe fragmentation (Bruner, Stover Wright, Gebhard, & Hibbard, 2004; Gallagher, Clifford, & Maxwell, 2004; Kagan & Cohen, 1997; Sugarman, 1991). They contend that such a systemic orientation, however complex to plan and implement, ultimately would evoke better quality programs, more equitable resource distribution, more effective use of scarce dollars, and improved outcomes for children. Yet, despite the lofty aspirations, calls for system building enunciated as early as the 1970s have been heard but not universally heeded.

Increasing Services/Increasing Accountability

Since these early calls for system building, early childhood education has experienced considerable growth, and with it, an increased focus on accountability. Egged on by well-known data from the neuro and social sciences, policymakers in states around the nation and in nations around the globe have seen fit to invest increasing resources in early childhood services. In many cases, these funds have supported the establishment or expansion of individual programs (e.g., state-funded prekindergarten, Early Head Start, parenting supports, home visiting). The resulting thicket of early childhood efforts, replete with expanding redundancies and inefficiencies, magnifies the need for greater cohesiveness. Compounding this challenge, severe resource constraints make policymakers highly desirous of getting full value for early childhood investments. Stated simply, they want to see concrete results from their investments and they want to see how such investments might save resources and/or leverage other fiscal commitments. Such demands for fiscal accountability focused initially on individual program effectiveness but, given the increasingly entwined nature of early childhood services, have become a press for cross-program planning, system building, and collective accountability.

Quality Crisis/Equity Crisis

Although research convincingly demonstrates that *high-quality* early childhood programs advance children's development and success in school (Campbell & Ramey, 1994; McCarton et al., 1997; Schweinhart, Barnes, Weikart, Barnett, & Epstein, 1993), the prevalence of such high-quality programs is limited (Cost, Quality, and Outcomes Study Team, 1995). Moreover, reflecting long-standing fragmentation, quality in early childhood programs varies by auspice. Early research found Head Start to be of higher quality than community center-based care (Lazar & Goodson, 1993); more recent data suggest that state-funded prekindergarten programs provide the highest quality care (Bellm, Burton, Whitebook, Broatch, & Young, 2002; Magnuson, Meyers, Ruhm, & Waldfogel, 2004). Although reasons for the higher quality found in prekindergarten programs are clear (e.g., more stringent state regulation regarding teacher qualifications, higher funding, infrastructure supports), such differences reveal the serious inequities in the nature of services young children receive. Indeed, disparities exist on virtually every measure associated with quality. With growing awareness of such inequitable distribution of resources within and between programs, planning bodies have been created to help redress the situation. Indeed, one of the goals of developing an integrated system is to elevate quality for all children while reducing service inequities.

Emerging Role of the States

Historically, the field of American early childhood has been dominated by community-based programs functioning with a high degree of autonomy and limited public accountability. A veritable panorama of micro-enterprises, early childhood education was regarded as a local service, not a state responsibility. Even the nation's premier early childhood program, Head Start, still bypasses the states with its federal-to-local structure. The establishment of the Child Care and Development Fund (CCDF) in the 1990s, however, changed the state–local balance, providing a major source of federal funding to the states. CCDF also gave states both the authority for setting program regulations and the flexibility to use set-aside dollars to improve quality and minimize system inconsistencies (Pittard, Zaslow, Lavelle, & Porter, 2006). The recent rise in state-funded prekindergarten programs has further positioned states as central players in planning and moving the early childhood agenda. With a need to improve the quality and the distribution of services within their borders, states have assumed a key role in system building, developing a plethora of efforts, including local and state partnerships, executive-level cabinets, consolidated early childhood governance, quality rating and improvement systems, and professional development systems (notable state examples are provided in Part IV of this volume). All different, such improvement efforts highlight why the state is an appropriate unit for planning and building an early childhood system.

KEY PRINCIPLES OF SYSTEM PLANNING

As the federal government devolved greater authority for early childhood services to the states, state policymakers began to shift their planning from a focus on individual programs to a more integrated approach. To do so, early childhood stakeholders from the public and private sectors within a given state often came together to create visions for their early childhood systems. Plans were debated and finalized; beautiful reports were written and disseminated. But sadly, once the initial buzz and the press conferences ended, the documents typically were left dormant, literally buried on bureaucrats' shelves. Despite their lack of direct implementation, however, the vision documents and the discourse associated with them did leave a positive platform for future work. Armed with a new clarity of intention, many individuals involved in these planning efforts craved concrete and action-oriented direction that would bring durable systemic change.

Seeking to support states as they refined their system-planning efforts, a team of scholar-practitioners at the National Center for Children and Families (NCCF) at Teachers College, Columbia University, developed a process and a set of tools that could be used in states to support system planning (Kagan & Rigby, 2003). Several key principles guided their thinking and continue to guide many systemic planning efforts today.

Principle #1: The Planning Process Must Be Inclusive, Transparent, and Influential

In order to have salience once the actual planning is complete, a system-planning process needs to involve an array of stakeholders, including those who have individual authority and collective influence. Everyone need not be involved in precisely the same way but, given the diverse nature of early childhood services in a state, participants in the planning process should include representatives from the governor's office; state legislature; departments of education, health, social services; child care subsidy administration; child care licensing; preschool special education; early intervention; Head Start–State Collaboration; state institutions of higher education; state chapter of the National Association for the Education of Young Children; KIDS COUNT organization; and community-based organizations. Moreover, because external recognition is critical for the process to be maximally effective, key leaders from the political, business, and advocacy communities need to endorse or be involved in the planning effort. In short, individuals with knowledge of, and influence to change, state policies need to be included.

Beyond having a solid representation of individuals, the planning process needs to be transparent to all involved. Specifically, the process should have a clear sequence and structure of activities with specified timelines and deliverables. It needs to delineate who will be responsible for what facets of the work, and who will be involved at each stage. It also must reflect a clear understanding of the mandates and timelines impacting its efforts. A diverse team and a transparent process accord heft to planning efforts.

Principle #2: The Planning Process Must Be Driven by Current Research and a Theory of Change

If a planning process is to generate accepted, reliable, and usable results, it must be grounded in the most current research related to child development, early education, and systems theory. Given the plethora of information on early brain development, coupled with data on the fadeout of many early education programs' effects, empirical findings suggest that a planning process focus not on one age within the early childhood continuum, but be guided by a goal of advancing a continuity of services for children from birth through the early years of schooling. The research is also clear that children do not develop in isolated domains so, for a planning framework to respect the comprehensiveness of early childhood, it should embrace families and communities, as well as the systemic elements described in the literature (financing, monitoring, professional development, accountability, quality programs, and governance).

In addition to being guided by research and data, a planning process needs to be driven by a theory of change. Sometimes referred to as a logic model, a theory of change enunciates an ultimate result—in this case, improved outcomes for children—and then "backward maps" the specific strategies whose cumulative effects produce this result. Rather than launch a planning process without a clear endpoint in mind, efforts built on a logic model are buttressed by a framework that guides policy decisions and provides discipline to evoke cogent actions that lead to desired results.

Principle #3: The Planning Process Must Account for the Realities of Each State's Policy and Political Context

Recognizing that an early childhood system will exist within a bevy of state policies and practices that vary dramatically, the planning process must be attentive to such contextual variables. Kingdon (2003) notes that when considering social change, the political and policy context is as influential as the policy problems themselves. Developing an approach to system planning, therefore, needs to take serious account of diverse state contexts.

To begin to do this, the planning process should be informed by the actual policies enacted in each state. By looking at the wording and nature of specific policies, rather than relying on myths or assumptions about what policy says, a planning effort can take realistic stock of the status of state early childhood policy. Further, the planning process should take stock of the diverse policy instruments that a state may use (e.g., legislation, administrative practices, memoranda of understanding, and executive orders). Within this context, a planning process should consider the authority of the governorship and the effectiveness of the bureaucracy supporting the governor's agenda. Moreover, to understand the political context, a planning process should examine the power and professionalism of the state's legislature, as well as the nature of and decisions made by the state's judicial branch.

The planning process also should systematically examine the public and political support for advancing an early childhood agenda, acknowledging data on the state's party composition, political ideology, and voter turnout, as well as early childhood demographic information. Stakeholders' opinions also need to be factored into this picture of the political context. Considering the diversity of the states, a process that intentionally discerns the unique political dynamics of each state is integral to the overall planning effort.

Principle #4: The Planning Process Must Result in a Set of Actionable Priorities

Any cogent planning effort involves the development of a politically feasible prioritization of policy changes. Given the scarcity of resources coupled with large needs, this is especially important for early childhood system building. To set priorities, a structured process with clearly identified criteria for evaluating potential policy changes is necessary. In other words, priorities need to emerge from a consensual process that represents more than a conglomeration of individuals' wish lists. A systematic approach to weighing policy proposals helps participants arrive at priorities in a thoughtful manner. Moreover, this consensus-driven process builds sustainable support for the team's policy priorities.

Among the prioritized policy changes, some need to be actionable in the short term while others can be long-term goals that require incremental progress. Gaining early policy "wins" builds momentum and serves to reinforce the importance and efficacy of the planning process. Establishing a way to discern the possible and probable early wins from the desirable but daunting long-term goals needs to be built into the planning process.

Principle #5: The Planning Process Must Have an Afterlife

Given that planning is an ongoing effort and that social change is highly incremental, the system planning process needs to be useful and adaptive over time. Once the initial planning is done, the process and its products need to be periodically revisited, updated, and used recurrently.

SYSTEM PLANNING AND THE POLICY MATTERS EFFORT

Using these five principles, scholars at NCCF developed a comprehensive approach to system planning. Known as *Policy Matters*, this approach used research in the field to identify 98 policies that, once in place, will support a comprehensive early childhood system. As of 2010, eight states have undertaken Policy Matters. Using the research-based framework, these states have analyzed their policies, reflected on their political context, and determined both long-term policy goals and more immediate policy priorities. For each participating state, the NCCF team produced an action-oriented deliverable, in accord with one of the state's policy priorities, to help attain system-relevant policy change. Highly inclusive and interactive, the Policy Matters process supports a state's efforts to assess, plan, and focus on the policies that, when implemented, will contribute meaningfully to building an early childhood system.

While Policy Matters is not the only approach to system planning, it is presented here, first, to illustrate how a set of principles can be brought to life, and, second, to provide a concrete example of a comprehensive and systematic approach that has been used effectively. Each of the principles will be discussed, explicating both the process and the content of the Policy Matters approach to early childhood system planning.

Policy Matters Principle #1: The Planning Process Must Be Inclusive, Transparent, and Influential

Policy Matters was designed to address this principle through its clear process and inclusive approach. Explicitly, the Policy Matters effort involves a four-stage process (see Figure 8.1). During the first phase, the state convenes a Policy Matters team, guided by recommendations from the NCCF team, and the planning process is introduced and launched.

While the state completes a self-analysis of the 98 policies, the NCCF team uses a protocol to profile the state's political context. During the second phase, the state team takes stock of the policy and political context analyses and, using this information, begins to determine its policy goals. To further inform these decisions, state leaders complete a survey that aug-

FIGURE 8.1. The Policy Matters Process

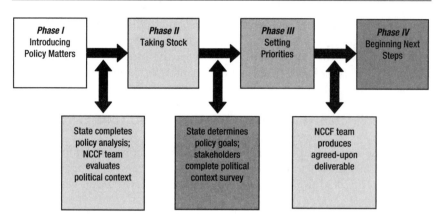

ments the data regarding the political context of the state. During the third phase, the state Policy Matters team reviews and refines its goals and determines its three top policy priorities. During the fourth phase, the NCCF team produces an agreed-upon deliverable that will support the state's policy priorities. Given this methodical organization, the planning process is both highly transparent and inclusive.

Policy Matters Principle #2: The Planning Process Must Be Driven by Current Research and a Theory of Change

Research drove the conceptualization of Policy Matters in several key ways. First, research on child development framed the scope of the Policy Matters effort to include children birth to age 8 and to address comprehensive services across key domains. In addition, a theory of change influenced the organizational structure of the Policy Matters process. Each will be addressed in turn.

Age Range. Policy Matters embraces all forms of nonparental care provided to young children, birth to school entry, within public or private settings. Our rationale for beginning with the birth to 5 age range is structural; it recognizes that the policy, administrative, and legislative structures that support children from birth to age 5 are, in many ways, different from those for children above formal school entry age. Additionally, driven by pedagogical and learning theory, the framework is designed to include children's education through age 8, addressing transitions to schools and education in the early elementary years. Overall, the nomenclature affirms a dedica-

FIGURE 8.2. Policy Matters Domains

Comprehensive Services	
VIII. Health, Mental Health, Oral Health	
Early Care and Education	**K–3 Education**
I. Quality ECE Settings	VII. Education in
II. ECE Professional and Workforce	the Early Grades
Development	
III. Informed Families, Informed Public	
IV. Accountability/Results Orientation	
V. Adequate ECE Financing	
Governance	
VI. Governance and Coordination	

← BIRTH   AGE 5   AGE 8 →

tion to conceptualizing an early childhood system as embracing a set of linked services that enhance children's early development and school readiness from birth to age 8, therein accommodating structural realities and pedagogical/developmental theory.

Content of the Key Domains. Based on a review of the literature, the 98 policies addressed by Policy Matters effort are comprehensive and fall within eight domains, as pictured below. Following Figure 8.2, each domain is described as well as the more specific subdomains each embraces.

Quality ECE Settings addresses those policies that directly target overall program quality. The first subdomain is titled *regulations and enforcement,* which includes the state licensing requirements for programs' group size and adult–child ratios. The policy score is calibrated based on the National Association for the Education of Young Children's program accreditation criteria. *Incentives for quality* is the second subdomain, including tiered reimbursement policies in which programs receive greater funding for providing higher quality care and having a robust Quality Rating and Improvement System. The third subdomain that falls under the umbrella of *Quality ECE Settings* is *facilities and capital.* Given the costs of opening and sustaining high-quality facilities and the significant impact of physical space on overall program quality, government strategies to support investments in capital are important elements of a high-functioning early childhood system.

ECE Professional and Workforce Development is the second domain. It begins by addressing states' requirements for teachers' *preservice and inservice training and education*. This domain also includes states' policies to raise teachers' *compensation*, including salaries and benefits. Finally, the domain assesses the status of *professional development systems*, such as articulation agreements to help teachers move easily from associate degree to bachelor degree programs.

The third domain is *Informed Families, Informed Public*. It examines *family information and involvement*, including a state's resource and referral capacities, as well as general parenting information campaigns. The domain also considers *family education and support*, the accessibility and overall funding allocation for home-visiting services. The third component of this domain is *public relations*, which addresses whether the state fosters public awareness of the importance of the early years.

Accountability/Results Orientation is the fourth domain. First, this domain gauges a state's *early learning standards and instructional assessments*, including the currency and comprehensiveness of the standards. Second, it considers *program accountability and evaluation*. This subdomain addresses the monitoring of trends in school readiness as well as use of longitudinal, outcome-based evaluations of all state-funded ECE programs to determine whether programs are effective in achieving intended outcomes. This domain concludes with the state's efforts regarding *data on the ECE system*, such as policies regarding state-level data collection infrastructure and coordination of data systems.

The fifth domain examines *Adequate ECE Financing* in five subdomains. *State-funded programs*, the first subdomain, includes overall investments as well as eligibility for preschool and infant and toddler programs. The second subdomain, *subsidy policies*, examines the eligibility for and adequacy of child care subsidies. The next subdomain is *child care tax provisions*—the overall value of a state's child care and dependent tax credit and its benefit and availability to low-income families. *Family leave* is the fourth subdomain, which includes duration of the leave benefit and the income-related payment for parents utilizing leave. The last subdomain, *revenue generation*, addresses the variety of strategies a state uses to generate resources dedicated to early care and education.

The sixth domain, *Governance and Coordination*, has four subdomains. This domain looks at the presence and authority of *state and local early childhood governance entities*. *Family and community involvement* in governance entities and early childhood *planning* also are addressed. The last subdomain concerns *alignment of ECE with other systems,* such as family support and health, to create an integrated and comprehensive early childhood system.

Education in the Early Grades is the seventh domain. The availability of *full-day kindergarten* is a key dimension of this domain. Next, *teacher certification* for kindergarten teachers and teachers in grades 1 through 3 and *class size* in kindergarten and in grades 1 through 3 are evaluated. Finally, this domain examines the *learning standards, assessments, and curriculum* used in kindergarten and 1st through 3rd grade.

The eighth and final domain in the framework is *Health, Oral Health, and Mental Health.* This broad domain focuses on the elements of the health, oral health, and mental health systems related specifically to early childhood. It begins with *health insurance,* the eligibility, financial coverage, enrollment procedures, and provider reimbursement rates of the state's Medicaid or State Children's Health Insurance Program. Second, the framework assesses the *accessibility of primary health and oral health services,* and, third, it looks at the *accessibility of mental health services.* The fourth subdomain, *prevention and health education,* considers, for example, requirements for early childhood screenings. Fifth, *qualified health/oral health/mental health professionals* covers health care providers' preservice and inservice training requirements related to child development. The domain concludes with an assessment of the state's *health/oral health/mental health system supports.*

Together, these eight domains, and the 98 policies across them, constitute a truly comprehensive early childhood system.

Theory of Change and the Structure of the Documents. It is important to note that the logic model used for Policy Matters is guided by the ultimate result: All children are ready for school and all schools are ready for children. Given this overarching goal, the logic model suggests that these eight domains comprise the means for achieving not only an effective early childhood system, but also results that will significantly enhance children's readiness for school and schools' readiness for children. In order to articulate the policy infrastructure necessary to achieve this goal, as well as the incremental and progressive nature of policy change, each domain and its subdomains are further subdivided into policy features, and each policy feature is then divided into policy levels (see Figure 8.3 for illustration). The Policy Matters domain framework is the analytic tool that breaks down the eight domains, the 31 subdomains, and the 98 policy features. For

FIGURE 8.3. Domain Framework Structure

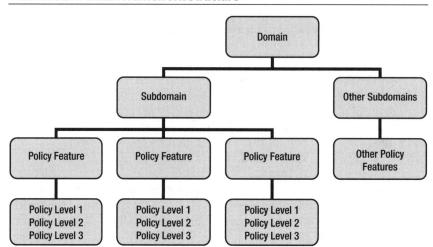

each policy feature, a set of mutually exclusive policy levels is delineated and ordered from most to least ideal, allowing each state both to identify where its current policies rank and to set a goal for improving the policy. Depending on the nature of each specific policy feature, its levels are based on a combination of the following criteria: Policy generosity refers to how generous policies are in terms of funding and eligibility (e.g., subsidy rates); policy comprehensiveness refers to the depth and breadth of programmatic offerings (e.g., scope of early learning guidelines); and policy approximation refers to the degree to which the feature addresses research-based best practices (e.g., requirements for teachers' formal education). Table 8.1 provides an example of one policy feature.

While the domain framework is a helpful analytic tool, it is most effective when used in conjunction with the well-articulated and conceptualized planning process that scaffolds an understanding of how to prioritize policy change. As a whole, Policy Matters exemplifies the actualization of Principle 2.

Policy Matters Principle #3: The Planning Process Must Account for the Realities of Each State's Policy and Political Context

In order to be responsive to political and policy diversity among states, Policy Matters incorporates a thorough process to help each state understand the dynamics of its context. Specifically, Policy Matters articulates the power of the governorship (not the individual governor), the power and professionalism of the legislature, and the scope of the judiciary, using met-

TABLE 8.1. Example of a Policy Feature

DOMAIN II: Professional and Workforce Development SUBDOMAIN A: Qualified ECE Professionals		State Self-Rankings	
Policy Feature	Policy Levels	Current Level	Desired Level
II.A.1 Professional Standards: State has established high standards for what ECE providers should know and be able to do	1. State has (1) conducted an updated review of curriculum; (2) developed standards/core competencies; (3) conducted a review of standards/core competencies; and (4) aligned professional development with these standards/core competencies	# 3 Notes: We have developed standards and reviewed them	# 1 Notes:
	2. State has completed three of the above		
	3. State has completed two of the above		
	4. State has completed one of the above		
	5. State has not completed any of the above		

rics familiar to political scientists. With this information, each state's Policy Matters team gains insight into potential avenues for systemic reform. In addition, an online survey is completed by scores of state leaders and advocates. Based on the results of these data, determinations are made regarding the nature and timing of key short- and long-term policy efforts.

States participating in Policy Matters differ dramatically on all of the variables, and consequently each has elected different policy priorities. Indeed, the analysis of the political context, often overlooked in system-building initiatives, is essential to the Policy Matters effort.

Policy Matters Principle #4: The Planning Process Must Result in a Set of Actionable Priorities

Each Policy Matters state team specified a deliverable it wished to have at the end of the project. Although the deliverables differed substantially, each met the principle of contributing to appreciable policy change. In some cases, the deliverable was oral (e.g., testimony before a state's legislature); in other cases, the deliverable was a written product (e.g., analyses of secondary data related to a policy priority; an analysis of governance structures that exist throughout the country, or a review of county-level policies, with an emphasis on their similarities and differences). In each state, the deliverable was aligned with the state's Policy Matters priority and used to impact policy construction or revision.

Policy Matters Principle #5: The Planning Process Must Have an Afterlife

The Policy Matters project—from the domain framework to the political context analysis—is a living process: It can be (and has been) used repeatedly by a state over time to review its policy accomplishments. Thus, Policy Matters leaves states with the capacity for reviewing and renewing the work down the line. It is clear that planning for system building is not a one-time exercise; it involves constant assessment and reassessment in light of state budgets, political climate changes, and the emergence of new data.

ISSUES RAISED BY POLICY MATTERS

As the previous discussion demonstrates, Policy Matters is a highly interactive and collaborative initiative. It is an innovative effort that systematically tackles the daunting task of planning an early childhood system. Accordingly, it raises many issues and provides many lessons for system-building efforts.

Several major policy issues regarding planning an early childhood system have been brought to light via the Policy Matters project. The first relates to the unit of policy construction. Some states adhere to strong and fairly universally applicable policies. In contrast, other states devolve much of their policymaking to substate entities, often county governments; in these cases, there tends to be considerable variation in the services provided. Moreover, when strong county variation exists, not only is it difficult to determine a state's overall performance on any policy feature, but it is challenging to carry out comprehensive state planning. In these cases, participating states have questioned whether a framework ought to be developed for the county level. Doing so would accommodate strong county-controlled states and would point out areas where policies are lacking and showcase pockets of excellence. At the same time, however, it violates a goal of fostering equitable policies statewide. This issue raises the challenge states face regarding the equitable (not necessarily equal) distribution of resources.

A second issue relates to prioritizing the policies. Given the lack of quality in the system and a large number of diverse policy shortfalls, participants face the Herculean task of discerning priorities from among a host of needed improvements. Complicating matters, within the domain framework, all policy features are weighted equally for planning purposes, yet they hold quite different implications for implementation. Some features are oriented to the overall system (e.g., establishing a governance entity with authority over all early childhood services), while others are more programmatic and directly related to children's well-being (e.g., providing home-visiting services). Some policy features require substantial resources but can greatly impact services across the state (e.g., raising child care subsidy reimbursement levels), while others are comparatively budget-neutral but have a less direct impact on the state's children and families (e.g., including families in the state governance entities). Participants must weigh impact and feasibility when developing their policy agenda and then accept the group process of arriving at the state's top choices. Simultaneously, they must maintain an eight-domain vision for their early childhood system as their long-term goal while focusing on more discrete quality elixirs.

A third issue relates to the chasm that routinely exists between policy and practice. In nearly every participating state, there has been an unexpected difference between extant policies and existing practice. For example, policies may be more generous than believed, given the services that actually are provided. Conversely, the policies may be weaker than believed, with localities and well-intentioned providers delivering services that exceed what is required by policy. Policy Matters reveals the fact that policy written is not policy implemented.

Lessons Learned from Policy Matters

Even though Policy Matters is designed to be a single-state planning process, having worked with eight states using Policy Matters, we can discern lessons learned that need to be considered as states move forward with their planning efforts. First, states vary dramatically in their processes and policies. No two states have the same policy profile, with variation characterizing how states elect to spend their limited early childhood capital.

Although some may applaud this variation, arguing that states should have the flexibility to create their early childhood destinies as they see fit, others might suggest that such uneven distribution patterns are the result of a set of forced choices, with scarcity as the only unifying bond. Moreover, such uneven distribution of resources suggests that states not only are making different investment choices, but are investing different amounts. Such differentiation in spending can be the antecedent of highly inequitable services, leaving poorer states and communities, often where the need is greatest, offering fewer services. The real question evoked by such variation relates to the equity of services that are provided across states. Are children in state X more advantaged than children in state Y because of policymakers' choices?

Context driven, a second lesson relates to the importance of, and the need for, adaptability in the planning process. Clearly, American early childhood is in a state of flux at federal, state, and local levels. With states exerting greater authority over early childhood policymaking and with options for early childhood investment increasing, policymakers have many decisions to make. Moreover, the options that exist today may not exist tomorrow, or may be increased tomorrow. New or modified funding streams may alter the amount and nature of available resources. New research or new foundation-funding priorities may advance different programmatic emphases. This dynamic context means that not only is planning an early childhood system critically important presently, but it must be envisioned as an ongoing process. Fueled by changing funds, mandates, or desires, system building is never going to be complete. To the contrary, it must be conceptualized as an ongoing component of the emerging early childhood system. This raises questions not only about how we enact planning, but about how we conceptualize, fund, and use its results most effectively.

Finally, we have learned the lesson of humility. In state after state, we have encountered early childhood heroes and heroines. We need to honor and respect those who have been engaged so diligently in the process of building an early childhood system, some for many years. In most fields, lacking policy nourishment, leaders would have given up long ago. Early childhood leaders, despite the miles of policy terrain still to be covered, remain devoted to creating a system. Their diligence, engagement, respect for others and for the process itself suggest that the field is fortunate, but we must take steps to stave off burn-out while making space for new voices and ideas.

Next Steps

Planning an early childhood system is a complex undertaking. Using a strategic and systematic approach guided by a logic model, Policy Matters has rendered this daunting process more accessible to a diverse range of state policymakers.

But it is not states alone that face challenges. Those who seek to support states, like the Policy Matters team, need to maintain currency within ever-shifting political and research landscapes. For the Policy Matters team, this means continuing two things: evaluation and expansion. With regard to evaluation, it would be important to conduct an impact evaluation of the Policy Matters planning process and states' system-building efforts. A first step in the process could involve revisiting each state's policy inventory and charting progress on all policy features. It could engage key stakeholders in each state to identify the underlying causes of progress to achieve a better understanding of whether and to what degree the Policy Matters planning process has contributed to states' progress. To carry out such efforts, support from those external to the process would be necessary. Such assistance could come in the form of federal legislation that supports infrastructure development and system building; it could come in the form of foundation commitments; or it could come in the form of formal institutions (e.g., schools, legislatures) recognizing that policy reviews are important components of planning.

With regard to expansion, Policy Matters has numerous options. It could expand into the international policy domain where early childhood development is now burgeoning. In developing countries, in particular, where early childhood policy and planning is a relatively recent development, Policy Matters could offer a helpful roadmap toward building a highly comprehensive early childhood system. It could expand its efforts to embrace more family support and allied domains. It could expand by working with more states. Moreover, such expansion is predicated on the need to keep the domain framework fresh and cognizant of emerging research.

Whether these efforts will be undertaken remains to be seen. What is clear, however, is that states have relied, and must continue to rely, on policy to achieve, solidify, and sustain early childhood systems. Moreover, with its policy focus and its strategies to make systemic planning more normative, objective, thorough, inclusive, and transparent, Policy Matters is one approach to facilitating policy change. While not perfect, it has been a used and respected strategy, one that has advanced early childhood system planning and that, hopefully, in turn will advance outcomes for America's young children.

REFERENCES

Bellm, D., Burton, A., Whitebook, M., Broatch, L., & Young, M. P. (2002). *Inside the preK classroom: A study of staffing and stability in state-funded prekindergarten programs*. Washington, DC: Center for the Child Care Workforce.

Bruner, C., Stover Wright, M., Gebhard, B., & Hibbard, S. (2004). *Building an early learning system: The ABCs of planning and governance structures*. Des Moines, IA: State Early Childhood Policy Technical Assistance Network and BUILD Initiative.

Campbell, F. A., & Ramey, C. T. (1994). Effects of early intervention on intellectual and academic achievement: A follow-up study of children from low-income families. *Child Development, 65*, 684–698.

Cost, Quality, and Outcomes Study Team. (1995). *Cost, quality and child outcomes in child care centers* (Executive summary, 2nd ed.). Denver: University of Colorado, Economics Department.

Gallagher, J. J., Clifford, R. M., & Maxwell, K. (2004). Getting from here to there: To an ideal early preschool system. *Early Childhood Research and Practice, 6*(1). Available on-line at http://ecrp.uiuc.edu/v6n1/clifford.html

Kagan, S. L., & Cohen, N. E. (1997). *Not by chance: Creating an early care and education system for America's children.* New Haven, CT: Yale University, Bush Center in Child Development and Social Policy.

Kagan, S. L., & Rigby, E. (2003). *Policy matters: Setting and measuring benchmarks for state policies.* Washington, DC: Center for the Study of Social Policy.

Kingdon, J. (2003). Agendas, alternatives, and public policies. New York: Longman.

Lazar, J., & Goodson, B. (1993). *Life in preschool: Volume one of an observational study of early childhood education programs for disadvantaged four year olds.* Dover, NH: Development Assistance Corporation.

Magnuson, K. A., Meyers, M. K., Ruhm, C. J., & Waldfogel, J. (2004). Inequality in preschool education and school readiness. *American Educational Research Journal, 41*(1), 115–157.

McCarton, C. M., Brooks-Gunn, J., Wallace, I. F., Bauer, C. R., Bennett, F. C., Bernbaum, J. C., et al. (1997). Results at age 8 years of early intervention for low-birth-weight premature infants: The infant health and development program. *Journal of the American Medical Association, 277*(2), 126–132.

Pittard, M., Zaslow, M., Lavelle, B., & Porter, T. (2006). *Investing in quality: A survey of state child care and development fund initiatives.* Washington, DC: American Public Human Services Association and Child Trends.

Schweinhart, L. J., Barnes, H. V., Weikart, D. P., Barnett, W. S., & Epstein, A. S. (1993). *Significant benefits: The High/Scope Perry Preschool study through age 2.* Ypsilanti, MI: High/Scope Press.

Sugarman, J. M. (1991). *Building early childhood systems: A resource handbook.* Washington, DC: Child Welfare League of America.

U.S. General Accounting Office. (1994). *Early childhood programs: Multiple programs and overlapping target groups.* Washington, DC: Author.

CHAPTER 9

Local-Level System Building

Dean Clifford

A system of effective, comprehensive, and well-integrated early childhood services is complex and multilayered. A system must not only integrate services provided to young children and their families across many domains, subsystems, and programs, but also improve and align policies, funding streams, and infrastructure across national, state, and local levels. To address some of these layers, in many states, system building has been planned and organized to occur simultaneously at state and local levels. This chapter examines the relationship and interface between state and local systems work, with particular emphasis on work at the local level.

The content of this chapter is informed by firsthand experience directing early childhood work at the local level in North Carolina, by lessons learned from work with a variety of other states and their local communities, and by a survey of local early childhood leaders in seven different states (Clifford, 2010). Resting on this wealth of real-world perspectives, this chapter provides a practical overview of early childhood system building at the local level.

ADMINISTERING AND OVERSEEING EARLY CHILDHOOD SYSTEMS WORK AT THE LOCAL LEVEL

Undertaking early childhood systems work at the local level is important, for obvious reasons. It is at the local level where the lives of children and their families intersect with community conditions and a vast array of early childhood services and programs. It is well understood that local and neighborhood conditions—both those that are positive and those that are negative—have tremendous impact on children's experiences, opportunities, and ultimate life chances (see, e.g., Shonkoff & Phillips, 2000). While policy and funding decisions most often emanate from the federal and state levels, their impacts are felt at the local level. Many communities express concerns over duplication and fragmentation in service delivery and the burden that families face when navigating a bewildering array of services and eligibility requirements.

Because the distance—both literal and figurative—between public policy and children's lives often is great, it is important to leverage local resources and engage local stakeholders in the work of system building. As goes an oft-quoted African proverb, "It takes a village to raise a child." Because community-based service providers and leaders have an on-the-ground perspective, they are best suited for assessing the quality and effectiveness of services at the local level, including the mechanisms that undergird those services and the gaps that allow children to fall through the cracks.

To establish vehicles for systems work at the local level, many states are creating and supporting a network of local councils that function in concert with early childhood system-building efforts at the state level. These models are built on the understanding that the state and local levels are not mutually exclusive but depend one on the other. For example, in reference to Arizona's early childhood system efforts, which are established at both state and local levels, it was said:

> First Things First would never have been approved by the voters without the promise of local flexibility by councils comprised of local citizens. It is also very clear that we would never realize the progress and promise from our early childhood system if local councils were not part of the governance and service delivery. (Karen Woodhouse, Deputy Director of First Things First, quoted in Clifford, 2010)

Effective and coordinated local early childhood systems work rests on clear conceptual vision and administrative organization.

Local Organizational Models

The term "local" usually corresponds to substate government units, most often counties, or other geographic areas that include some minimum number of children. In some states, "local" refers to a region that corresponds with pre-existing patterns of cooperation across county lines.

Any definition of local must incorporate and adapt to the challenges presented by variable population levels (e.g., low-density rural areas and densely populated urban areas). For example, Arizona's early childhood system includes large low-density areas represented by a single regional council, and densely populated metropolitan areas, such as Phoenix, that are represented by more than one local council. Similarly, in North Carolina, where Smart Start Partnerships were formed primarily at the county level, some multicounty partnerships have been formed. In this model, certain partnership functions (e.g., accounting) have been moved to the regional level, with several county-based partnerships placing one or more functions in a single partnership office. Regional organization may create a sufficient population base for efficient service delivery, as well as a reduction in administrative costs.

In order to structure and streamline the linkages between state and local systems work, various governance models are being adopted and adapted around the country. At the state level, they include new early childhood departments, interagency management teams, new not-for-profit organizations authorized to oversee comprehensive early childhood work, and others (see Chapters 5, 16, and 17 in this volume for more in-depth discussion of state-level governance models). Just as important, and just as innovative, there are a variety of local governance models emerging around the country.

Most often, the state both requests and supports the development of local governance structures. Three primary variations in local-level structures exist across the United States: (1) collaborative early childhood councils and task forces; (2) new not-for-profit organizations; and (3) existing agencies providing leadership and fiscal management, with collaboration in planning and service delivery. The following examples illustrate the range of models in use. In Michigan, local Great Start collaborative councils exist, each with a public fiscal agent. North Carolina, in its creation of Smart Start at both the state and local levels, established new, private, not-for-profit agencies that are vested with authority from the legislature to direct collaborative early childhood work. In Arizona, a new quasi-governmental entity, First Things First, was established at the state level with regional councils; here, the regional councils function not as separate entities but as direct agents of the state organization.

The feasibility and desirability of each model vary depending on the history, political climate, and overall bureaucratic structure of government in each state. In addition, each model offers particular advantages and disadvantages in terms of establishing trust and reducing turf, developing fiscal and data management across systems, start-up and continuing costs, and balancing flexibility with organizational restrictions and requirements. For example, more loosely formed coalitions may offer advantages such as low overhead and time to build trusting relationships, but they also may have the disadvantage of not being imbued with any real authority. In contrast, more structured organizations may provide established mechanisms for management of finances and data, as well as greater authority and structural strength, but may be perceived to be a threat or competitor by other local organizations and partners.

Local early childhood system-building entities tend to begin informally and evolve into increasingly formal structures. For example, when local early childhood systems work began in Colorado in 1997, each participating Consolidated Child Care Pilot community formed a loosely structured collaborative council that focused on planning. One or more fiscal agents were identified to manage funds secured by the council. Over time, as funding was secured from a variety of sources and as the work became more complex, several of these communities established independent 501(c)3 nonprofit agencies to manage the work. Others function as a division of an existing not-for-profit entity; still others continue to function as a collaborative council, but with formal memoranda of understanding among the various partners. Similar patterns of organizational evolution have occurred in Virginia and Iowa.

Across the varied organizational structures, without exception local-level systems efforts rely on broad-based involvement from parents; child care, Head Start, and other preschool educators; K–12 and postsecondary educators; officials from public health, social services, mental health, libraries, and nonprofit agencies serving families; the business and faith sectors; local elected officials; foundations; and, in some communities, tribal representatives, medical practitioners, and civic groups.

Common Responsibilities

Beyond the involvement of many partners, the various local organizational models share common goals and responsibilities. One common goal is to develop local assessments and plans that reflect and respond to both state mandates and local needs; these can include demographic profiles, needs assessments, and asset maps. The involvement of multiple partners often allows for a "divide and conquer" approach to conducting community assessments. Participating local agencies and organizations already collect or can share in collecting information such as: (a) basic census and KIDS COUNT data; (b) descriptions of services available in the community, including number of clients served, program budgets, and waiting lists; (c) parent surveys; (d) surveys of the early childhood workforce, as well as resource and referral data; and (e) focus group discussions with parents, professionals, community leaders, and specific target groups. These data can then be used to develop comprehensive community reports.

A second common responsibility shared by local early childhood collaboratives, built on the community-based assessments, is the development of an overarching vision for the work, supported by goals, objectives, strategies, responsibilities to be shared among partners, and anticipated results.

These plans must reflect and support a statewide vision and goals. When surveyed (Clifford, 2010), community leaders agreed on the critical importance of careful planning, with one saying, "We spent a long time listening to our stakeholders and engaged in a comprehensive planning stage," and another saying, "If we were starting over, we should have taken a much more careful approach to planning." To keep all partners working for the same goals and to reduce ongoing turf conflicts, it is essential to reach and sustain agreement on the vision, goals, and key strategies.

Just as the organizational structures evolve, so, too, do the community plans. In early stages, community plans have a limited focus on programs. In later stages, the plans become more sophisticated, addressing an integrated system of services, tracking the availability of services for all children, monitoring impact for participating families and children, working to apply quality standards across programs, and evaluating not only the impact of specific services, but also the combination of services.

Creating a Collective Voice

Yet another common organizational tactic of local system-building efforts is the coordination, across a single state, of the leaders of local efforts to become both a "learning community" and a source of mutual support. In most cases, no other person in the local community must negotiate and coordinate the interests and responsibilities of as many groups, organizations, and personalities, and this is demanding and often lonely work. Thus, it is important to build networks of support and shared expertise and experiences among local council leaders. In *Beyond Parallel Play*, Coffman, Stover Wright, and Bruner (2006) point out that local organizations serve "as 'laboratories' to test new ideas and aid in technology transfer across communities" (p. 4). In several states, "tool kits" have been developed for sharing ideas, strategies proven effective, and lessons learned across communities. Face-to-face meetings during which local system-building leaders from across a state can interact and engage in collective work have proven essential in most states; additionally, password-protected internet sites, conference calls, and other technologically advanced strategies have been employed.

THE INTERSECTION OF STATE AND LOCAL WORK

Building an early childhood system requires establishing service components and infrastructure at both the state and local levels; at the same time, leaders at both the state and local levels must manage and oversee systems work. As a result, building a system requires creating vertical linkages between the two levels so that each level's policies and programs complement and align with, rather than contradict or compete with, one another. Two key questions must first be answered: (1) How are the state and local responsibilities defined? and (2) How will their responsibilities interface? Local-level systems work is not a simple replication of state-level systems work. There are both distinct differences and similarities between the two levels.

Take, for example, fiscal development. Providing adequate and sustainable resources for the early childhood system requires careful long-range planning at both state and local levels to garner and effectively use diversified public and private support. At both the state and local levels, leaders should be responsible for mapping available resources; identifying strategies for blending, braiding, and leveraging of funds; demonstrating accountability for the use of all funds; and securing additional funds. However, in addition to these shared responsibilities, each level has unique roles to play.

At the state level, leaders should be responsible for ensuring that the state provides the matching funds required by various federal funding streams, thereby maximizing the amount of federal dollars coming into the state. In addition, state-level leaders should assume primary responsibility for working with the governor's office and the state legislature to increase general fund appropriations, to maximize efficiencies and economies of scale across state agencies' budgets, and to secure cross-agency commitment to early childhood goals. State-level early childhood system leaders also hold primary responsibility for soliciting broad partnerships with and large donations from business and corporate entities.

In contrast, related to fiscal development, leaders at the local level have responsibility to identify local efficiencies and economies of scale across organizations; to diversify and expand resources—both public and private—by seeking foundation and United Way grants, as well as corporate and individual contributions; and to coordinate grassroots advocacy for additional funding from the state legislature. The local level also holds primary responsibility for sharing in-kind resources, including such contributions as donated office space, use of church facilities for meetings, corporate training for child care providers in business and management skills, and donated equipment. Further, system-building efforts can be bolstered when local councils build early childhood endowments; establish planned giving efforts, special local taxes, or fees; and employ other creative financing strategies.

Table 9.1 highlights the intersection and mutuality of various other aspects of state- and local-level responsibilities for system building. While Table 9.1 does not present a comprehensive listing of the many roles and

TABLE 9.1. Examples of Differences Between State- and Local-Level Responsibilities for System Building

	State Responsibilities	Local Responsibilities
Policy Development and Improvement	• Establish rules and regulations to guide the work • Address barriers imposed by complicated or conflicting policies • Establish accountability procedures that ensure compliance with state policy	• Establish procedures for delivering services • Avoid duplication of state-funded infrastructure or services • Identify difficulties experienced by families or service providers caused by state policy requirements • Track expenditures without supplanting funds
Service Creation and Delivery	• Develop program standards, performance standards, and professional credentials • Improve coordination of staff and alignment of standards across state-level organizations and agencies • Maximize the federal, state, and private funding for services	• Conduct assessments of available resources and needs • Develop collaborative plans for coordinating, improving, revising, and/or expanding services • Support improved professional development among service providers • Maintain communication across partner agencies
Evaluation and Reporting of Outcomes	• Identify outcomes that all communities will measure, providing flexibility for local priorities • Create mechanisms to collect, store, and track data • Report statewide benefits and return on investment	• Measure both state-mandated outcomes and additional local indicators • Collect and aggregate data • Report changes to both the state and the local community
Public Engagement and Advocacy	• To avoid multiple or competing branding, create a "brand identity" for the early childhood work • Lead top-down and broad-based public engagement efforts and media campaigns, enlisting highly visible champions • Create materials that can be adapted and used locally • Organize statewide advocacy opportunities and messages • Provide training to local leaders	• Identify specific messages to ensure that the local community understands the importance of early childhood, the nature of quality services, and the benefits to local children of the systems work • Marshal the energy of grassroots advocates • Engage a broad base of volunteers in meaningful work for children

responsibilities related to system building at state and local levels, it makes clear that mutuality between the two levels is crucial.

Beyond shared and mutual responsibilities, there are additional system-building roles and responsibilities that are held primarily at the state level—and others that are held primarily at the local level. Both are discussed next.

From State to Local: Communities' Expectations of the State

When asked (Clifford, 2010), leaders of local early childhood system-building efforts identified several key areas in which they need help from the state.

Respectful Partnership and Transparent Communication. As partners in building statewide early childhood systems, local councils and leaders need transparent and clear communications from the state. Progress in systems thinking and work at both national and state levels, shifts in the political environment, and new federal or state mandates all require timely, continual, and respectful sharing of information by the state with a wide variety of local leaders.

Flexible Data Collection Requirements. Local leaders point to tension between a state's need for statewide measurements of progress and the local desire to measure progress on unique local priorities and children's needs. Often, the local perception is that the state is overly prescriptive in what data are to be collected. This tension is best resolved by open communication and negotiation between state and local representatives whereby they reach agreement on the essentials to be addressed statewide and the flexibility provided to local communities to measure other benchmarks.

"Reflective" Supervision. Local leaders understand the need for monitoring by the state, but abhor micromanagement. As one leader stated (Clifford, 2010), locals want "reflective supervision" from the state. In other words, local leaders desire supervision from the state that demonstrates that local perspectives have been fully heard, reflected upon, and balanced against such factors as state priorities, emerging research and best practices, and political necessities.

Technical Assistance Provision. A key part of the state–local interface is the provision of technical assistance (TA) by the state to local entities. The need for TA is ongoing. TA includes a variety of topic areas, strategies to be used, frequency of contact, and assigned responsibilities for providing assistance. Often, it has proven beneficial to provide training opportunities to both local staff and the entire local board or council.

Frequently cited topics for TA from the state to the local level include organizational development, collaboration, community assessments, strategic planning, evaluation, data collection, resource development, public engagement, advocacy, best practices, involving parents, partnering with the business and/or faith sectors, and addressing cultural differences.

From Local to State: States' Expectations of Communities

Just as locals rely on the state to provide certain things, the state relies on local communities as well. Below are some of the unique ways that local communities and early childhood councils contribute to a state's overall system-building endeavor.

Policy Guidance. As described in *Beyond Parallel Play*, one of the expectations in systems work is that the local units will provide "guidance back to the state on how the state can effectively manage resources and ensure quality" (Coffman et al., 2006, p. 4). For example, the authors point to Colorado's innovative system of waivers that "provides for the flow of information to the state on needed changes to regulation and policy. Local pilots can petition the state for waivers to existing state rules and regulations that are barriers to achieving local results" (p. 9). Subsequently, waivers demonstrated as effective lead to revisions in state policies and processes. Similarly, in North Carolina, as the state moved to implement a five-star system for rating quality in all licensed child care programs, the local Smart Start Partnerships proved to be crucial in providing the necessary relationships, incentives, and support structure for widespread acceptance of, participation in, and advancement upward in the statewide star system.

Public Awareness. Local communities play important roles in raising public awareness among a variety of target audiences. Local entities are uniquely positioned to "tell the story" as children are served, appealing to the head with data and to the heart with stories about individual children to demonstrate the positive impact of effective services or the negative impact of lack of services. Among local organizations surveyed (Clifford, 2010), public awareness efforts included speakers' bureaus, media campaigns, websites, newsletters, a variety of special events, and information distributed by parents and service providers. Local groups involve volunteers as an additional tool for public engagement.

Advocacy. Local organizations have the benefit of long-term relationships with parents, service providers, and their own elected officials, creating an advocacy base for state-level reforms and investments. Local leaders have learned to quickly launch an avalanche of contacts from the grassroots level when policy or funding decisions are being debated in the state capitol.

Impact. Measuring progress and direct impact of system-building efforts on children and families at the local level is essential in order for state leaders to make the case for additional funding and policy changes.

As the examples cited throughout this chapter illustrate, effective early childhood systems work involves an ongoing dance of cooperation and collaboration between state and local entities.

CHALLENGES IN IMPLEMENTING EARLY CHILDHOOD SYSTEMS WORK

The work of building early childhood systems is always complex and often laborious. While challenges exist at both state and local levels, there are some issues that are especially problematic at the local level.

Exercising Authority

One of the greatest organizational challenges is to gain sufficient and appropriate authority—both real and perceived—to direct and integrate collaborative planning and service delivery. Organizational efforts emerging from cross-agency relationships have little genuine authority and may disappear when a given individual leaves a position. Creating state or local organizations by executive order may offer the advantage of speed in implementation; however, changes in the governor's office may terminate these structures. Organizations created by legislation appear more difficult to overturn, but are more arduous to initiate and face the prospect of changes from subsequent legislative bodies.

Building and Sustaining Strong Leadership and Staffing

Building and sustaining effective leadership is a second challenge. Strong leadership, in terms of both paid staff and volunteer leadership on the local board or council, is critically important for creating continuity in early childhood system-building efforts. The collaboration involved in building an early childhood system requires sophisticated skills, including knowledge in the service areas, organizational and financial management, human relations, diplomacy and negotiation, communications, marketing, resource development, advocacy, planning, evaluation, and data management. Even with limited funding, those local organizations with skilled leadership flourish, continually expanding and deepening their impact. Absent strong leadership, progress is limited.

The challenge is to identify strategies to either develop leadership from within or attract skilled individuals from outside. At the council level, this may require extensive governance and board development training. Building staff leadership may require particularly creative approaches in rural or isolated areas, such as designing leadership development programs for local directors, with assigned mentors to give ongoing coaching; developing incentives to attract skilled leaders to rural areas; enlarging the definition and geographic scope of "local"; or merging several local units under the leadership of one highly skilled executive director.

Not only are skill levels often underestimated, but there may be unrealistic expectations about the number of staff positions necessary to lead, manage, and support early childhood systems work. Many communities have only one part- or full-time coordinator, relying on additional contributions from partner agencies or contracted services. One way to address this challenge is to intentionally and continually recognize the need for dedicated funding for staff and leadership development. For example, from the inception of Smart Start in North Carolina, Smart Start funds included both administrative and service funding for the local level, allowing for more appropriate staffing in every local partnership. As the number of partnerships grew, cost-saving strategies were introduced to allow for regional staffing of certain functions.

Dealing with Diverse Interests

Another challenge relates to collaboration. Collaboration among many stakeholders is essential for success in early childhood system building. Collaboration brings together a wealth of expertise and in-kind resources that, together, can have greater impact and influence than the expertise and resources of any single organization. At the same time, however, many communities refer to "turf battles" in the process of their collaborative work.

Not only are there conflicts between the interests of participating agencies and organizations, but there also can be challenges associated with involving other sectors. For example, while the business sector may bring expertise related to strategies for demonstrating the return on investment and influence with the legislature, it also may bring different notions of how to organize the work and of how quickly work can progress. Similarly, engaging the faith sector provides access to families in congregational settings and opportunities for service delivery, but may present philosophical differences. Expanding the participation of parents is essential, but not easy to implement, requiring such strategies as ensuring convenience in time and location of meetings, transportation, and child care.

Two keys to overcoming challenges related to collaboration require establishing and focusing on a shared vision and goals for the work, and devoting time and attention to building trusting relationships. However, because people move in and out of positions, relationships change, underscoring the importance of formal collaborative agreements that clearly spell out partners' respective roles and responsibilities. Some states have responded to these challenges by establishing specific supports for engaging different sectors and participants. For example, Michigan created parent liaison positions at both the state and local levels to create and staff Parent Advisory Councils in each Great Start community. Similarly, the Down East Partnership in North Carolina provides a year of leadership training to parents, many of whom move on to become community leaders.

Inadequate and Episodic Funding

A major challenge at both the state and local levels is the simple fact that there is never enough funding to fully implement plans; thus, it is vital to establish priorities for the work. What will be done first? Next? As new opportunities arise? The inadequacy of funding also underscores the necessity for unrelenting advocacy, making the case in a variety of ways relevant to the political environment at that moment and/or to the audience being addressed.

Balancing Proven Practices and Innovation

Systems work—especially taking it to scale across an entire state—requires an emphasis on using proven practices with a track record in achieving desired outcomes. Fueled by a heavy federal emphasis on rigorous research, there has been continued evolution, across states and communities, toward implementing evidence-based practices in early care and education. The expansion of quality rating systems, with targeted efforts to support and measure improvements in quality, is one example of this trend. Likewise, many states are stressing model fidelity to well-evaluated programs in family support and health. A challenge, though, is that the very nature of "local" work leads to variations in the delivery of proven practices.

At least two things can help to address these challenges. First, there needs to be ongoing monitoring and/or coaching provided to local communities to support their efforts to implement evidence-based models. Second, there needs to be acceptance of, and meaningful financial support for, local communities that implement unique and perhaps unproven efforts, particularly in more isolated areas. For example, in Ashe County, a rural mountain county in North Carolina, the partnership departed from more standard Smart Start approaches to seize an opportunity to adapt a vacated school building as a one-stop center for families, including child care and family support services, adult education, the community recreation program, and job training in baking and welding—using the former cafeteria and shop. Other rural counties have found it important to develop mobile delivery mechanisms for health and dental services. Projects such as these are well-suited to their geographic locations and should be considered as important contributors to early childhood system building, just as are evidence-based practices.

How to Ensure Accountability

Yet another challenge related to system building at the local level relates to ensuring accountability. There has been an evolution toward increasingly sophisticated approaches to ensure accountability for the public and private dollars invested in systemic early childhood work. State and local organizations must demonstrate efficiency in the use of funds, a clear positive impact of services delivered, and the return on investments.

States are not only encouraging, but requiring, communities to demonstrate results, such as measurement of improved quality in early childhood programs, percentages of children served in higher quality programs, changing levels of public support for early childhood, reduced duplication and fragmentation in service delivery, improved levels of professional development, increasing numbers of children with health insurance and/or enrolled in a medical home, and other outcomes. Ultimately, as services move to scale, evaluation must measure direct and lasting impact on children, such as improved school readiness and higher levels of performance during the K–3 years in school. Given the diversity of local demographics, resources, and priorities, there should be balance between "carrot and stick" approaches to accountability. The challenge is to strike a balance between state-imposed mandates and state-offered incentives to local communities. It is also important for local and state levels to collaborate in developing systems for collecting and aggregating data across programs, agencies, systems, and communities.

LESSONS LEARNED

Both experience and surveys of local early childhood systems leaders point to ten key lessons learned about this shared state and local early childhood systems journey (Clifford, 2010). These lessons can be used to guide ongoing and future efforts to build and sustain system-building work at the local level.

Lesson 1: Recognize that collaboration is essential and requires continuous and time-consuming attention to building trusting relationships among partners, while also managing conflicts of interest. As one survey respondent stated, "At the local level, the relationships are the most important part of the work."

Lesson 2: Take a comprehensive approach to ensure universally positive impact and sustainability. Even as the system is built, however, concentrate some efforts on addressing those most at risk. To ensure maximum support for system-building efforts, it is necessary to take a comprehensive approach that demonstrates universal positive impact, such as improved quality for *all* children in child care. However, it is also essential to target some of the work for those children most at risk for school failure and other problems, in order to maximize efficient use of limited resources.

Lesson 3: Establish effective local and state governance structures, with authority to effect change across systems. Maintain the public/private aspect of decision making, in order to build upon, improve, and integrate existing services, both public and private.

Lesson 4: Ensure adequate staffing and skilled leadership for the work.

Lesson 5: Take a strategic approach from the beginning, with broad-based community involvement in shaping a shared vision and clear priorities, in harmony with state-level planning. Allow sufficient flexibility to respond to unique local needs, to respond to "low-hanging fruit" for some early successes, and to take advantage of unexpected opportunities that may emerge.

Lesson 6: Clearly define expected outcomes early in the process and build capacity to measure and track these.

Lesson 7: Emphasize public awareness and involvement from all sectors from the beginning.

Lesson 8: Give attention early in the process to building a diversified funding base, drawing from every conceivable public and private resource available, always with an eye on sustainability.

Lesson 9: Publicize and celebrate successes along the way.

Lesson 10: View building an early childhood system as an endeavor that demands slow, steady progress toward the vision. Change will come gradually, and perseverance over the long haul is essential. This work is not for the faint of heart!

THE ROAD AHEAD

There is reason for both optimism and pessimism in considering the prospects for building an effective early childhood system. The severity of the recent economic recession dampens the prospects for advancing the early childhood agenda, bringing reductions in both public and private resources. Yet, there is recognition among an increasing number of leaders at both state and local levels of the importance of early and primary education as critical factors in local, national, and global development.

Of particular relevance to the interface of local and state early childhood systems work, there is a growing army of grassroots advocates who have seen the benefit of improved services and are finding their collective voice in speaking on behalf of young children. Many corporate leaders enlisted by their local coalitions have become effective advocates for an early childhood system that prepares the workforce for a global economy. Where early childhood systems work has brought positive change for children, parent voices are being heard, asking for maintenance of these efforts.

To sustain and improve systems work that is aligned between state and local levels, as well as aligned across different local organizations, will require intentional capacity building on multiple levels. First, there must be individual professional development, both for the staff of the collaborative entities and for those delivering services. Second, local coalitions must provide technical assistance to participating partner agencies, encouraging increasing knowledge of evidence-based practices and expanding skills in such areas as advocacy, evaluation, and data collection. Third, the state must provide technical assistance to the local coalitions.

As local system-building efforts emerge, strengthen, and stabilize, their collaborative efforts must progress gradually from coordination to institutionalization through policy changes. Strong partnerships across the local and state levels offer bright prospects for building a sustainable system of high-quality early childhood services for all children, provided practitioners and advocates work together to present incontrovertible evidence that a system of excellent services in early childhood offers a high return on investment and a solid foundation for success in education and life. All of this work at both state and local levels—the work of building an effective early childhood system—is a journey, not a destination, requiring continuous attention and improvement.

REFERENCES

Clifford, D. (2010). *Survey: Relationship between state- and local-level early childhood systems work*. Unpublished work.

Coffman, J., Stover Wright, M. S., & Bruner, C. (2006). *Beyond parallel play: Emerging state and community planning roles in building early learning systems*. Des Moines, IA: State Early Childhood Policy Technical Assistance Network and BUILD Initiative.

Shonkoff, J. P., & Phillips, D. A. (Eds.). (2000). *From neurons to neighborhoods*. Washington, DC: National Academy Press.

ADDITIONAL READINGS

Anderson, L. (2009). Unpublished paper developed for training Early Partnerships in Alaska.

Benson, P. (2006). *All kids are our kids*. San Francisco: Jossey-Bass.

Bruner, C., Coffman, J., & Stover Wright, M. (2006). *Building connections: Six state case studies of early childhood system building at the state and local levels*. Cross Lanes, WV: BUILD Initiative.

Bruner, C., Stover Wright, M., Gebhard, B., & Hibbard, S. (2004). *Building an early learning system: The ABCs of planning and governance structures*. Des Moines, IA: State Early Childhood Policy Technical Assistance Network and BUILD Initiative.

Coffman, J. (2007). *A framework for evaluating systems initiatives*. Retrieved from the BUILD Initiative website: http://www.buildinitiative.org/content/evaluation-systems-change

Karr-Morse, R., & Wiley, M. S. (1997). *Ghosts from the nursery*. New York: The Atlantic Monthly Press.

Kroll, C., & Rivest, M. (2000). *Sharing the stories: Lessons learned from five years of Smart Start*. Durham, NC: Smart Start.

Ramey, C. T., & Ramey, S. L. (2004). Early learning and school readiness: Can early intervention make a difference? *Merrill-Palmer Quarterly, 50*(4), 471–491.

Schorr, L. B., & Marchand, V. (2007). *Children ready for school and succeeding at third grade*. Cambridge, MA: Pathways Mapping Initiative.

Schweinhart, L. J., Montie, J., Xiang, Z., Barnett, W. S., Belfield, C. R., & Nores, M. (2005). Lifetime effects: The High/Scope Perry Preschool study through age 40. *Monographs of the High/Scope Educational Research Foundation, 14*. Ypsilanti, MI: High/Scope Press.

CHAPTER 10

How Do We Get There from Here?

Financing the Transformation from a Collection of Programs to an Early Childhood System

Helene M. Stebbins

An early childhood system coordinates multiple programs and funding streams to meet the diverse developmental needs of young children. While the debate continues over which programs and which funding streams should be part of an early childhood system, there is an emerging knowledge base on what it takes to transform a disparate array of programs and funding streams into a coherent system of service delivery that meets the comprehensive needs of young children. This chapter examines how states are financing this transformation through the act of system building. It begins by defining the pieces of a system, and distinguishes the pieces from the act of putting the pieces together (*What is the definition of system building?*). It then describes system building using examples from three states (*What does it look like?*), identifies public and private funding streams explicitly focused on system building (*How is it funded?*), and concludes with some of the challenges of financing system building.

WHAT IS THE DEFINITION OF SYSTEM BUILDING?

For the purposes of this chapter, the pieces of an early childhood system fall into two categories: direct services and infrastructure supports. These pieces are described in greater detail to distinguish them from the act of system building.

Direct services are the programs that directly touch children and families. These may include early care and education programs (e.g., child care, prekindergarten, Head Start, Early Head Start), as well as health care, family support, and early intervention programs. Early childhood direct services are severely underfunded, so research on financing traditionally examines how to increase funding for direct services, including how to make existing funding streams more flexible.

Infrastructure supports enhance quality and improve access to direct services. Elements of infrastructure include program standards and the alignment of those standards across different types of programs; common data elements and the collection of longitudinal data across program types; a professional development system for the workforce; a Quality Rating and Improvement System for programs; and evaluation for accountability and continuous improvement. These infrastructure elements are subsystems of the larger early childhood system, requiring coordination across programs and funding streams. All of them require financing. These infrastructure elements are necessary for system building, and they are described in greater detail in other chapters of this book.

System building is the process that transforms the discrete pieces of direct services and infrastructure into a coherent early childhood system. System building has the potential to improve service delivery, raise quality, maximize outcomes, and maintain accountability for the use of public and private funds. System building includes four core activities: strategic planning, coordination, leadership development, and technical assistance/monitoring. Each activity requires financing. This chapter examines these four activities of system building with a focus on how they are financed in three states.

WHAT DOES SYSTEM BUILDING LOOK LIKE?

North Carolina, Michigan, and Arizona are three states with clearly defined early childhood system-building efforts. The states are diverse in their geographic representation, the political make-up of their state legislatures, and the longevity of their system-building efforts. They are similar in that all three have a state-level entity that oversees local system-building activities, and state resources fund the majority of the work. Table 10.1 compares the three initiatives at a glance, followed by highlights of what strategic planning, coordination, leadership development, and technical assistance/monitoring look like in these states.

TABLE 10.1. Comparison of Three State Early Childhood Initiatives

	Arizona	Michigan	North Carolina
Early Childhood Initiative	First Things First	Great Start	Smart Start
Year of Inception	2008	2003	1993
State-Level System-Building Entity	Arizona Early Childhood Development and Health Board	Early Childhood Investment Corporation (ECIC)	North Carolina Partnership for Children
Number of Local System-Building Entities	31 Regional Partnerships	55 Great Start Collaboratives	77 Local Partnerships for Children
Financing for System-Building Activities (FY 2009)			
State Funding	$9.7 million	$6 million	$4 million + local $
Federal Funding	$140,000	$2.75 million	
Private Funding		$1.6 million	$2 million

Strategic Planning

Strategic planning provides a common foundation for everyone working to build the system. With the multiple stakeholders involved in early childhood programs and policy, it can be a lengthy but important process. It involves stakeholders who discuss and create a common vision for the system, educate one another about existing supports and services, analyze data on the population of young children (including who is and is not accessing direct services), identify inefficiencies as well as service gaps, and develop an action plan to achieve shared outcomes.

Arizona, Michigan, and North Carolina do extensive strategic planning. Each has a statewide system vision with parameters that guide local system-building efforts. In Arizona, the initial strategic plan was a collaborative process that engaged state leaders and local representatives from all 31 of the state's regions. The result was the First Things First Strategic Roadmap, which includes system goals and measurements on coordination and communications that regional partnerships must follow. The state also commissioned a statewide needs and assets assessment to establish a baseline and to guide future investments. In more mature initiatives, like Michigan's, local collaboratives must update their strategic plan annually, which includes both an early childhood action agenda as well as a communications plan. All three states periodically update their strategic plans to ensure that system-building activities reflect current state needs and priorities.

Coordination

Implementing the strategic plan requires convening those who can integrate and transform a collection of programs into a coherent system. It shifts the focus from meeting program requirements to meeting shared outcomes for children and families. Coordination relies on some of the infrastructure supports of the system, such as common standards and data collection, in order to allow for smoother transitions, referrals, and reimbursements between services and their corresponding funding streams.

Coordination looks different at the state and local levels. At the state level the focus is more likely to be on the infrastructure elements of the system. It may include coordinating the statewide professional development or quality rating and improvement systems, and ensuring that these pieces support better access to quality programs. It also may include working with state administrators to align program policies or make state funds more flexible. The North Carolina Partnership for Children, for example, works closely with state agency administrators to ensure that state policies and funding streams support the work of the local partnerships. Interagency agreements are in place to promote communication and support a common vision among the state-level entities that administer funding for early childhood programs and/or monitor compliance with standards.

At the local level, coordination is more likely to occur among the programs that directly serve children. For example, several regional partnerships in Arizona focused on how to streamline the delivery of home-visiting programs in their communities. In North Carolina, one local partnership has a Program Development Coordinator who acts as a networking link between programs to promote coordination of services. The coordinator works with all partnership-funded programs to ensure that the services they provide are of high quality, meet the needs of children and families, use evidence-based and family support best practices, and adhere to the partnership's vision, mission, and goals.

Leadership Development

System building requires leaders at all levels—from civic and business leaders to parents and care providers—to help develop, carry out, and evaluate the strategic plan. Strong leadership also helps build the public and political will that is necessary to achieve the shared outcomes that are the goal of the system. Developing leaders requires strategic communications, education, advocacy, and outreach to support the system.

Leadership within the ranks of elected and appointed policy decision makers is crucial. In Michigan, the Early Childhood Investment Corporation promotes leadership development through candidate education and an annual event at the state capitol. Leadership development also includes cultivating the grassroots support needed to do the work of system building.

At the Downeast Partnership for Children, a partnership of Edgecombe and Nash Counties in North Carolina, the Ready Communities program provides three levels of leadership development. First, the Champions Workshop Series empowers and connects more parents and community members to schools. Second, Community Voices empowers grassroots leaders to develop a shared vision and become involved in solving issues in their community through a 10-week workshop. And third, Community Fellows engages grassroots leaders focused on early care and education from birth to 3rd grade in a 2- to 3-year leadership development program. The partnership's strategic plan states, "We build leaders, particularly those grassroots leaders who can serve as the 'hands and arms' of [our partnership] and link the people in their neighborhoods with the community-wide continuum of services for children and families."[1]

Technical Assistance and Monitoring

Statewide early childhood systems that have a local component also must support system-building activities at the local level. The statewide system provides technical assistance and monitoring of local coalitions in start-up, implementation, and continuous improvement. This requires a set of performance standards and a process for measuring and evaluating performance on those standards.

All three states have staff dedicated to helping local partnerships develop and implement their strategic plans. In Michigan, the state-level ECIC enters into a performance-based contract with each local Great Start Collaborative (GSC), and every contract specifies performance measures for "service system integration." In 2005, North Carolina instituted a performance-based incentive system to track progress and objectively evaluate local Smart Start partnerships based on common outcome measures. Unlike in Arizona and Michigan, there are no system-building measures. Instead, the measures focus on child and program outcomes, such as access to high-quality programs and the healthy development of young children. Implicit is the assumption that system building leads to better program and child outcomes, and that the value of system building is best measured by these outcomes.

In 2006, the Early Childhood Investment Corporation was established to lead the development of a comprehensive early childhood system in Michigan. ECIC enters into a performance-based contract with each local GSC. The scope of work for the contract must address establishing a collaborative governance structure; parent and community engagement; results, accountability, and standards; data and information systems; financing and fund development; communications and public will building; local and state leader education; and service system integration. Two examples of performance measures on service system integration include:

- At least two new examples of increased coordination and service integration (e.g., common forms, processes, agencies/organizations changing policies and procedures to better serve families and children, collection and integration of parent input into service delivery, etc.).
- The implementation of at least two written agreements (e.g., memoranda of understanding, interagency agreements, contracts, letters of agreement, etc.) that establish connections among the components of the local Great Start system and facilitate access, interface, coordination, and inclusion for all young children. These agreements are reviewed and updated on an annual basis.

ECIC manages the system-building activities, but unlike in North Carolina and Arizona, neither the ECIC nor the GSCs receive any funding for direct services.

HOW IS SYSTEM BUILDING FUNDED?

The three state examples profiled in this chapter rely primarily on state revenues to fund their system building. All three states leverage additional private and federal funds, but the state funds provide the anchor for their work.

State Revenue

While all three states dedicate funding to system building, each has different funding mechanisms to do so. In Michigan, local partnerships receive funding through the state aid formula that funds public education (K–12). The North Carolina Partnership for Children has an appropriation from the state general fund. Arizona has a dedicated revenue stream generated by a state excise tax on cigarettes.

- *Michigan:* $55,000 for statewide system building, plus $6 million for local system building
- *North Carolina:* $4 million for statewide system building, plus

TABLE 10.2. Arizona's Spending on Early Childhood System Building, 2009

Staffing of 31 regional partnership councils and local strategic planning	$5.8 million
State-level strategic planning	$25,000
Conducting and communicating a needs and assets survey	$2 million
Coordination strategies implemented by regional partnerships	$450,000
Policy and research staff dedicated to coordination with state and federal agencies and other partners	$1 million
Communications	$442,000
Total costs for system building	$9.7 million

> additional state funds for local system building that vary by local
> partnership
> • *Arizona:* $3.45 million for state and $6.25 million for local system
>   building

Financing System Building Through Arizona's First Things First.
In 2006, Arizona voters approved Proposition 203 and created a dedicated revenue stream to support the healthy development of young children, as well as the Arizona Early Childhood Development and Health Board to oversee the implementation of the First Things First system-building initiative. Arizona's system-building efforts are in the early stages of implementation, but a closer look at the spending of Proposition 203 funds during 2009 highlights some of the early costs of system building (see Table 10.2). The total cost, $9.7 million, represents 7% of the revenue budgeted in 2009.

Federal Revenue

All three states receive an Early Childhood Comprehensive Systems (ECCS) grant from the federal government. The state-level system-building entities in Michigan and Arizona manage the ECCS grants. Michigan also allocates quality set-aside funds from the Child Care and Development Block Grant. (See Appendix to this chapter for a full description.)

• *Arizona:* The Early Childhood Development and Health Board receives the $140,000 ECCS grant. The Board has been designated as the State Advisory Council on Early Childhood Education and Care and will manage this grant once the application is approved.
• *Michigan:* At the local level, the GSCs receive $1 million from the quality set-aside of the federal Child Care and Development Block Grant (CCDBG). At the state level, the Early Childhood Investment Corporation receives $140,000 from the ECCS grant,

$225,000 from the Head Start State Collaboration grant, and a little more than $1 million from CCDBG.

- *North Carolina:* The North Carolina Department of Health and Human Services receives the ECCS grant and works in close partnership with the North Carolina Partnership for Children.

Private Revenue

All three state early childhood initiatives are public/private partnerships. North Carolina and Michigan must generate private investments to match state funds, and the authorizing statute for Arizona requires the Board to cultivate private resources. While Arizona receives private funds, it does not use these resources to fund system-building activities.

- *North Carolina:* The North Carolina Partnership for Children must raise 10% of its state allocation from private sources, and three-quarters of the match must be in cash. In 2009, the Partnership raised 30% of its budget ($2 million) from private foundations. Local partnerships also must raise 10% of their state funds from private sources.
- *Michigan:* One million dollars in foundation funds goes directly to designated local collaboratives, and $600,000 supports the ECIC. While there is no requirement to raise private funds for system building at the state level, every local collaborative must raise 5% in cash and 5% in-kind to draw down state funding.

THE CHALLENGES OF FINANCING SYSTEM BUILDING

System building is an essential ingredient of an early childhood system, but it is hard to explain, difficult to evaluate, and thus challenging to finance. It is not a tangible service, or part of an infrastructure that supports the delivery of high-quality services. It is a process, or a set of activities, that contribute to improved child outcomes without actually touching a child. Arizona, Michigan, and North Carolina offer three examples of system building because they elevated the act of system building within their early childhood initiatives and dedicate funding for this purpose. But this approach comes with several risks.

First, it raises the expectations for accountability and results, and early childhood leaders and advocates struggle to demonstrate compelling results for system building. Michigan and Arizona include system building in their performance measures, but these are largely process measures such as implementing an effective collaborative governance structure, actively engaging local stakeholders, cultivating new leaders, implementing a communications plan, and implementing policies and procedures that facilitate service access and coordination. These are accurate measures of system building, but they are too far removed from the goal of improving shared outcomes for children. In contrast, North Carolina's performance measures are almost entirely focused on child and program outcomes, making it difficult to disaggregate the effect of system building from direct services and infrastructure supports. While this strategy leads to more compelling results, system building is only one piece of the equation. And, in states like Michigan where the system-building initiative receives no funding for direct services, it may be unreasonable to hold the ECIC and GSCs accountable for child outcomes.

Second, dependence on state revenues also puts system-building efforts at risk. With state revenues declining as much as 40% in some states in the past few years, every recipient of state funds has had to justify its value. Some have been more successful than others. Michigan held onto its funding for the local Great Start Collaboratives, which receive funding through the state education aid formula, in 2010, but it may have benefited from the state protecting education funding. Arizona's First Things First escaped elimination when the voters defeated the ballot initiative offered by the legislature to redirect revenue from the dedicated tax on cigarettes to the general fund. In contrast, in North Carolina, total funding (including direct services) dropped to the lowest level in the past 10 years.

The instability of state funds, combined with an inability to make the case for system building, makes the financing of these efforts especially fragile. System builders are constantly defending their work. They must answer to critics who see system building as ancillary, an added layer of bureaucracy, or an administrative function that should be minimized so as to maximize funding for direct services or infrastructure supports. Several directors of system-building activities acknowledge that they intentionally work under the radar. Some fund system building by including small line items in every funding request, just like fringe benefits and indirect costs. This stealth strategy has the potential to undermine system building by perpetuating a general lack of understanding about what it is. It also means funding for system building remains small, scattered among multiple pots of money, with little or no dedicated funding.

Given the challenges of financing system building, we need three things to promote its role in the development of early childhood systems. First, we need to be more articulate about what we mean by system building so that we can justify its expense. We must see it as distinct from both direct services and infrastructure supports, but as necessary to transform these pieces into a coherent system. We must be better communicators of *what* needs to be funded so that we can make a better case for *why* it needs funding to those who make funding decisions.

Second, we need better measures to demonstrate the value of system building. In this era of accountability, we need something more compelling than process measures to show that investing in system building is worthwhile. We also must be able to disaggregate the added value of system building from direct services and infrastructure.

Third, we need to overcome the zero-sum thinking that funding one aspect of the early childhood system comes at the expense of another, and that funding programs is more valuable than funding system building. One local partnership in North Carolina claims its system-building activities are cost neutral because of the efficiencies identified through the process of coordination and outreach. Regardless of the cost, children need more than any one program can provide. If the system vision includes improving shared outcomes for children, system building is needed to transform individual programs into an integrated system.

This chapter takes the first step in improving the financing of system building by clearly defining it and raising its visibility. The next step is to demonstrate accountability for investments in system building. We need better ways to measure investments in system building so we can justify the expense. Unfortunately, system-building measures are mostly process measures. While these measures can be quantified and met, they fail to be as compelling as outcome measures. We have an implicit assumption that system building leads to better programs and child outcomes, but until we make this explicit, we will continue to struggle to raise funding for system-building activities.

APPENDIX: FEDERAL EARLY CHILDHOOD SYSTEM-BUILDING FUNDING STREAMS

There are a few small federal grants that some states use for early childhood system-building activities.

Early Childhood Comprehensive Systems Grants (ECCS)

The Maternal and Child Health Bureau (MCHB) launched ECCS in 2002. Its purpose is "to help States plan, develop, and ultimately implement collaborations and partnerships to support families and communities to raise children that are healthy and ready to learn at school entry."[2] In 2009, this $7.3 million program provided 49 states, the District of Columbia, and four territories with annual grants of $100,000 for planning and $140,000 for implementation. Grantees are working to build and integrate early childhood service systems that address five critical components: access to comprehensive health services and medical homes; social-emotional development and mental health of young children; early care and education; parenting education; and family support. More information is available at http://www.state-eccs.org/index.htm.

State Advisory Council on Early Childhood Education and Care

The Improving Head Start for School Readiness Act of 2007 requires governors to create or designate an entity dedicated to improving the coordination and quality of programs and services for children from birth to school entry. While authorized through the Head Start legislation, the councils are intended to focus broadly on the comprehensive needs of young children and must include representatives from health, education, child care, Head Start, and early intervention (IDEA, Part C) programs or agencies. One of the responsibilities of the councils listed in the legislation is to "identify opportunities for, and barriers to, collaboration and coordination among federally funded and state-funded programs and agencies responsible for child development, child care, and early childhood education programs and services."[3] Council responsibilities also include providing advice on other parts of an early childhood system, such as professional development systems, standards, and data for accountability.

States may apply for a one-time, start-up grant of not less than $500,000 from the federal government, but must provide a 70% state match to receive funds. In-kind funds may be counted toward the match. More information is available at http://nccic.acf.hhs.gov/poptopics/advisorycouncils.html.

Project LAUNCH

The federal Substance Abuse and Mental Health Services Administration funds Project LAUNCH (Linking Actions for Unmet Needs in Children's Health) in 24 communities. Project LAUNCH grantees implement evidence-based public health strategies to support the wellness of young children, ages birth to 8 years of age, by addressing the physical, emotional, social, and behavioral aspects of their development. Grantees will work to improve coordination among child-serving systems, build infrastructure, and improve methods for providing services.

LAUNCH grantees each receive approximately $850,000 per year, over the course of 5 years. The majority of the funds (approximately $700,000) will be passed from the state and tribal level to an identified locality where the grant will support the enhancement and integration of services in addition to system coordination and development. The state receives $150,000 for coordination. More information is available at http://projectlaunch. promoteprevent.org.

Head Start State Collaboration Grants

In 1990, the federal government began funding Head Start State Collaboration offices in each state. These grants were intended to create partnerships that helped build early childhood systems that promote access to comprehensive services. Each state appointed a State Director of Head Start Collaboration to encourage collaboration between Head Start and other programs or services working to promote the healthy development of the Head Start target population and other low-income families. These positions continue to receive an annual amount of $125,000, $175,000, or $225,000, depending on the size of the state and the number of children in poverty. More information is available at http://eclkc.ohs.acf.hhs.gov/hslc/ hsd/SCO.

NOTES

The primary source of information for this chapter was interviews with the leaders of the early childhood system initiatives in Arizona, Michigan, and North Carolina. Thank you to Joan Blough, Stephanie Fanjul, Elliott Hibbs, Pauline McKee, Karen Woodhouse, and Henrietta Zalkind for their time and insights.

1. Down East Partnership for Children. (2007). Strategic Plan. Retrieved November 20, 2009, from http://www.depc.org/images/stories/pdfs/depcstrategicplan07.pdf

2. State MCH Early Childhood Comprehensive System Implementation Grants. (2009). Retrieved November 14, 2009, from https://grants.hrsa.gov/webExternal/ SFO.asp?ID=C659EDD3-65E1-4E3C-B2B1-D8C404E8651D

3. 42 U.S.C. § 9837b (2007 through Pub. L. No. 110-134)

CHAPTER 11

Estimating the Costs of Early Childhood Systems

Andrew Brodsky

Comprehensive early childhood systems are interconnected sets of supports available to all young children, comprising early childhood education, family supports, and medical and behavioral health care. Comprehensive early childhood systems help ensure that young children are physically, emotionally, socially, and academically prepared to succeed as they move to school and beyond. To be effective, they must encompass a range of services and programs for young children, place importance on quality standards, and incorporate collaborative relationships among local organizations, parents, and service providers (Kagan & Cohen, 1997; Ruderman & Grason, 2004; Stoney, Mitchell, & Warner, 2006). Quantifying the costs to build such systems is key to ensuring that they are comprehensive, high quality, logistically feasible, and politically viable.

Cost estimation work comprises a number of interlocking elements. These can include identifying the current range of services and resources available for young children, providing a justification for increased funding, defining the extent of a comprehensive system, and helping policymakers balance competing policy options when available funding is limited. Cost estimation also can encompass budgeting, planning, feasibility assessments, program monitoring, and public accountability (Myers, 2008).

In this chapter, I investigate the integral role cost estimation plays in system building. I begin by exploring the boundaries and parameters of the field, surveying current work, and contrasting various approaches. Next, I discuss findings and implications of this work. Finally, I offer several principles for effective use of cost estimation for system building and conclude with a look forward in the field.

WHAT DOES COST ESTIMATION
FOR SYSTEM BUILDING LOOK LIKE?

Early childhood system cost models vary widely in scope. They may estimate costs for an individual community or county, for a state, or for the nation as a whole. They may estimate costs for an individual program, such as a state's universal preschool program; for a set of programs or services in a particular early childhood domain, such as early education; or for an entire comprehensive early childhood system (e.g., Brandon, Maher, Li, & Joesch, 2004; Brodsky & Medler, 2006; Brodsky, Rooney, & Silverstein, 2010; Golin, Muenchow, Wang, & Lam, 2004).

Much of the work of cost estimation overlaps with the work of early childhood finance, although the two approaches are distinct. Cost estimation models typically calculate the costs necessary to achieve a specific status level of the system, such as coverage, participation, or quality. Financing, on the other hand, addresses cost inputs, such as the share of costs borne by parents or by the state, or the identification of sustained revenue streams (e.g., Calman & Tarr-Whelan, 2005; Gomby & Krantzler, 1996; Mitchell & Stoney, 2006; Stoney, Groginsky, & Poppe, 2002; Stoney et al., 2006). Financing projects often include cost estimation as a critical component, especially in identifying how to use finite resources most effectively (Hayes, Flynn, & Stebbins, 2004).

Cost estimation is also distinct from estimating the economic effectiveness of early childhood programs, although these two goals may overlap. Estimates of economic effectiveness typically evaluate long-term cost savings from public investments in early childhood systems. These savings may be realized through a range of positive outcomes for children who attend early childhood programs, such as higher graduation rates, lower incarceration rates, and higher college-going rates (e.g., Belfield, 2004; Galinsky, 2006). These effectiveness estimates may be driven at least in part by a cost estimation process. For example, the RAND Corporation studied the economic returns of a high-quality universal preschool program in California (Karoly & Bigelow, 2005). In order to determine the "cost" portion of this cost–benefit analysis, the researchers estimated the costs of the program based on a range of assumptions, including enrollment patterns, instructional and administrative staff required, and child/staff ratios.

Current Work in Early Childhood Cost Estimation

While individual government agencies and child care programs typically are required to produce budget and cost estimates, cost estimation within the larger frame of early childhood system building is relatively new. The systems frame requires moving beyond a narrow programmatic approach and embracing more ambitious goals.

A number of distinct approaches to cost estimation are currently in use. In this section, I review four such approaches: (1) the cost simulation approach developed by Rick Brandon and colleagues at the University of Washington Human Services Policy Center (HSPC); (2) the cost of quality approach developed by the Institute for Women's Policy Research (IWPR); (3) the interactive approach developed by Andrew Brodsky, Alex Medler, and colleagues at Augenblick, Palaich and Associates (APA) and the Colorado Children's Campaign (CCC); and (4) the cost estimation process for quality early childhood education (ECE) developed by the Finance Project. These approaches have been selected to exemplify the range of current practice, but they are not intended to represent all work in the field.

Brandon Cost Simulation Approach. Richard Brandon and colleagues at the University of Washington use a computer simulation to estimate the costs of providing financial access to high-quality ECE services for children from birth through age 5. In this approach, partners specify a wide range of parameters regarding both the services to be delivered and the mechanisms by which families of different income levels are to be assisted in affording those services. In the course of the cost estimation process, HSPC provides results for a number of preset scenarios, and then adjusts scenarios in partnership with stakeholders (Brandon et al., 2004; Brandon, Scarpa, Maher, & Li, 2005; Brandon & Stutman, 2008; Human Services Policy Center, 2005). For example, in Shelby County, Tennessee, researchers generated cost estimates for three policy options, including two market-based approaches that would support about half the cost of high-quality ECE through financial assistance to providers, and a public school type system that would replace the current ECE market with a publicly funded service. These costs were based on a range of factors, including teacher qualifications and compensation, and child income eligibility (Brandon et al., 2005).

Institute for Women's Policy Research Cost of Quality Approach. The IWPR and Early Childhood Policy Research developed a model to estimate the cost of implementing a state-based, voluntary, universally accessible program to provide quality early childhood education to preschool-age children. This approach determines a per-child-hour estimate based on a set of predetermined quality levels, which in turn are based on a wide range of variables, including teacher qualifications, teacher-to-child ratios, and parent involvement (Gault, Mitchell, Williams, Dey, & Sorokina, 2008; Golin,

Mitchell, & Wallen, 2003, 2004; Golin, Muenchow, et al., 2004; Mitchell & Stoney, 2004). For example, an IWPR study of the cost of preschool in Illinois was built on a series of estimates, including the need for universally accessible preschool, the number of 3- and 4-year-olds likely to participate, how much the program would cost based on each of the four quality levels, and what components should be included in direct service costs or in infrastructure costs (Golin et al., 2003).

APA/CCC Interactive Approach. Augenblick, Palaich and Associates developed an interactive, web-based model that estimates costs for a comprehensive early childhood system under a variety of user-defined settings. The current model's predecessor was developed for Colorado in partnership with the CCC and Anne Mitchell, using some of the cost of quality methodology described in the IWPR approach, and has since been expanded. In this approach, a set of programs and services that serves children birth through age 5 is identified within each of several domains, such as early care and education, family support, and health care. For each program or service, current and projected enrollment figures are determined for children, who are categorized by age and income. The figures are multiplied by estimated costs, which can vary by age, quality level, or intensity. A web-based interface allows users to change a range of assumptions, such as participation rates and eligibility levels, and to view the resulting cost changes instantly (Brodsky, 2010; Brodsky & Mitchell, 2007; Brodsky et al., 2010; Colorado Children's Campaign, 2007).

In Ohio, APA worked with the Governor's Early Childhood Cabinet to create a comprehensive early childhood cost model for the state. Users can adjust variables that affect projections—such as participation rates or days of service per year—and then view cost estimates for each program and for the system as a whole. Results of this study will be used to inform the state's ongoing policy debate about early childhood funding (Brodsky, 2010).

Finance Project Cost Estimation Approach. The Finance Project's cost modeling approach estimates the cost of high-quality ECE programs for children birth through age 5, based on three categories of costs: direct services, infrastructure costs, and capital improvements. Researchers use five steps to estimate costs: (1) determine the scope and definition of what is being estimated; (2) identify the level of quality improvements stakeholders seek to achieve; (3) determine a baseline of cost estimates, using the costs of a hypothetical child care center multiplied by the number of children in the community projected to need services; (4) estimate the cost of improving quality based on quality improvement goals; and (5) determine how long it will take to phase in various components of the plan (Stebbins & Langford, 2006).

For example, the Finance Project's cost model for Kansas City determined an average cost per slot for a hypothetical child care center or home, relying on current salary and budget information, and using a set of assumptions of current services. Once a baseline had been established, quality parameters were adjusted to reflect a specific standard level. The result was an estimate of the total annual cost for a fully implemented improved level of quality for the city (Stebbins & Langford, 2006).

Comparing Approaches

The four approaches described above all estimate the costs for various system components based on per-child or per-provider costs for various quality levels. They provide results for a range of scenarios, either based on predetermined settings (such as Brandon's work in Boulder), or through a dynamic interface with a range of user options (such as APA's work in Ohio).

The models vary in the specific methodology used to determine cost estimates. For example, the IWPR and APA models create cost estimates by multiplying a matrix of hourly costs by the number of children enrolled, while the HSPC model uses a more complex proprietary formula to derive cost estimates, incorporating a range of parameter estimates. The Finance Project's work in Kansas City was based in part on current budget data, while APA's work on a national early childhood cost model derived per-child cost estimates from scratch (Brodsky et al., 2010; Stebbins & Langford, 2006).

These approaches also vary in scope: Some are designed to estimate the costs of universal preschool programs, while others explicitly aim to derive a comprehensive systems cost. Both approaches are useful in system-building work. Cost estimates for universal preschool programs are useful because these programs may form the core of a comprehensive system, and because they may be the most politically or practically viable component of the system to improve. In comparison, the more comprehensive approaches explicitly seek to model an entire system, including preschool, ECE costs for younger children, family supports, mental health, and health care costs.

Cost estimation approaches can be categorized as aspirational or incremental. An *aspirational* approach seeks to determine the cost of a full-scale, high-quality program or system, based on a specified set of standards. For example, a national estimate of the cost of high-quality preschool for all children, a modification of APA's interactive approach, based its analysis on predetermined national quality standards (Brodsky et al., 2010; National Association for the Education of Young Children, 2007). Brandon's (2000) estimate for a national universal preschool program incorporated its own set of standards, which included minimum levels for staff qualifications, compensation, staff/child ratios, and a number of other factors. A cost estimate for universal preschool in California used a predetermined definition of a comprehensive universal preschool program, including assumptions about family contributions and staff/child ratios (Golin et al., 2004).

An aspirational approach can work well within a system-building frame. For example, it can provide a rationale for funding increases, it can help set ambitious goals for a comprehensive system, or it can demonstrate the magnitude of current funding gaps. Aspirational models provide valuable information about the current and desired status of the system and can dramatically illustrate the urgency for an improved system.

An *incremental* approach, on the other hand, takes a more practical tack. In this approach, a model estimates the costs associated with a small, politically viable change in the current system. This approach can be used if stakeholders determine that it is politically or financially impossible to create a truly universal program or system, but that smaller steps are feasible. For example, a cost estimate for a taxpayer-funded preschool program in Denver varied participation rates, parental co-pays, and target quality levels to work within the constraints of the projected funding that would be available for the project (Brodsky & Medler, 2006).

The incremental approach may be useful in working with policymakers and budgeters who are concerned about logistics and the political realities of increasing funding. For example, the additional costs of creating a truly comprehensive, universal early childhood system for a large state could run into the billions of dollars. Legislators who see only this number may balk at considering *any* increased funding. However, an estimate for an incremental and intermediate goal, such as increasing the number of publicly funded preschool slots by 10%, might be more palatable.

The aspirational and incremental approaches can be combined in a single modeling exercise. An interactive model "pre-loaded" with current enrollment and funding rates, and costs per child, can accomplish this goal. Using an interactive model, users can manipulate such variables as participation rates and quality levels either to reflect a high-quality, universal program (an aspirational system) or to model a more practical, incremental change from the current system. Examples include a cost estimator for California's Preschool for All program, which allows users to adjust participation rates and per-child costs, and a statewide early childhood cost model for Colorado, which allows users to estimate the costs of any level of system between the current level of services and a comprehensive, universal system (American Institutes for Research, 2009; Colorado Children's Campaign, 2007).

Implications of Existing Cost Estimation Work

Several themes can be drawn from recent cost estimation studies. One recurrent theme is that in the short term, creating a high-quality early education system is expensive relative to current public funding. For example, national cost estimates range from about $8 to $12 billion to provide a free preschool education to all children (Barnett & Robin, 2006), to $50 billion nationally to provide families with a substantial voucher to buy quality child care and to fund higher reimbursement fees to providers serving subsidized children (Helburn, 2002). A universal preschool program to serve all 4-year-olds in California would cost about $1.9 billion a year, and would cost almost $700 million to serve only free-and-reduced-lunch-eligible children (Golin et al., 2004). A high-quality universal preschool program for 200,000 children in Illinois would cost about $440 million annually (Golin et al., 2003), and a free, high-quality universal preschool program serving all children in Shelby County, Kentucky—a county with a population of just under 1,000,000—would cost, under current utilization assumptions, up to $524 million, about five times the current funding level (Brandon et al., 2005).

A caveat to these findings is that they represent additional costs to the early childhood system from a public perspective only. They may not show the associated public or private economic benefits of system building. For example, a strong system of family supports may increase academic outcomes for children and reduce social problems, thus creating long-term economic benefits. These estimates may reflect cost shifting from parents, who currently bear much of the cost of child care, to public financing. While this initially will result in greater public costs, increased access to child care will allow more parents to participate in the workforce, providing broad economic benefits. Cost estimates also may mask cost shifting from one public financing method to another. For example, Denver's publicly funded preschool program increased sales taxes in the city (thereby costing taxpayers), but some of these funds went to Denver public school classrooms, thereby offsetting budgets in the school district, which also is publicly funded.

A second theme that emerges from recent work is that per-child public funding for early childhood systems is much smaller than that of K–12 systems. For example, on a per-child basis, the United States spent only one-tenth as much on early education as on elementary and secondary education (Brandon, 2000). Brodsky (2008) found that average public per-child spending for 0- to 5-year-olds in Colorado was $1,130, including publicly funded health insurance programs, compared with about $8,700 spent per K–12 child in the public school system alone. Other research also indicates that substantially fewer resources are available to children under 3 compared with older children (e.g., Kagan & Neuman, 2003).

These findings suggest that significant public commitment is required to build early childhood systems. However, these investments result in benefits that are not always immediately visible. In order to generate public support for system building, policymakers and advocates should communicate not only the costs of system building, but also its broader societal benefits as well.

PRINCIPLES FOR EFFECTIVE USE OF COST ESTIMATION FOR SYSTEM BUILDING

In order to be most effective at helping to foster early childhood systems, cost estimation work must adhere to a number of key principles. In this section, I enumerate three principles and discuss some common pitfalls that may hamper success.

Principle 1: Cost Estimates Should Represent Comprehensive and Inclusive Systems

Building comprehensive early childhood systems involves more than simply piecing together a hodgepodge of individual programs. Creating systems that provide effective and comprehensive care for all children involves planning, funding, and coordination across a wide range of services. These direct services can be categorized in a number of ways, often termed domains. For example, the Early Childhood Systems Working Group proposes four interlocking domains, including early learning; health, mental health, and nutrition; family support; and special needs/early intervention (Coffman, Wright, & Bruner, 2006; Ruderman & Grason, 2004). Early childhood cost models for Colorado were defined slightly differently: early childhood education, family support, mental health, and health (Colorado Children's Campaign, 2007). A cost estimation model within a systems frame, therefore, should cost out the wide range of direct services that constitute a system (Kagan & Neuman, 2003). Infrastructure elements also should be accounted for, including supports such as professional development, regulation, quality assurance mechanisms, finance, and governance.

A true comprehensive early childhood system also should aim to support all children, regardless of age or income. Cost estimates should expand beyond the traditional domain of preschool and incorporate children starting from birth. This may require models to account for different per-child costs for younger children due to higher staff/child ratios, lower participation rates, and other factors. At the other end of the early childhood age continuum, kindergarten might be incorporated, especially if free full-day kindergarten is not provided by the state or district.

A system should aim services not only at children in poverty, but also at mainstream American families (Calman & Tarr-Whelan, 2005; Stoney et al., 2006). Therefore, cost models should estimate the costs of providing ECE to all children who may participate, not only those below a given income level. Focusing only on low-income children fails to acknowledge that preschool benefits all children (Stoney et al., 2006). Incorporating more-affluent children in public programs also can provide political momentum for these programs, which are funded largely by taxpayer money. Varying expected participation rates by parents' income tier can provide a more nuanced cost estimate. This approach was used by the Colorado Children's Campaign (2007) in the creation of a cost estimation model for the Preschool Matters Initiative in Denver, a successful ballot initiative that led to the passage of a citywide universal preschool program. This model incorporated all children but assumed a higher participation rate, and a lower parental co-pay rate, for lower income children (Augenblick, Palaich and Associates, 2009a).

A system input that frequently is omitted from cost estimations is private contributions, such as parent fees. Parent fees not only help pay for services, but also can help parents feel greater investment in ECE programs. If parents are required to have some "skin in the game," they may be more likely to support the program and may provide political support as well. The effect of parent contributions can be captured by incorporating them into cost models and allowing them to vary by family characteristics, such as size or income. More sophisticated models also could use existing data to statistically model how changing parent fees affects participation rates and, in turn, costs.

Principle 2: Cost Estimates Should Assume High Quality

A wide body of literature increasingly points to the importance of measurable quality levels in creating positive outcomes for children, especially in the early learning domain, where current quality levels are inconsistent (e.g., Campbell, Ramey, Pungello, Sparling, & Miller-Johnson, 2002; Espinosa, 2002; Loeb, Fuller, Kagan, & Carrol, 2004; Shonkoff & Phillips, 2000). A system cost estimate can contribute to quality improvement by quantifying the relative costs of quality.

Quality itself can be defined in various ways, and these definitions can vary for different programs or services. For example, a cost model for an early childhood system for Colorado defined quality differently for different parts of the system. In this model, the costs of quality for child care and early childhood education programs were tied to four predetermined quality levels based on assumptions about staff qualifications, staff/child ratios, and other dimensions. Costs of quality for mental health services were defined using a simpler formula based primarily on the intensity level of services offered (Colorado Children's Campaign, 2007). Brandon and colleagues base their cost-modeling methodology on a market-oriented approach in which improving the supply of ECE will lead to increased demand, which in turn will lead to quality improvement. The cost estimation approach associated with this orientation suggests that quality standards will change provider costs, which will change parent prices, and require different assistance to families (Brandon et al., 2004).

Cost estimation also can help identify how much money would be needed to fix the "broken" market, in which inadequate money exists in the system to produce high-quality outcomes and inadequate information is available on the relative costs of quality (McCartney, 2002; Mocan & Blau, 2002; Vandell & Wolf, 2000). Rectifying the situation requires more than simply allowing parents choice within the market, assuming that they will make appropriate trade-offs between quality and cost in their decision making. Rather, additional resources need to be injected into the system to produce high-quality options.

Principle 3: Researchers Should Articulate How Cost Models Will Contribute to System Building

Without a clearly defined vision for how a cost model's results will be used to effect systemic change, the work may have little real-world effect. Cost models that are most effective at promoting system building are based on clear thinking about how they will be used in the policy arena.

While cost models must be built on a solid foundation of theory and methodology, the need to build high-quality systems is too urgent for cost estimation to remain an academic exercise. Researchers and stakeholders should ask how, specifically, results will be used once the research is completed. A plan should exist so that the results of the model are communicated to policymakers, and model results should have specific, real-world policy applications, such as expansion of a state's preschool program. Other goals might include creating pressure for legislation, providing an argument for increased funding, or promoting discussion among stakeholders about the best ways to spend limited funds.

One way to help ensure that cost estimates gain traction is to ensure stakeholder buy-in throughout the model development process and to strive for consensus among partners. However, balancing the interests of various stakeholders with the integrity of the research can be challenging. Stakeholders may exert pressure for cost estimates to be either higher or lower than the research justifies. For example, a cost model might return a politically unfeasible cost estimate for a comprehensive preschool program, resulting in pressure from legislators involved in the project to argue for changing the cost of program quality rather than accepting the model's implication that fewer children can be covered. Advocacy groups may be motivated to exaggerate the costs of a system in order to make rhetorical points about the urgent need for increased funding, or, conversely, they may be motivated to portray costs as less than they are, in order to build public will and demonstrate feasibility for programmatic changes. When the cost model is completed, access to it may be vulnerable to "turf wars," in which one group or another wishes to control access. Building a broad coalition beforehand and clearly establishing rules for distribution and access can help prevent these pitfalls.

In navigating this maze, researchers must ensure that the project retains its integrity and that the model is not changed to meet individual interests that are counterproductive to the project's stated goals. Rather than compromise the model's essential structure and data, project partners in this example should work with legislators to ensure that the model provides clear, useful results and should help advocate for the types of policy change implied by model results.

THE FUTURE OF EARLY CHILDHOOD SYSTEMS COST ESTIMATION

Cost estimation for early childhood systems is still a relatively new field. Much of the well-known work in the field has been undertaken since 2000. But with increased emphasis on system building and increased public funding directed toward early childhood finance and cost estimation, the field is expanding quickly.

Cost estimation work has already driven policy and programmatic change. Cost estimates frequently are used to advocate for policy at the national level. Advocacy organizations such as the National Association of Child Care Resource and Referral Agencies (NACCRRA), the National Institute for Early Education Research, and the National Center for Children in Poverty routinely use estimates of early care costs to advocate for public spending and quality improvement. Government-affiliated agencies such as the National Child Care Information and Technical Assistance Center assist states in setting child care policies, in part based on cost estimates.

Other examples of cost models helping to drive policy change exist at both local and state levels. Cost estimates for a proposed Denver preschool program—which later passed—helped determine whether the proposed tax increase would be adequate to fund the program. This work was modified for use in Boulder County, which utilized the results to help establish the feasibility and structure of a similar county-wide preschool program. A model in Washington estimated the costs of providing continuous care to children through the state child care program, and was used by policymakers in discussions about changing state regulations (Augenblick, Palaich and Associates, 2009b).

More states may soon undertake cost estimation projects in conjunction with Early Childhood Comprehensive Systems (ECCS) planning grants. These federal grants, first issued in 2003, allow states to engage in strategic planning and collaboration-building efforts needed to promote the development of comprehensive early childhood systems. One requirement for each state's ECCS plan is to include a sustainability plan that encourages financing and resource-leveraging strategies for carrying out the follow-up implementation of the project. A number of states have identified resource mapping and cost modeling as an important component of their early childhood reform plan. For example, one of the goals of New York's Early Childhood Comprehensive Systems plan is to assess the capacity of the current systems serving young children and their families, and to identify existing gaps or challenges (New York State Council on Children and Families, 2009). Colorado's state early childhood plan identified a goal of "an early childhood system [with] adequate, sustainable, and flexible funding and resources from a broad array of public and private partners." To meet this goal, stated objectives included identifying cost models and financing plans for high-quality early childhood systems (Smart Start Colorado, 2007). In North Carolina, one goal of the state's early childhood system plan is to build broad-based support for investing in efforts to produce positive child outcomes. One strategy identified to implement this goal is to educate families, stakeholders, and policymakers about the costs and benefits of building (or neglecting to build) a comprehensive, integrated early childhood system (Nelson, n.d.), a task that would incorporate a cost estimate. Federal investments through the American Recovery and Reinvestment Act (ARRA) of 2009, which directs $2 billion to the child care block grant program, also may provide opportunities for states and counties to undertake cost estimation models. A portion of ARRA funds are directed specifically at evaluation and system monitoring, making cost estimation projects more financially feasible.

While the field is developing rapidly, few national estimates exist for the cost of a truly comprehensive early childhood system, spanning the key domains and extending from birth through age 5. Such a model might have broad policy applications. A number of technical issues need to be considered; for example, the model would need to take into account varying costs of the components, such as personnel and infrastructure costs, across states. While the scope of such work is ambitious, it could have significant utility in articulating a cohesive national vision for an early childhood system.

As the technical computing capabilities and skills of cost-modeling teams have improved, a new range of possibilities has opened up for cost estimation projects. Using existing programs and proprietary or custom-designed software, cost modelers can create more complex analyses and offer users more flexibility in creating scenarios and receiving results. For example, APA's cost-modeling work for NACCRRA uses a customized software system and web-based interface. This platform allows users a great deal of flexibility in adjusting model parameters and viewing and saving multiple scenarios, and allows the project team to control access to the model using unique usernames and passwords.

The integrated data systems being developed in many states are technical advances that also will greatly enhance the accuracy and scope of cost estimation work. Often conceived as part of an integrated "P–16" (prenatal through grade 16, or college graduation) system, an integrated data system facilitates the sharing of child-level data across social systems. Such data might include information on public education, health insurance program enrollment, parental employment status, and other data points. As such systems become more accurate and efficient, a wealth of information will be available to researchers. For example, a data system that integrates preschool attendance and developmental indicators with social services data and school district data could be used to create more nuanced examinations of the relationship between cost inputs and outcomes.

Ultimately, as the body of experience around early childhood cost estimation grows, researchers and local stakeholders will be better able to share knowledge; and as more and more states and counties engage in cost estimation projects, models will become more nuanced and sophisticated. Child advocates should take advantage of a unique combination of new funding opportunities, enhanced data systems, improved technology, and political inertia to expand and improve the work of early childhood cost estimation and, in turn, ensure successful outcomes for all young children.

REFERENCES

American Institutes for Research. (2009). *The preschool for all cost estimator*. Palo Alto, CA: AIR. Retrieved from http://www.earlylearningsystems.org/budget-planning/estimator

Augenblick, Palaich and Associates. (2009a). *Denver preschool program year two evaluation report*. Denver, CO: APA Consulting.

Augenblick, Palaich and Associates. (2009b). *Washington department of early learning continuity of care cost model.* Denver, CO: APA Consulting.

Barnett, W. S., & Robin, K. B. (2006). *How much does quality preschool cost?* New Brunswick, NJ: National Institute for Early Education Research, Rutgers University.

Belfield, C. (2004). *Early childhood education: How important are the cost-savings to the school system?* New York: Center for Early Care and Education.

Brandon, R. N. (2000, June). *Design choices: Universal financing for early care and education* (Human Services Policy Center Policy Brief). Seattle: University of Washington.

Brandon, R. N., Maher, E. J., Li, G., & Joesch, J. M. (2004). *Financing access to high quality early care and education for all of Illinois' children* (Public Report of the Illinois Task Force). Seattle: University of Washington.

Brandon, R. N., Scarpa, J., Maher, E., & Li, G. (2005). *Early care and education cost estimates for Shelby County, Tennessee* (Report to the First Years Institute ECE Initiative Planning Committee). Seattle: University of Washington.

Brandon, R. N., & Stutman, T. J. (2008, April 12). *A "policy cluster" approach to allocating resources to improve student performance.* Paper presented at the annual conference of the American Education Finance Association, Denver, CO.

Brodsky, A. (2008, April). *Public funding for Colorado's early childhood system* (Report submitted to the Colorado Children's Campaign). Denver, CO: Augenblick, Palaich and Associates.

Brodsky, A. (2010). *An early childhood cost model for Ohio.* Denver, CO: Augenblick, Palaich and Associates.

Brodsky, A., & Medler, A. (2006). *Early childhood education in Denver: A needs assessment.* Denver: Colorado Children's Campaign.

Brodsky, A., & Mitchell, A. (2007). *Colorado early childhood systems cost model: Technical manual.* Denver: Smart Start Colorado, Colorado Children's Campaign, & Augenblick, Palaich and Associates.

Brodsky, A., Rooney, K., & Silverstein, J. (2010). *A national early childhood education cost model.* Washington, DC: NACCRRA.

Calman, L. J., & Tarr-Whelan, L. (2005). *Early childhood education for all: A wise investment.* Recommendations arising from "The economic impacts of child care and early education: Financing solutions for the future." New York: Legal Momentum.

Campbell, F. A., Ramey, C. T., Pungello, E., Sparling, J., & Miller-Johnson, S. (2002). Early childhood education: Young adult outcomes from the Abecedarian Project. *Applied Developmental Science, 6*(1), 42–57.

Coffman, J., Wright, M. S., & Bruner, C. (2006). *Beyond parallel play: Emerging state and community planning roles in building early learning systems.* Des Moines, IA: State Early Childhood Policy Technical Assistance Network and Build Initiative.

Colorado Children's Campaign. (2007). *An early childhood cost model for Colorado* (Interactive Excel model). Denver, CO: Author.

Espinosa, L. M. (2002). *High-quality preschool: Why we need it and what it looks like.* New Brunswick, NJ: National Institute for Early Education Research, Rutgers University.

Galinsky, E. (2006). *The economic benefits of high-quality early childhood programs: What makes the difference?* Washington, DC: Committee for Economic Development.

Gault, B., Mitchell, A. W., Williams, E., Dey, J., & Sorokina, O. (2008). *Meaningful investments in pre-K: Estimating the per-child costs of quality programs.* Washington, DC: Institute for Women's Policy Research.

Golin, S. C., Mitchell, A.W., & Wallen, M. (2003). *The cost of universal access to quality preschool in Illinois: A report to Governor George H. Ryan's task force on universal access to preschool.* Washington, DC: Institute for Women's Policy Research.

Golin, S. C., Mitchell, A.W., & Wallen, M. (2004). *The price of school readiness: A tool for estimating the cost of universal preschool in the states.* Washington, DC: Institute for Women's Policy Research.

Golin, S. C., Muenchow, S., Wang, H., & Lam, I. (2004). *Estimating the cost of preschool for all in California: A policy brief.* Prepared for the David and Lucile Packard Foundation. Palo Alto, CA: American Institutes for Research.

Gomby, D., & Krantzler, N. (Eds.). (1996, Summer/Fall). Financing child care. In *The future of children,* Vol. 6, No. 2. Los Altos, CA: Center for the Future of Children & David and Lucile Packard Foundation.

Hayes, C., Flynn, M., & Stebbins, H. (2004). Strategic financing: Making the most of the state early childhood comprehensive systems initiative. *No. 5. Building state early childhood comprehensive systems series.* Los Angeles: National Center for Infant and Early Childhood Health Policy.

Helburn, S. W. (2002). Measuring classroom costs in early education programs. In *Measuring preschool costs and revenues: Issues and answers. A summary report of the 2002 Early Education Cost Symposium* (W. S. Barnett & P. J. Kelley, Eds.). New Brunswick, NJ: National Institute of Early Education Research, Rutgers University.

Human Services Policy Center. (2005). *Estimating the cost of a high quality early care and education system for a state or local area: Simplified approach.* Seattle: University of Washington.

Improving Head Start for School Readiness Act of 2007, 42 U.S.C. § 9801 *et seq.* (2007).

Kagan, S. L., & Cohen, N. E. (1997). *Solving the quality problem: A vision for America's early care and education system. A final report of the Quality 2000 initiative.* New Haven, CT: Yale University.

Kagan, S. L., & Neuman, M. J. (2003). Back to basics: Building an early care and education system. In F. Jacobs, D. Wertlieb, & R. M. Lerner (Eds.), *Handbook of applied developmental science: Vol. 2. Enhancing the life chances of youth and families: Contributions of programs, policies, and service systems* (pp. 329–345). Thousand Oaks, CA: Sage.

Karoly, L. A., & Bigelow, J. E. (2005). *The economics of investing in universal preschool education in California.* Santa Monica, CA: RAND Corporation.

Loeb, S., Fuller, B., Kagan, S. L., & Carrol, B. (2004). Child care in poor communities: Early learning effects of type, quality, and stability. *Child Development, 75*(1), 47–65.

McCartney, K. (2002). *HGSE alumni weekend lecture.* Retrieved from http://www.gse.harvard.edu/news/features/mccartney08012002.html

Mitchell, A., & Stoney, L. (2004). *Costing out the system: How can we develop a comprehensive, cross-system approach to determining a per-child cost for early care and education?* Raleigh, NC: Alliance on Early Childhood Finance for the Smart Start National Technical Assistance Center.

Mitchell, A., & Stoney, L. (2006). *Financing early childhood care and education systems in the states: A standards-based approach*. Houston: Rice University Baker Policy Institute, Texas Program for Society and Health.

Mocan, H. N., & Blau, D. M. (2002). The supply of quality in child care centers. *The Review of Economics and Statistics, 84*(3), 483–496.

Myers, R. G. (2008). A note on costs and costing of early childhood care and development programmes. In *Coordinator's notebook: An international resource for early childhood*, No. 3. Toronto, Ontario, Canada: Consultive Group on Early Childhood Care and Development.

National Association for the Education of Young Children. (2007). *NAEYC early childhood program standards and accreditation criteria: The mark of quality in early childhood education*. Washington, DC: Author.

Nelson, D. C. (n.d.) *North Carolina's plan for a comprehensive early childhood system*. Retrieved from http://eccs.hrsa.gov/PlansModels/stateplans/docs/northcarolinastateplan.pdf

New York State Council on Children and Families. (2009). *Early childhood comprehensive systems (ECCS) plan*. Retrieved from http://www.ccf.state.ny.us/Initiatives/EccsRelate/EccsPlan.htm

Ruderman, M., & Grason, H. (2004). *Early childhood system building tool*. Baltimore, MD: Johns Hopkins Bloomberg School of Public Health & Los Angeles: National Center for Infant and Early Childhood Health Policy.

Shonkoff, J. P., & Phillips, D. A. (2000). *From neurons to neighborhoods: The science of early childhood development*. Washington, DC: National Academies Press.

Smart Start Colorado. (2007). Smart Start Colorado strategic plan and implementation schedule. Denver: Smart Start Colorado.

Stebbins, H., & Langford, B. H. (2006). *A guide to calculating the cost of quality early care and education*. Financing Strategies Series. Washington, DC: Finance Project.

Stoney, L., Groginsky, S., & Poppe, J. (2002). *Investing in our future: A guide to child care financing*. Denver, CO: National Conference of State Legislatures.

Stoney, L., Mitchell, A., & Warner, M. (2006). Smarter reform: Moving beyond single-program solutions to an early care and education system. *Community Development: Journal of the Community Development Society, 37*(2), 101–115.

Vandell, D. L., & Wolf, B. (2000). *Child care quality: Does it matter and does it need to be improved?* (Special Report No. 78). Madison: Institute for Research on Poverty, University of Wisconsin.

CHAPTER 12

Evaluating System-Building Efforts

Julia Coffman

System-building efforts are complex and notoriously hard to evaluate. They feature multiple programs and players and aim for outcomes at multiple levels (child, family, community, state, and national). They involve numerous public or private funding streams administered through different agencies and decision-making structures, and require that goals and actions be aligned and coordinated across programs with different political cultures. System-building efforts also tackle difficult and deep-rooted problems such as gaps in services and outcomes based on race, income, culture, and language, making them complicated and long-term endeavors. Finally, all efforts to improve systems necessarily evolve over time in response to the political, economic, and social contexts around them. These many complexities place system building directly outside of the more familiar and more traditional program evaluation comfort zone, which prefers programs and their environments to be more controlled, static, and straightforward.

Adding to this complexity is the fact that several longstanding questions still loom large in discussions about how to evaluate both system-building efforts and the systems they are trying to build. These questions include whether experimental designs (or other counterfactuals) are appropriate or even possible in this context, and under what conditions efforts to build early childhood systems should be held accountable for demonstrating child- and family-level impacts. While these questions have been asked many times, the debate over how they should be answered continues.

This chapter aims to help clarify discussions about how to evaluate *efforts to build early childhood systems*. It presents an evaluation framework that explains what system-building efforts do and the types of outcomes and impacts they produce. In doing this, it moves the conversation from a macro level where the concept of evaluating early childhood systems in their entirety can be either overwhelming or premature, to a more manageable discussion of the concrete concepts and practical steps that should be involved in evaluating the system-building process.

This chapter does *not* focus on how to evaluate early childhood systems once they have been built. While this question is also of critical importance, this chapter responds to the needs of states and communities that are deeply engaged in constructing comprehensive and coordinated early childhood systems, but are not yet at a place where they are ready to be accountable for the kinds of child and family impacts that are expected from fully constructed systems. These states and communities are "in process" with their system-building efforts and want to know what data they can and should collect to both track their progress at a system level and capture what they are accomplishing for children and families.

FIVE AREAS OF SYSTEM BUILDING

The next step in advancing the evaluation conversation is defining what it means to engage in building the kinds of early childhood systems defined above. *System building* refers to organized efforts to improve early childhood systems and their impacts. It is the process used to achieve the end goal of integrated early childhood systems. System building is necessary because few places can claim that they have achieved fully functioning and comprehensive systems. For example, parts that would greatly improve a system's functioning may be missing, or the system's parts may be disconnected and working toward inconsistent goals. This is especially true with early childhood systems, where programs are often disconnected or "siloed."

All system-building efforts do not look the same. In different places they may be focused at different levels (local, state, or federal), have different goals and objectives, work on different timelines, or focus on different aspects or stages of systems development. Because system-building efforts mean different things to different people, it can be difficult to have clear conversations about how to evaluate them. In addition, because there are many aspects and stages of systems development, no one evaluation approach is appropriate for all. Multiple evaluation approaches can be appropriate and useful, with different approaches fitting certain efforts better than others. Until a way of talking about different kinds of system-building efforts exists, it will be difficult to sort out what evaluation approaches to use and when.

The five-part typology below was developed in 2007 for the BUILD Initiative, a collaboration of funders that supports states' efforts to create comprehensive early childhood systems (Coffman, 2007). The typology was developed to address the need for a common understanding and language about what system-building efforts do. It posits that these efforts are best understood by their *focus* or by what they are trying to change. A system-building effort might focus on one or more of these five areas.

- *Context:* Improving the *political environment* that surrounds systems so it produces the policy and funding changes needed to create and sustain systems
- *Components:* Establishing *high-performance programs and services* within systems that produce results for children and families
- *Connections:* Creating strong and effective *linkages* within and between systems that further improve results for children and families
- *Infrastructure:* Developing the *supports* that systems need to function effectively and with quality
- *Scale:* Ensuring that *comprehensive systems* are available to as many people as possible so they produce broad and inclusive results for children and families

System-building efforts that focus on all five areas will, ultimately, result in comprehensive early childhood systems that produce broad impacts for children and their families. In reality, however, many states and communities are not yet at a point where they are tackling all five simultaneously, or where they have done enough work in each area to claim this result. Because resources are often limited, some efforts can focus on only one or two areas at a time. In addition, tackling the fifth area of scale generally takes a considerable amount of time and resources.

Also, there is no linear sequence to the five focus areas and, in fact, system-building efforts can focus on multiple areas simultaneously. They generally do not, however, place an equal emphasis on all areas at once. Some areas receive more attention than others at any given point in time, depending on the opportunities available and where the needs are greatest.

This emphasizes again that while system-building efforts share similarities in focus, each is constructed differently. Before evaluations are designed, then, it is important to have a clear sense of what the effort is doing, as its focus will drive the kinds of outcomes and impacts that can be expected.

EVALUATION FRAMEWORK FOR SYSTEM-BUILDING EFFORTS

Building from the typology above, Table 12.1 offers an evaluation framework for early childhood system-building efforts. The framework identifies

TABLE 12.1. Evaluation Framework for System Building

System-Building Focus	Examples of Activities	Examples of System-Level Outcomes	Child and Family Impacts	Examples of Evaluation Approaches
Context Improving the political context that surrounds the system so that the policy and funding changes needed to create and sustain the system exist	• Developing a shared vision for the system • Educating policymakers, public • Developing leaders • Engaging the media • Building coalitions • Grassroots/grasstops mobilization	• Public will or engagement in support of the system • Advocates or champions for the system • Policy changes that strengthen the system • Less categorical funding streams	Context outcomes should not be expected to show a direct causal link to child and family impacts	*System-Level Outcomes* • Public polling • Policy tracking • Key informant surveys • Policymaker interviews • Media tracking
Components Establishing high-performance programs and services within the system that produce results for system beneficiaries	• Developing new programs • Expanding high-quality programs • Increasing access and availability • Involving parents in program development	• New system programs/ services • Expanded program coverage • Improved program quality • Increased operational efficiency	Better impacts for children and families *related to specific programs or practices*	*System-Level Outcomes* • Program monitoring • Quality assessments • Efficiency analyses • Customer (parent) surveys *Impacts* • Quasi-experimental designs • Experimental designs
Connections Creating strong and effective linkages across system components that further improve results for system beneficiaries	• Aligning standards • Fostering cross-sector planning • Smoothing developmental transitions • Connecting data systems • Promoting collaboration and referrals	• Coordinated eligibility assessments • Referrals across the system • State–local connections • Joint planning across system components • Shared data systems • Cost efficiencies	Better child and family impacts *where or when connections exist compared with when they do not*	*System-Level Outcomes* • System mapping • Network mapping/analysis • Customer (parent) surveys *Impacts* • Quasi-experimental designs • Experimental designs

TABLE 12.1. Evaluation Framework for System Building, continued

System-Building Focus	Examples of Activities	Examples of System-Level Outcomes	Child and Family Impacts	Examples of Evaluation Approaches
Infrastructure Developing the supports systems need to function effectively and with quality	• Developing governance structures • Improving quality • Improving education, training, and professional development • Creating state–local connections • Monitoring the system	• Governance entities to oversee and coordinate systems • Quality improvement systems • Cross-system certifications • Professional development systems based on aligned standards and curricula	Infrastructure outcomes should not be expected to show a direct causal link to child and family impacts	*System-Level Outcomes* • Case studies • Performance audits • Quality assessments • Management information systems • Practitioner surveys/interviews
Scale Ensuring that a comprehensive system is available to as many children and families as possible so it produces broad and inclusive results	• Establishing policies that institutionalize the system and make it available to all children and families who need it	• Availability of comprehensive programs and services throughout a geographic region • Institutionalized practice-level change • Long-term financial system security • Shifts to collective responsibility for maintaining the system	Better child and family impacts *across a broad spectrum of domains and on a system-wide population level (e.g., on community or state indicators)*	*System-Level Outcomes* • Population-based demographic and service analysis • Results-based accountability *Impacts* • Quasi-experimental designs • Experimental designs

what can be measured, and how, for efforts focused on enhancing a system's context, components, connections, infrastructure, or scale.

For each focus area, the framework offers examples of *activities* that might be part of a system-building effort, followed by the *systems-level outcomes* those activities might generate, and then what those outcomes, if achieved, might produce in terms of *impacts* for children and families. While all system-building efforts have their eyes on the ultimate prize—better impacts for children and families—these results can take many years to achieve and may require major new investments or changes in the current system's operations. Consequently, it is important to identify system-level outcomes that are precursors to longer term impact. Unless early childhood systems themselves change as evidenced by system-level outcomes, child and family impacts cannot be expected to occur. While better impacts for children and families should remain the ultimate goal, and system-building efforts should be clear about how they contribute to that goal, system-level outcomes are important measures of progress along the way.

The framework's final column adds possible *evaluation approaches* that can be used to capture outcomes and impacts. It identifies methods for capturing system-level outcomes, as well as designs for capturing impacts.

The framework is neither exhaustive nor prescriptive. It offers ideas, but does not spell out how evaluations should look. Those decisions must be based on a careful consideration of the specific system-building effort in question and what it is designed to do. The next sections describe each focus area in more detail.

Evaluating Context

System-building efforts focused on context attempt to change the policy and funding environment that surrounds and affects a system's development and ultimate success. Early childhood systems require substantial public investments. They cannot be built entirely on private resources, nor can they be scaled up or sustained without public funding (Bruner, 2004b). Securing these public investments typically requires public and political will—a willingness by the public and policymakers to act in support of systems issues or policy proposals. Some system-building efforts, therefore, focus on building that support and the elements that influence it. Activities may include public or policymaker education and awareness building, leadership development, media advocacy, coalition building, or grassroots or grasstops mobilization.

A focus on the policy and funding context tends to come earlier in a system's developmental trajectory, as it can help pave the way for the system's construction. At the same time, systems require that context be a continuous focus, as sustaining support for system building requires constant vigilance in a regularly shifting political environment.

System-Level Outcomes. It is useful to ground evaluations of system-building efforts that focus on context in theories about the policy process, as these theories point to the factors that influence the policy environment and signal what outcomes to measure (e.g., Sabatier, 1999). For example, basic agenda-setting theory says that the policy agenda is influenced by what the public thinks, cares about, and is willing to act on. Public will, in turn, is influenced by what the media reports and how it frames issues (McCombs & Shaw, 1972). It follows, then, that system-building efforts wanting to get particular issues onto the policy agenda might use the media as a vehicle for doing so. An evaluation to track success in influencing the policy agenda would then track progress toward this goal by looking at the shorter term outcomes of both media attention and public will. It also may be possible to produce context changes through other approaches, including interest group pressure and advocacy independent from broad public opinion (Bruner, 2004a).

For efforts focused on context, an array of system-level outcomes is possible. Those outcomes include, but are not limited to, increases in target audience awareness or understanding of system issues, increases in public will or political will, new advocates or champions, policy changes that strengthen the system, or new or more diversified system funding.

Impacts. While better impacts for children and families are always the end goal, system-building efforts that focus on context should not be expected to demonstrate that context-related outcomes causally connect to child and family impacts. Evaluations of systems work in this area should focus instead on outcomes that are "closer" to context-related work (i.e., the system-level outcomes described above).

Evaluation Approaches for Assessing Context. The key evaluation questions for system-building efforts focused on context are: (a) Has public or political support for the system changed? and (b) Have investments or policies changed to enable improvements in the system's components, connections, infrastructure, or scale?

Because they interact with the policy process, system-building efforts focused on context primarily involve some form of policy advocacy. They use similar strategies and tactics and can be challenging to measure, both because they evolve over time and because their activities and outcomes can shift quickly (Harvard Family Research Project, 2007).

These similarities in strategy and purpose allow system-building efforts focused on context to draw from the now growing body of work on advocacy and policy change evaluation to identify useful evaluation approaches. For example, evaluation methods that are applicable to both advocacy and system-building efforts focused on context include public polling, media tracking, policy tracking, systems mapping, policymaker or bellwether interviews, or intense-period debriefs (Coffman, 2009; Coffman & Reed, 2009).

Evaluating Components

While a system is made up of interconnected parts and those connections are critical, sometimes a system's problem is not so much that it lacks connections, but that it lacks the parts to connect in the first place. System-building efforts focused on components concentrate on putting in place high-quality supports for children and families. The emphasis is on building or enhancing programs and services in each of the four ovals in Figure 2.1 that make up the early childhood system—early learning; health, mental health, and nutrition; early intervention; and family support. Although systems must contain more than independently operating programs, ensuring that a sufficient and comprehensive supply of quality and affordable programs and services are in place is an important part of systems work (Bruner, 2004b).

System-Level Outcomes. Outcomes for system-building efforts focused on components relate to the programs or services themselves and how they are implemented (e.g., better participation, quality, or operational efficiency). System-level outcomes in this area can include new programs or services developed within the system or expanded program reach or coverage. Sometimes, however, new programs are not necessary and the focus instead is on improving the quality of existing programs or services, or on increasing their operational efficiency.

Impacts. System-building efforts focused on increasing the access or quality of individual programs can be expected to demonstrate measurable impacts for children and families. For example, the addition of a nutrition program should result in better health outcomes for participants. Or a high-quality pre-K program should lead to improved school readiness. But in contrast to evaluations of more comprehensive systems where impacts are expected across a broad array of domains (discussed more in the section on scale), expected impacts should be specific to the program or intervention being evaluated.

Evaluation Approaches for Assessing Components. Evaluations of system-building efforts focused on components share much in common with traditional program evaluations—both assess individual programs or interventions. Also like program evaluations, systems evaluations focused on components address questions about both program implementation and program impacts. Key questions include: (a) Were specific components designed and implemented as intended? and (b) Did those components produce their intended impacts for children and families?

Again, because the focus is on individual programs, evaluations here can use traditional program evaluation approaches that feature the application of social science research designs and methods to assess program implementation and effectiveness. Evaluations that examine implementation can use some form of program monitoring or process evaluation. Program monitoring addresses questions about the extent to which the program is reaching its target population, whether program delivery matches design expectations, and what resources have been used to deliver the program (Rossi & Freeman, 1993). Program monitoring often goes hand in hand with impact assessments, as monitoring addresses questions about *why* a program was or was not effective. A wide array of both quantitative and qualitative methods can be used for program monitoring, such as observations, participant surveys or focus groups, staff member interviews, or document and record reviews.

Evaluations that examine program impacts can use experimental or quasi-experimental designs that employ a range of possible quantitative or qualitative methods, although quantitative data generally prevail in impact assessments. These designs assign (randomly or nonrandomly) individuals to participant and nonparticipant groups and then compare those groups. Experimental designs generally provide the most definitive attributions of causality and remain the program evaluation "gold standard." They are expensive to construct and implement, however, and random assignment may not be appropriate for programs that feature enrollment inclusivity because such programs violate experimental designs.

Evaluating Connections

System-building efforts that concentrate on connections focus on what makes a system a *system*—the integration, linkages, and alignment among its parts. They attempt to connect the four ovals in Figure 2.1 in meaningful ways, or to increase connections within those ovals. On the frontlines, those connections may include, for example, sharing professional development, staffing, facilities, technology and communication, data collection, or funding. At the administrative level, such connections may include aligned eligibility requirements and enrollment processes, streamlined reporting procedures, coordinated case management, and established protocols and memoranda of understanding for referrals.

System-Level Outcomes. Outcomes here relate to connections themselves in the form of increased system coordination, alignment, integration, or linkages. The challenge is to operationalize these concepts so they are measurable and relevant to the system-building effort at hand. Ways of operationalizing connections include, for example, referrals occurring from one program to another, activities to ease developmental transitions, connections between state- and local-level system building, joint planning across system components, or cross-system competencies or skills standards.

System-level outcomes also may take the form of cost savings. Particularly when they make systems more efficient, connections may be expected to accrue tangible financial returns.

Impacts. System-building efforts focused on connections may be expected to demonstrate impacts for children and families. Better results for children and families are expected when systems are connected compared with when they are not. The specific child- and family-level impacts measured will depend on the level at which connections are expected. If many connections are expected across the system, then impacts can be expected across a wide array of domains (e.g., health, literacy, mental health, etc.). If they are expected within or between particular areas, then expected impacts should be specific to those areas.

Evaluation Approaches for Assessing Connections. Evaluations in this area tend to focus on two main questions: (a) Did the system-building effort design and implement connections and linkages as intended? and (b) Did the connections and linkages produce their intended (or perhaps unintended) impacts?

If the evaluation is assessing the first question about whether connections exist within the system, several methodological choices are available. For example, network mapping or social network analysis is one option. This method explores whether connections or relationships exist, and it indicates their nature and strength. It identifies the nodes (people, groups, or institutions) that make up the network or system, and then examines the relationships between them. Results are depicted visually to reveal the network's connections (Durland & Fredericks, 2005). Pre- and post-analyses can determine whether the network and its connections look different over time.

If the evaluation's focus is on assessing the second question about whether systems that feature connections produce better results for children and families, then evaluations can compare conditions where connections exist with conditions where they do not. Evaluations that examine connections and their impacts for children and families are particularly important for system-building efforts that feature connections focused on improving developmental transitions (e.g., from preschool to kindergarten).

Evaluating Infrastructure

Sometimes a system's main problems or needs do not exist as much at the actual point of service as at the level of governance, financing, or other critical supports that challenge their performance or existence (Chynoweth, Philliber, & Oakley, 2000; Gonzalez & Gardner, 2003). System-building efforts focused on infrastructure make changes that facilitate a system's development and functioning. Infrastructure development helps to ensure that systems have the supports they need to function effectively and with quality.

System-Level Outcomes. System-level outcomes for efforts focused on infrastructure depend on the kinds of supports being established or enhanced. For example, infrastructure outcomes may include governance entities that oversee and coordinate subsystems, quality improvement systems, system-level or aligned standards, or training, education, and professional development organizations or programs that include and align curricula across early childhood systems.

Impacts. Like system-building efforts focused on context, infrastructure efforts should not be expected to show a direct causal link to impacts for children and families. Again, the kinds of outcomes listed above tend to be the evaluation's focus because they are "closer" to what system-building efforts actually are doing.

Evaluation Approaches for Assessing Infrastructure. Evaluations of infrastructure-focused efforts explore two main questions: (a) Did the system-building effort establish infrastructure or supports that are consistent with its needs? and (b) Is the infrastructure that was developed effective and efficient?

For evaluations that address the first question regarding whether the system has the supports it needs, case studies offer a useful methodological option. Case studies use multiple methods (quantitative or qualitative) to examine how an infrastructure initiative played out and the factors that contributed to its success or lack thereof. For example, the success case method is a particular type of case study that is relatively cost-effective. It is a post-hoc analysis of success (or failure) that combines systematic case study methodology with storytelling and reports results that stakeholders easily can understand and believe (Brinkerhoff, 2003).

Evaluations focused on the second question about whether supports are effective once they are in place should examine those supports' benefits for the system itself or for the individuals who receive them. For example, evaluations might examine how practitioner supports in the form of aligned training curricula benefit the system and its workforce. They might examine the extent to which alignment results in greater efficiencies for training organizations because their curricula can include modularized content that is transportable across different contexts (i.e., the four ovals in Figure 2.1). Evaluations also might focus on benefits for practitioners themselves, examining whether aligned curricula result, for example, in more portable skills or the use of a common frame of reference and language across practitioners working in different areas of the system.

These evaluations also can draw on a range of methodological options. For example, a performance audit can determine how well a governance entity or state agency is functioning. Customer satisfaction surveys can determine whether particular supports are accessible and user-friendly. Program evaluations can determine whether new education and training programs or policies have an impact on the workforce.

Evaluating Scale

System-building efforts focused on scale aim to ensure that early childhood systems are as comprehensive as possible and available to all children and families who need them. These efforts may attempt to scale up systems by increasing services and the numbers of individuals served, ensuring program integrity and service quality are high enough to produce results, and making sure systems are sustainable in terms of institutionalized policies and funding (Coburn, 2003).

System-building efforts attempting to scale up a system usually require a high level of funding. This funding can come from both public and private investments, but the lion's share must come from public sources, especially if the goal is to scale up the system over a large geographic area.

System-Level Outcomes. Outcomes for system-building efforts focused on scale might include system spread, system depth, system sustainability, or shifts in system ownership. For early childhood systems, traditional definitions of scale concentrate on the system's *spread,* or the availability of comprehensive programs and services throughout a geographic region. But this definition alone is limited; it says little about how scale-up has affected the services people receive. The concept of spread should expand beyond simply "upping the numbers" to include the spread of ideas, beliefs, values, and principles that support bringing systems to scale. *Depth,* or the nature and quality of change that takes place at the practice level, is another important dimension of scale, as is *sustainability* or whether the system financially can be maintained over time. Finally, the definition of scale can include a *shift in ownership*, meaning that a broad array of stakeholders, especially those on the frontlines, assume responsibility for maintaining the scaled-up system (Coburn, 2003).

Impacts. System-building efforts that concentrate on scale should demonstrate positive results for children and families. Because the system is, by definition, comprehensive, these impacts should exist across a wide range of domains (e.g., health, education, literacy, and mental health).

Evaluation Approaches for Assessing Scale. Evaluations of system-building efforts focused on scale concentrate on two key questions: (a) Was the system scaled up with quality and fidelity? and (b) Did scale-up result in broad impacts for children and families at a system-wide population level?

For the first question, evaluations explore the scale-up process itself. Because there are many historical examples of system-building efforts that "demonstrated, researched, and died" during scale-up, or that experienced model drift and ended up offering lesser services and benefits than intended, evaluations that focus on this process and continuously feed back findings to inform midcourse corrections can be critical to system-building success (Weiss, 1995).

Evaluating the scale-up process, particularly when systems are designed to be available to all children and families (e.g., community-wide or statewide), involves some statistical analysis of the size of that population and the degree to which systems reach and serve it. When a system's ultimate goal is to produce population-wide outcomes and impacts, it is essential that the system reach a sufficient number of individuals to show results at that level (Bruner, 1996). This requires a clarified definition of participants and the system components and connections that they will use (children and families may use only a part of the system). Methods such as polls and random sample surveys can then assess the degree to which the population is aware of and uses relevant system components. Such surveys also can provide valuable feedback to systems practitioners on where outreach, engagement, and additional focus are needed (e.g., by neighborhood, socioeconomic status, ethnicity, etc.).

For the second question, evaluations determine whether systems are producing comprehensive impacts for children and families. Like the evaluation design options described under the section on evaluating components, these evaluations generally use experimental or quasi-experimental approaches. The difference is that here the system, rather than a single program, is the intervention. In other words, under components, the evaluation might look at the child-level impacts of a statewide pre-K program, focusing on school readiness measures. With scale, the focus is the broader early childhood system, which is made up of multiple programs linked and aligned across early learning; health, mental health, and nutrition; special needs/early intervention; and family support. Consequently, evaluations focused on scale should examine a broad array of child-level measures across these different domains.

Evaluations focused on the second question also can use a results-based accountability approach. This approach requires institutions at the state, community, agency, program, *or system* level to articulate clearly their expected results (or goals). Once results are identified in the form of outcomes, indicators, and benchmarks, they are tracked at regular intervals to determine whether results have been achieved. With a results-based accountability approach, it is still important to construct a counterfactual or basis of comparison, as broader societal factors may influence these outcomes independent of system-building efforts. Trend data from other communities or states on similar outcome and impact measures can provide such a counterfactual for assessing whether system-building efforts themselves have "turned the curve" on results or whether the changes were part of broader societal trends.

ANSWERING THE BIG QUESTIONS

This chapter grew from the observation that the dialogue about how to evaluate system-building efforts was stalled, at least in part, because the field lacked a way to think and talk clearly about what system-building efforts do and are trying to accomplish. To address this challenge, the chapter offered a framework that defined five system-building areas of focus and the system-level outcomes, impacts, and evaluation approaches that fit with those areas. The framework is designed to be a resource when developing evaluations of system-building efforts. It also can be a useful tool when planning those efforts. Practitioners can use it to think about where early childhood systems are strong, where they are not, and where their priorities should be in the short and long term.

The chapter began by articulating some of the "big" questions that have long persisted in discussions about evaluating system building. These questions include: Are experimental designs (or other counterfactuals) appropriate or even possible in this context? And under what conditions should efforts to build early childhood systems be held accountable for demonstrating child-level impacts? To close out the chapter, below are several overarching conclusions that have emerged in response to these questions and others.

Decisions about outcomes and impacts should be based on the focus of the system-building effort. These efforts are diverse and can mean different things to different people. Because they focus on different things and vary greatly in both resources and design, it is not possible to discuss or decide generally the outcomes and impacts to which they all should be held accountable. These decisions should be tailored to each effort. The evaluation framework was designed to facilitate these decisions, but choices about outcomes and impacts should be determined on a case-by-case basis.

There is no one right or "best" approach or methodology for evaluating system building. This point follows from the one above. Choices about evaluation methodology should be based on the system-building effort and the questions being asked about it. Just as with all research and evaluation, the questions being asked should determine the methodological approaches selected. Experimental or quasi-experimental designs can be used with system-building efforts (although experimental designs are difficult to use with system building), but they are not appropriate or even needed for answering many important evaluation questions about system building.

System-level outcomes precede child and family impacts and should be an important evaluation focus. A tendency exists with system building to expect too much, too soon, and for too little effort. Child and family impacts take time to emerge, and the system first has to change, and change enough, before they can be seen. Evaluations of system-building efforts need to pay attention to system-level outcomes as important precursors of child and family impacts. Because they represent the results that are generally the closest to system-building work, they are important and meaningful measures of progress.

Some system-building efforts, but not all, should be held accountable for demonstrating child and family impacts. Building on the point above, this chapter showed that for some system-building efforts, the expectation that they be able to show child and family impacts is warranted. For example, efforts that scale up early childhood systems should be able and expected to demonstrate such impacts. Every effort to build an early childhood system, however, should not be held to this measurement expectation. For some—namely, those focused primarily on context or infrastructure—child and family impacts are far removed from the actual work that is occurring. While the hope is that any positive outcomes achieved by these efforts will play out later in the form of child and family impacts, and there should be a clear sense of how that process will occur, it makes little sense for these evaluations to collect data that document such impacts.

System-building efforts should not be accountable for producing child and family impacts simply because participants agree that they would like to see such impacts occur. Measurable changes in such impacts should be expected only when a system-building effort makes investments in strategies that are powerful enough to produce them.

Finally, the question of how to evaluate early childhood systems themselves remains unanswered. This chapter focused on how to evaluate the process of building early childhood systems, as that is where the majority of states and communities across the nation currently are in their work. They have visions of comprehensive and integrated systems, but are still on the journey to making those visions a reality. But questions about the point at which early childhood systems are sufficiently "ready" to be evaluated, and ready to be accountable for the child and family impacts they promise, have yet to be addressed, as are questions about how to approach such evaluations once systems are deemed ready. This chapter addressed how to evaluate the process leading up to this point; future work must focus on how to evaluate systems once they are in place and ready.

REFERENCES

Brinkerhoff, R. (2003). *The success case method: Find out quickly what's working and what's not.* San Francisco: Berrett-Koehler.

Bruner, C. (1996). Where's the beef? Getting real about what comprehensive means. In R. Stone (Ed.), *Core issues in comprehensive community-building initiatives* (pp. 85–86). Chicago: Chapin Hall Center for Children.

Bruner, C. (2004a). *Beyond the usual suspects: Developing new allies to invest in school readiness.* Des Moines, IA: State Early Childhood Policy Technical Assistance Network.

Bruner, C. (2004b). *Toward a theory of change for the BUILD Initiative: A discussion paper.* Retrieved from http://www.buildinitiative.org/docs/TowardaTheoryofChange.doc

Chynoweth, J., Philliber, S., & Oakley, M. (2000). *Systems change in California: Progress at the Millennium.* Sacramento, CA: Foundation Consortium.

Coburn, C. (2003). Rethinking scale: Moving beyond the numbers to deep and lasting change. *Educational Researcher, 32*(6), 3–12.

Coffman, J. (2007). *A framework for evaluating systems initiatives.* Retrieved from the BUILD Initiative website: http://www.buildinitiative.org/content/evaluation-systems-change

Coffman, J. (2009). *A user's guide to advocacy evaluation planning.* Cambridge, MA: Harvard Family Research Project.

Coffman, J., & Reed, E. (2009). *Unique methods in advocacy evaluation.* Washington, DC: Center for Evaluation Innovation.

Durland, M., & Fredericks, K. (Eds.). (2005). *New directions for evaluation: Social network analysis in program evaluation* (Vol. 107). San Francisco: Jossey-Bass.

Gonzalez, R., & Gardner, S. (2003). *Systems change and school readiness* [Electronic version]. UCLA Center for Healthier Children, Families, and Communities.

Harvard Family Research Project. (2007). Advocacy and policy change. *The Evaluation Exchange, 13*(1). Cambridge, MA: Author.

McCombs, M., & Shaw, D. L. (1972). The agenda-setting function of the mass media. *Public Opinion Quarterly, 36,* 176–185.

Rossi, P., & Freeman, H. (1993). *Evaluation: A systematic approach.* Newbury Park, CA: Sage.

Sabatier, P. A. (Ed.). (1999). *Theories of the policy process.* Boulder, CO: Westview Press.

Weiss, H. (1995). New approaches to evaluating systems: The Gwen R. Iding Brogden distinguished lecture series. In C. Liberton, K. Kutash, & R. Friedman (Eds.), *8th annual research conference proceedings on a system of care for children's mental health: Expanding the research base* (p. 412). Tampa, FL: Research and Training Center for Children's Mental Health.

Part IV

SNAPSHOTS OF SYSTEM BUILDING IN ACTION

CHAPTER 13

Establishing a Common Vision for Colorado's Early Childhood System

Jeanine Coleman and Jodi Hardin

Early childhood system-building work has existed in Colorado since the early 1990s. While system-building leaders, partners, and priorities have evolved over time, the consistent vision has always been to make Colorado a great place to raise healthy and thriving children. Colorado's early childhood system building has included both state-level and local-level efforts demonstrated by a statewide system of local Early Childhood Councils, solidified in 2007 legislation, that work in collaboration with state-level partners. This chapter will address the development of a common vision for early childhood system-building efforts in Colorado.

THE EARLY CHILDHOOD COLORADO FRAMEWORK

In 2008, early childhood partners in Colorado identified the need to synthesize and integrate multiple years' system-building efforts into a plan that would provide a collective vision, guide next steps in systems work, and link system-building efforts to outcomes. The Early Childhood Colorado Framework was developed to provide that common vision within which both public and private, and state- and local-level, partners could see their work and invest in the future. It connected many pieces of work while outlining the efforts needed by all partners to make positive change in the lives of young children and their families. The mission was for both state and local early childhood systems work to promote the development of a comprehensive, sustainable early childhood system encompassing health, mental health, early learning, family support and parent education with an overall vision that all children are valued, healthy, and thriving. The Early Childhood Colorado Framework is a one-page document (see Figure 13.1 and http://earlychildhoodcolorado.org/inc/uploads/CO_EC_Framework.pdf) that is supported, embraced, and used by a multitude of governmental and non-governmental partners; there is no individual proprietary ownership of the document.

The Early Childhood Colorado Framework aimed to foster collaborative system building because of Colorado's commitment to:

- *Recognize the needs of the whole child and family* by including outcomes that cut across the early learning, family support, mental health, and health sectors
- *Communicate the vision for comprehensive early childhood work* by helping early childhood partners see how their work, individually and collectively, contributes to the greater picture of all children in Colorado being valued, healthy, and thriving
- *Connect "comprehensive system-building" language to specific strategies for action and measurable outcomes* for children, families, and early childhood professionals
- *Provide a framework to guide and focus the actions* of public and private stakeholders who work with or on behalf of young children and their families
- *Promote an outcomes-based approach* to early childhood system-building efforts

Additionally, a core set of *guiding principles* provided the foundation for the Early Childhood Colorado Framework and resulting efforts. These guiding principles reflect commonly held values within the field of early childhood. Partners agreed to:

- Be child-focused and family-centered
- Recognize and respond to variations in cultures, languages, and abilities
- Use data to inform decisions
- Build on strengths of communities and families
- Focus on children from birth to age 8
- Promote partnerships
- Act at state, local, and statewide[1] levels

The Promise of the Framework

Colorado early childhood partners recognized that efforts must be taken to better coordinate, align, and integrate resources to make early childhood services more efficient and effective for families. The Framework underscores the collective work of all partners, across levels (e.g., state/local, policy/programs) so that Colorado could make the Framework's vision a reality. Concurrent state-level and local-level systems work was essential, along with strong linkages between the two.

The Framework provides the opportunity to integrate state and local efforts, resulting in several significant accomplishments. First, the Framework encompassed diverse perspectives and partners across system sectors. More than 20 logic models, strategic plans, and blueprints, previously developed by a wide range of Colorado early childhood initiatives, served as building blocks for the Framework. Consequently, there was tremendous buy-in and support from stakeholders because they could see past work, decisions, and priorities within the Framework. In their "transfer of commitment" theory, Hicks, Larson, Nelson, Olds, and Johnston (2008) described the importance of this kind of commitment from stakeholders for meaningfully creating systems change. They stated, "Cooperation and commitment, like other patterns of authentic behavior, are contagious. Behaviors signaling both high cooperation and low cooperation are transferable despite a high turnover of members" (p. 472). The depth and breadth within the Framework supported both state and local systems efforts to build new partnerships, diversified activities across broader networks of stakeholders, and provided the context for contagious behavior so that a transfer of commitment to the Framework transpired.

Next, the Framework provides common language for state and local partners. State- and community-elected officials, agency personnel, nonprofit leaders, service providers, and family leaders use the Framework as a common reference to guide planning, discussion, and/or decision making related to young children. A shared vision and common language give state and local early childhood partners a foundation from which to strategize and align actions.

Moreover, the Framework promotes mutual accountability for shared results. The outcomes within the Framework clearly identify what Colorado is committed to and striving for in terms of early learning, family support and parent education, mental health, and health for young children and their families. Through the statewide system of Early Childhood Councils, the Framework provides a vehicle for long-established councils to expand the lens for strategic planning and monitoring to include a cross-sector approach, as well as providing newer councils with a foundation from which to build. The Framework also has given state-level partners a structured base from which to identify and measure system enhancements and improved outcomes for children and families. The Framework, developed at the 50,000-foot level, allows for flexibility and adaptability by partners and communities so that they can build from a common foundation and still

FIGURE 13.1 Early Childhood Colorado Framework

Goals: Children have high quality early learning supports and environments and comprehensive health care; Families have meaningful community and parenting supports; Early childhood professionals have the knowledge, skills, and supports to work effectively with and on behalf of families and children; All children are valued, healthy, and thriving

	Early Learning	Family Support and Parent Education	Social, Emotional, and Mental Health	Health
Access Outcomes	Increased availability of formal education and professional development opportunities for early childhood professionals related to early learning standards. Increased access to high quality early learning, birth through third grade.	Increased availability and family use of high quality parenting/child development information, services, and supports. Increased parent engagement and leadership at program, community, and policy levels.	Increased availability and use of high quality social, emotional, and mental health training and support. Increased number of supportive and nurturing environments that promote children's healthy social and emotional development.	Increased access to preventive oral and medical health care. Increased number of children covered by consistent health insurance.
Quality Outcomes	Increased number of children meeting developmental milestones to promote school readiness. Increased number of programs that are accredited and/or quality rated. Increased number of schools that have leadership and educational environments that support young children's success. Increased availability of community resources and support networks for early childhood practitioners, professionals, and programs.	Increased number of children who live in safe, stable, and supportive families. Improved family and community knowledge and skills to support children's health and development. Increased family ability to identify and select high quality early childhood services and supports.	Increased number of environments, including early learning settings, providing early identification and mental health consultation. Improved knowledge and practice of nurturing behaviors among families and early childhood professionals.	Increased number of children who receive a Medical Home approach. Increased number of children who are fully immunized. Increased knowledge of the importance of health and wellness (including nutrition, physical activity, medical, oral, and mental health).

	Early Learning	Family Support	Mental Health	Health
Equity Outcomes	Increased number of children with special needs who receive consistent early learning services and supports. Decreased gaps in school readiness and academic achievement between populations of children.	Increased availability and use of family literacy services and supports. Increased availability of resources and supports, including financial and legal, to promote family self-sufficiency. Increased coordination of services and supports for families and children who are at-risk or have special needs.	Increased number of mental health services for children with persistent, serious challenging behaviors. Decreased number of out-of-home placements of children.	Increased percentage of primary care physicians and dentists who accept Medicaid and Child Health Plan Plus. Increased percentage of women giving birth with timely, appropriate prenatal care. Decreased number of underinsured children.
Strategies for Action	Develop and support use of early learning standards by families, programs, and professionals. Evaluate and recognize high-quality programs with a comprehensive rating and reimbursement system. Develop, promote, and support high-quality professional development and formal education for adults who work with young children. Monitor children's learning and development through screening and ongoing assessments. Improve financial sustainability and governing efficiency of early learning programs and infrastructure.	Strengthen coordinated efforts of public and private stakeholders to meet the needs of children and families. Strengthen and support family leadership through effective training models. Provide tools and information to families to strengthen their own engagement and involvement in their children's lives. Provide information to families to facilitate connection to services and supports.	Promote caregivers' knowledge of the social, emotional, and mental health of young children. Provide early childhood professionals with effective practices that promote children's social-emotional development and mental health. Strengthen and support community-based mental health services that identify and serve young children.	Enroll more children in health insurance programs. Promote and support use of standards for a Medical Home approach (including medical, oral, and mental health, as well as developmental, vision, and hearing screening and services). Strengthen coordinated efforts of public and private stakeholders to support health and wellness.

Note. This is a modified version of the original Framework. The original can be found at http://www.earlychildhoodcolorado.org

account for their unique differences. As one local partner stated, "This is a great document; I am glad to see how we as local communities can align with the statewide systems Framework in the work that we do."

The Framework in Action

The Early Childhood Colorado Framework has accelerated comprehensive systems efforts by establishing and enhancing new and existing partnerships, leveraging new and existing resources, guiding planning and alignment, and communicating to a wide audience. The examples below illustrate how some partners in Colorado have put their own unique stamp on the Framework and focused on their priorities.

To begin, the Framework provides the context to strengthen existing partnerships and create new and unusual partnerships. For example, agencies and departments that work on child abuse and neglect prevention and child welfare have become engaged in early childhood systems efforts and are taking leadership roles in cross-sector initiatives such as Strengthening Families (http://www.strengtheningfamilies.net/).

The Framework also has had an impact on how resources are used, as illustrated by the investment from a local, health-focused philanthropic foundation. The foundation invested in the existing system infrastructure by providing grants to the system of Early Childhood Councils with the common goal of promoting the child health outcomes with the Framework. The foundation saw its mission within the Framework, made a financial commitment to Colorado's early childhood system, and leveraged its investment by promoting common goals across grantees.

Additionally, the Framework aligned state and local systems efforts and changed the way partners approached collaborative processes so that they could identify priorities and link decisions to outcomes. For instance, the state agency that administers Medicaid and the Child Health Plan Plus references the Framework in legislative reports and national presentations, identifying its agency-specific contributions to and alignment with broader early childhood efforts. Moreover, the state partners managing the local Early Childhood Councils aligned their work with the Framework and reorganized their technical assistance system so that local communities are more effective and efficient in meeting the needs of children and families.

Finally, in terms of providing a communication tool for a broad audience, the Framework has been used by the lieutenant governor's office, legislators, state agency personnel, private partners, and communities across the state to convey what is meant by comprehensive early childhood systems efforts. A community partner stated the following about the Framework: "After 9 years of work, something is now available that defines and illustrates what early childhood councils' and systems work is all about."

PROGRESS AND POSSIBILITIES

Early childhood systems efforts are evolutionary and dynamic. Colorado is no different from other states in that nurturing state and local partnerships and connections takes time and sustained effort. Colorado has found that the commitment to a shared vision for children and families facilitates collaborative work between state partners and communities, while honoring individual community needs and priorities. Effective system building requires that state and local levels work in tandem to connect and align public and private services for all children and families.

The Early Childhood Colorado Framework has been much more than a simple visual depiction of what Colorado strives to achieve on behalf of young children and families. It has truly been a catalyst for early childhood systems efforts across a diverse state and numerous partners. The benefits of this long-term strategic vision have yet to be fully realized. Colorado has just begun to reap the rewards from this unifying vision that promotes shared leadership and ownership to ensure all Colorado's children are valued, healthy, and thriving.

NOTE

1. *State* refers to issues for which the state has direct jurisdiction (e.g., eligibility for state-funded PreK program). Since Colorado is a local control state. *Local* refers to issues for which individual localities have direct jurisdiction (e.g., eligibility for child care subsidies). *Statewide* relates to efforts to ensure that localities' policies and practices align as much as possible, even though there is no state authority to mandate as much (e.g., incentive funding for all counties to have local early childhood councils).

REFERENCE

Hicks, D., Larson, C., Nelson, C., Olds, D. L., & Johnston, E. (2008). The influence of collaboration on program outcomes: The Colorado Nurse Family Partnership. *Evaluation Review, 23*(5), 453–477.

CHAPTER 14

Washington State's Early Learning and Development Benchmarks

A Foundation for an Aligned System

Sangree Froelicher

In Washington State, our goal is to create a "world-class" early learning system that serves the full range of children's needs, prenatal through 3rd grade. Development of this system is not happening by chance. It necessitates coordinated brainstorming, planning, advocacy, and sustained collaboration across multiple groups and institutions. It calls for a willingness to rethink longstanding finance and governance structures. It requires our best efforts to create high-quality programs, strengthen accountability, and deepen our knowledge about children's learning and development.

One of the cornerstones of these efforts is a comprehensive set of early learning standards—the Washington State Early Learning and Development Benchmarks (State of Washington, Kagan, Britto, Kauerz, & Tarrant, 2005). This chapter outlines how the Benchmarks are being used by leaders in Washington State to guide a unified vision of early learning, aligning ideas, infrastructure, and resources to effectively and comprehensively support the development of young children and their families.

THE PURPOSE FOR WASHINGTON STATE'S EARLY LEARNING AND DEVELOPMENT BENCHMARKS

Published in 2005, the Benchmarks were designed for three purposes. First, they establish a common set of standards that support each child's early learning and development, that promote reasonable expectations, and that suggest practical strategies for parents and others who care for and teach young children. Second, by aligning with Washington State's K–3 standards

(Essential Academic Learning Requirements) and K–3 Grade Level Expectations, the Benchmarks establish the foundation for a continuum of learning that links early learning and development to later success in school and life. Third, and perhaps most important, the Benchmarks contribute to a unified vision for Washington State's early learning system.

Three key state-level institutions lead Washington State's early learning system and use the Benchmarks as a source for alignment and coordination: the Department of Early Learning (DEL), Office of the Superintendent of Public Instruction (OSPI), and Thrive by Five Washington (Thrive). These organizations agree that early learning is a shared responsibility and collectively represent a strongly aligned and invested partnership across the public and private sectors. Together, these entities have committed to collaborate on behalf of all young children, prenatal through 3rd grade, and jointly produced a comprehensive strategic 10-year roadmap, the Early Learning Plan, for building the early childhood system in Washington State (Washington State Early Learning Plan, 2010). The Plan is organized around five categories of effort: (1) ready and successful children; (2) ready and successful parents, families, and caregivers; (3) ready and successful early learning professionals; (4) ready and successful schools; and (5) ready and successful systems and communities. Together, these components establish a ready and successful state. We recognize that families, communities, schools, early learning coalitions, public/private partnerships, and all of those who care for and teach young children have pivotal roles to play in children's healthy development and early learning. The remainder of this chapter highlights how the Benchmarks are being used to support each of these priority areas.

SUPPORTING VARIOUS COMPONENTS OF THE SYSTEM

The Benchmarks represent an important and pioneering effort to create a guiding framework for various cross-purposed efforts on behalf of young children and their families. Because of the importance of children's early years, and because it is beneficial for children to experience consistency from the many adults and organizations that contribute to their learning and development, the Benchmarks provide essential information for those who love, care for, and educate young children. We believe that a key strategy for achieving school readiness and success is to align various components of our early learning system with the Benchmarks. To this end, the Benchmarks can and should be used for a variety of purposes to drive broad systems change.

Ready and Successful Children

Ready and successful children are healthy and socially, emotionally, and cognitively prepared for success in school and in life. The Benchmarks provide essential information and a common understanding about how young children grow and acquire knowledge. Specifically, the Benchmarks provide a set of standards that describe what young children should know and be able to do by the time they reach the end of each of four critical stages of development: 18 months, 36 months, 60 months, and entry to kindergarten. The Benchmarks reflect a comprehensive approach to child development and cover five major dimensions of children's overall development: (1) physical well-being, health, and motor development; (2) social and emotional development; (3) approaches toward learning; (4) cognition and general knowledge; and (5) language, literacy, and communication.

Given the many people who play a part in young children's development, it is not surprising that there is often little alignment in what is expected for children across the various settings in which they spend their days. Washington's Early Learning and Development Benchmarks provide a common understanding about expectations for children's development and learning.

Ready and Successful Parents, Families, and Caregivers

Ready and successful parents, families, and caregivers have the information and resources needed to be their children's first and most important teachers. Because, as the commonly used adage states, "babies don't come with how-to manuals," the Benchmarks can be used in a manner that provides families and parents with guidance and information to recognize, understand, and nurture the growth and development of their young children.

Parents may use the voluntary Benchmarks in several ways. First-time parents will find them especially helpful as they observe their children's development and watch them learn over time. In addition, parents can use the Benchmarks to learn what to expect from their children at certain ages and how to help their children learn important new skills.

Caregivers in a variety of early learning settings can use the Benchmarks for similar purposes. In this way, the Benchmarks help to establish and strengthen continuity of high-quality experiences for children at home and elsewhere. To accomplish this, the state-level partners are creating an outreach plan and related resources to inform parents and other family members about the Benchmarks, as well as tools and materials for professionals who teach parent and family education workshops and classes.

Ready and Successful Early Learning Professionals

Ready and successful early learning professionals have the knowledge and skills to be responsive to children's different learning processes, capabilities, and developmental goals. Across schools, center-based classrooms, and homes, teachers and other early childhood professionals face the important challenge of meeting the educational and nurturance needs of all children.

Formal education and training in early childhood development and learning have been linked consistently to positive teacher/caregiver behaviors and knowledge. To promote and support early learning professionals' preparation and ongoing education, personnel in higher education and both formal and informal professional development trainers in Washington State are beginning to provide early childhood teachers with a stronger and more specific knowledge of children's learning and development based on the Benchmarks. This is being accomplished through incremental efforts to use the Benchmarks to drive the content of teacher preparation programs and professional development curriculum, by eliminating discontinuities between what is taught and what children are expected to know and be able to do, and by using the Benchmarks to influence the nature of state credentialing and licensing criteria related to teacher preparation.

Ready and Successful Schools

Ready and successful schools are prepared to support the learning and development of every child in their community. K–3 teachers, administrators, and specialists are not strangers to standards-based education. In order to promote and support continuity of learning expectations across the early childhood and elementary school years, it is especially important for school leaders and teachers to be familiar with the Benchmarks and to integrate into their own policies and practices the Benchmarks' principles and approaches to nurturing and supporting all children.

Moreover, it is critical for those who teach children younger than school age to be equally familiar with K–3 learning standards. The intention is that all educators have a clear understanding of the expectations that frame learning and development for children from birth through age 8.

The ultimate goal is for the state to establish a continuum of learning and development for later success in school, by aligning early learning standards with K–3 standards, thereby creating a coordinated system of early learning for young children. To support and strengthen ready schools, Washington State is developing a series of documents that clearly show the linkages and continuity between the Benchmarks and K–3 standards and grade-level expectations. We also are improving strategies and mechanisms that address educational policies and practices on school transitions, and beginning to provide joint professional development opportunities for K–3 staff and early childhood professionals.

Ready and Successful Systems and Communities

Ready and successful systems and communities have the resources and information needed to provide high-quality governance, financing, accountability, planning, and communication for the programs and services that support children, parents, and schools. There is now broad consensus that inconsistent policies and fragmented programs result in a higher risk of duplication, inefficient spending, a lower quality of service, difficulty in meeting goals, and, ultimately, a reduced capacity for high-quality service delivery. The need for and benefits of improved coherence are widely accepted today in the Washington State early learning context. The Benchmarks provide a crucial point of reference for building broad consensus and increasing the capacity of the system to effectively serve children and parents.

SUPPORTING SYSTEM-LEVEL COHERENCE

The concept of coherence clarifies what work is most important and should be prioritized. Coherence also clarifies how success will be achieved, reminding stakeholders that the system's priorities should work together in a sensible, transparent, and well-coordinated manner. The Benchmarks are being used to support four elements of coherence at the system level:

- *Agency coherence*—The Benchmarks are guiding efforts to ensure consistency among the policies and actions of individual agencies, including the internal consistency of a specific policy or program.
- *Whole-of-government coherence*—The Benchmarks are guiding efforts to ensure consistency among the policies and actions of the different government agencies within the state.
- *External coherence*—The Benchmarks are guiding efforts to ensure consistency among the policies pursued by the various external players/actors in Washington State.
- *Internal-to-external coherence*—The Benchmarks are guiding efforts to ensure consistency and alignment between the policies of the internal and external actors in Washington.

Our theory of change related to successful system building is simple. We believe that:

- Sustained and strategic use of the Benchmarks for multiple purposes *will lead to*
- Coherence of strategy and commitment system-wide, *which leads to*
- Alignment of partnerships, policies, and programs, *which results in*
- A sustainable commitment of resources to support a statewide system.

While Washington continues to refine and revise the Benchmarks as different communities and cultures explore how to adapt them to support their own approaches to learning and human development, the Benchmarks provide the focus for long-term coherence and alignment across Washington State's early learning system.

REFERENCES

State of Washington, Kagan, S. L., Britto, P. R., Kauerz, K., & Tarrant, K. (2005). *Washington early learning and development benchmarks: A guide to young children's learning and development from birth to kindergarten entry.* Olympia: State of Washington.

Washington State Early Learning Plan. (2010). State of Washington: Department of Early Learning, Office of the Superintendent of Public Instruction, Thrive by Five. Retrieved from http://www.del.wa.gov/publications/elac-qris/docs/ELP_Exec.pdf

CHAPTER 15

The Missouri Quality Rating System

Kathy R. Thornburg and Denise Mauzy

Missouri, similar to many other states, built early childhood and school-age supports, standards, and guidelines in a piecemeal fashion, responding to specific needs or implementing projects based on funding availability. Three different state departments—Social Services, Education, and Health—have responsibilities for these activities. The result of these piecemeal efforts, although well intended, is a statewide "nonsystem."

Several years prior to the Quality Rating System (QRS) "movement," Missouri leaders discussed the need for a streamlined, efficient, and accountable system for early childhood and school-age programs. Meetings were held to develop a vision, but the work lacked an organizing structure for assessing quality improvement activities. As we studied information from other states and as funding opportunities were made available, we realized that a QRS could be the organizing tool to address some of the larger systemic issues, such as streamlined data collection, equitable distribution of resources, and consumer education. In addition, we realized that the QRS must be designed for each type of licensed program. The Missouri Quality Rating System (MO QRS) State Committee, consisting of key stakeholders, was convened to provide oversight for the project and developed shared expectations for the MO QRS to guide development and decision making. Those shared expectations for the MO QRS included:

- Utilizing Missouri's existing early childhood and after-school infrastructure;
- Being voluntary and including incentives for programs to participate;
- Applying to all licensed early childhood and after-school programs;

FIGURE 15.1. MO QRS Models: Common Categories and Components

Program Personnel

1. Director Education and Training
2. Staff Education
3. Annual Training
4. Education Specialization

Program Content

5. Learning Environment
6. Intentional Teaching

Program Management

7. Family Involvement
8. Business and Administrative Practices

- Providing a number of tiers starting with licensing and progressing to the top tier, which includes program accreditation;
- Assessing all aspects of program quality using verified data and on-site observations by reliable assessors;
- Offering programs constructive feedback based on the assessment;
- Providing opportunities for all programs to increase program ratings prior to publicizing; and
- Allowing programs to appeal their QRS rating.

The Committee's efforts resulted in three MO QRS models for licensed programs: early childhood centers/group homes; family child care homes; and school-age only programs. Although each model is specific to the type of program rated in relation to licensing, accreditation, and classroom/group assessments, all three models share the same eight components organized into three categories (see Figure 15.1). Within each component, requirements are progressive, building upon the previous tier. A program's overall rating is determined by the total number of points earned across the eight components. Programs are awarded one to five stars for an 18-month period.

Now, 5 years into this process, we reflect on the process, successes achieved, and challenges encountered. The most significant insight we have to offer is to strongly urge others to include pilot and demonstration periods in the QRS development. We believe that initial planning efforts, while important for the development of a model(s) based on a state's unique infrastructure, are limited without a pilot effort to allow for extensive data collection to "test" the models and subsequent measures included in the rating. This process allows stakeholders to review the data and further balance the need to "raise the bar" with the reality of current levels of quality being provided, thus creating achievable criteria. Additionally, it allows decision makers to be responsive to certain program issues that can be identified only through actual pilot/implementation activities. Examples from the Missouri pilot include selection of suitable classroom/group measures and establishing appropriate thresholds for staff education in small, medium, and large programs. Based on the Missouri experience, we advise states to expect extensive revisions that will produce stronger, more relevant models to rate quality. Once the revised models have been approved by appropriate authorities, a demonstration period will allow states to prepare for large-scale recruitment, data collection, assessment, and implementation. Missouri's demonstration phase allowed us to identify data collection gaps, inconsistent interpretation of state and/or QRS policies, and partnerships necessary to support large-scale implementation.

A ROADMAP TO QUALITY

Initially, Missouri's success was defined by two things: (1) the development of three MO QRS models that serve as a "roadmap to quality" for programs; and (2) advancements in data collection processes and interfaces.

The MO QRS State Committee understood that in order for MO QRS to be successful, it must be relevant and the progression of requirements must be within reach of programs pursuing quality. Relevance was achieved by integrating pertinent pieces of the current infrastructure, quality improvement processes, and state standards into the system. QRS requirements were designed to provide steps to quality, beginning with licensing and culminating with program accreditation. State standards and the state registry, both key infrastructure supports, also were incorporated. The following state standards and resources were incorporated into the criteria for the model to further promote their use in quality improvement efforts and to provide a common framework of standards for professionals and children that aligns with the standards established by QRS for programs.

- Core Competencies (Early Childhood and Youth): Criteria from the competencies can be found in the director education and training and the business and administrative practices components.
- Missouri Early Learning Standards: Criteria from the standards can be found in the family involvement and the business and administrative practices components.

- Missouri After-School Program Standards: Criteria related to these standards are included in the after-school intentional teaching checklist, which is part of the classroom/group assessment.

Finally, the state-supported practitioner registry tracks all staff requirements, both formal education and annual training hours. Tabulations for the program personnel criteria are determined using registry data, thus reducing the data collection costs for the QRS.

ADVANCEMENTS IN DATA COLLECTION PROCESSES AND INTERFACES

The QRS State Committee members were steadfast in their belief that verified and reliable data are the cornerstone to a valid rating. The MO QRS requires extensive, time-intensive data collection, which resulted in significant personnel time during the pilot period. Therefore, the demonstration period was a critical time for technological advancements in order to create a process that is manageable and cost effective. The three examples below illustrate how technologies have been created to help manage MO QRS.

First, the registry operating system has been upgraded to include a web-based interface that allows directors to add/edit/terminate staff, add/edit/close classrooms, and assign staff to classrooms. Given the frequency of these types of changes at the program level and the amount of personnel time it takes to process changes, this functionality increased the cost effectiveness of the QRS process.

Second, a data-sharing partnership is being finalized so that the state registry will receive training attendance data from the state training calendar system after they are entered by the trainer, eliminating the need to enter training information for each individual. This partnership will result in a significant cost savings.

Third, the registry quickly is becoming a central repository for data that are accepted by many agencies and organizations (e.g., licensing and accrediting entities), which helps to streamline the QRS and other quality initiative processes.

In addition to these important successes, the ultimate success was the results of the child outcome study, the Missouri Quality Rating System School Readiness Study (Thornburg et al., 2009), in determining the predictive validity of the QRS. The data from the child outcome study are compelling for all children, but especially for children living in poverty. Children make greater gains in higher quality programs as compared with lower quality programs, when controlling for many relevant variables.

CHALLENGES

The pilot and demonstration periods supported our success and helped further clarify the challenges that still need to be resolved at the program and systems levels. For the purpose of this chapter, we will focus on three broad systems-level issues—infrastructure, the "partial" system, and funding.

Infrastructure

The QRS pilot and demonstration phases highlighted significant issues related to the state infrastructure that must be addressed in order to ensure the success of the QRS. Specifically, our current coaching system is fragmented and some coaches are not adequately prepared to support programs in two QRS components: intentional teaching and business and administrative practices. Additionally, it is necessary to determine, possibly through a testing process, that coaches understand the state career development system (e.g., career lattice and registry process), standards (e.g., core competencies and early learning guidelines), and QRS requirements and assessment tools (e.g., Environment Rating Scales and checklists). Another infrastructure issue is related to the assessor system. Although individual assessors were reliable with others in their region, much work was needed to develop a reliable system statewide. To address this issue, one entity is now responsible for the assessment system and maintaining the rigor of the assessment process. Finally, we continue to encounter and resolve issues that have to be addressed regarding licensure requirements and documentation of noncompliance.

The "Partial" System

The MO QRS State Committee wants to improve the quality of all programs serving children, but, by making the decision to use the state licensing structure as the baseline criterion, we leave out thousands of children in unlicensed programs. It is our understanding that Missouri is not alone in regard to this issue and that many states are grappling with what to do with the programs that are not licensed or do not meet the requirements for QRS participation.

Funding

It is difficult to accurately project the true cost of piloting and operating a QRS. Year after year, we have needed more funding to complete the various phases of the project. Our advice to others, in order to have sufficient funds to support the work, is to connect with states that are implementing similar models to determine costs and to get a sense of potential roadblocks.

THE IMPACT OF QRS ON MISSOURI'S SYSTEMS REFORM EFFORTS

Missouri began this work roughly 5 years before the writing of this chapter, which is a short time in terms of systems development work. However, the children born that year, who are now entering kindergarten, did not have the benefit of improved programs based on the new system. We know that although the MO QRS has contributed significantly to the system-level organization efforts in Missouri, its ultimate effectiveness is limited by our inability to secure support for statewide implementation. Although the MO QRS models have been endorsed by the appropriate authorities, legislative efforts have failed during the past three sessions. There has been significant support from legislators, the lobbying community, and state department personnel, but due to the political and economic climate, a bill has not passed. Early childhood and school-age leaders, with support from the business and philanthropic communities, continue to support local QRS projects. Administrative support is necessary to achieve statewide implementation, and only then can Missouri begin to address issues related to consumer education and equitable distribution of resources based on shared standards of practice. It is our hope that the results of the MO QRS School Readiness Study will be the final piece of data needed to convince the administration and legislature that QRS is a necessary part of the system. The data definitely support the notion that the MO QRS is a valid measure, and it is our belief that with the information from the rating and additional supports, programs can improve in quality and, therefore, help children be more successful as they enter and progress through school.

REFERENCE

Thornburg, K. R., Mayfield, W. A., Hawks, J. S., & Fuger, K. L. (2009). *The Missouri quality rating system school readiness study*. Columbia, MO: Center for Family Policy & Research. Available at http://CFPR.missouri.edu/MOQRSreport.pdf

ADDITIONAL RESOURCES

For more information about the Missouri QRS, visit www.OPENInitiative.org

To review more information about the development of MO QRS in general, see

Thornburg, K., Mauzy, D., Mayfield, W., Scott, J., Sparks, A., Mumford, J., et al. (2011). Data-driven decision making in preparation for large scale QRS implementation. In M. Zaslow, I. Martinez-Beck, K. Tout, & T. Halle (Eds.), *Quality measurement in early childhood settings*. Baltimore: Brookes.

CHAPTER 16

Changing Governance and Governing Change

The Massachusetts Department of Early Education and Care

Amy Kershaw and Ann Reale

Merging separate parts of state government is no small task. It can take such a Herculean effort to get to the bill-signing ceremony that it is tempting to think the rest will fall into place. And it can. But it takes constant, focused attention on what it really means to have a system. It takes the energy and discipline necessary to rebuild the old pieces into something new, to ensure that every agency action reflects that newness, and to keep informing, refining, supporting, and building out from all of those actions into solutions that are even better and more interconnected. For governance change to live up to its promise, the process of change must become a constant.

Thus, the key to building "a system" is in knowing that *what* you choose to do—whichever agencies or programs or pieces are put closer together—must be grounded in a deep understanding of *how* you choose to continuously reshape those pieces to fit better. To develop truly sustainable and thriving early childhood systems, the focus must be both on the need to develop new institutions that can provide the catalyst for change, and also on the process of change itself: to take advantage of the countless opportunities to build positive relationships, to learn from honest assessment and analysis, to share information and resources, to trust, and to become comfortable with more change.

This is the story of how one agency in one state made systems change happen—and learned that it was only just beginning.

CREATING THE WILL FOR GOVERNANCE CHANGE

First there was the Task Force, then the Summit, then the Work Group, then the Advisory Council—one produced the purple book, another the green book, another the red book, and yet another the blue one with the cute baby on the front. They were all charged with figuring out how to bring together multiple state agencies with responsibility for educating and caring for young children. Each held the promise of alleviating the infighting among the "education" and "care" factions in the field, but not much changed.

Then came "the campaign." In 2001, Strategies for Children, a Massachusetts-based nonprofit, launched the Early Education for All Campaign, bringing together leaders from across sectors to advocate for greater investments in early education. Early on, it became clear to the organizers that the lack of a coherent vision for the delivery of early childhood services was a barrier and had to change if the state was ever going to capitalize on the potential benefits of early education and care for young children, their families, and the commonwealth as a whole. And so the creation of a new, integrated governance structure became a companion goal in the campaign's push for universally accessible early childhood education. Without the first, the campaign made clear, it would be impossible to achieve the second.

Leaders in the field, as well as in the legislative and executive branches, eventually agreed and legislation was passed to establish the new department and lay the foundation for universal prekindergarten in Massachusetts.[1]

BUILDING THE CAPACITY TO GOVERN CHANGE

The Department of Early Education and Care (EEC) became officially operational on July 1, 2005. All of the state's child care line items and functions, and the Head Start–State Collaboration Office, were transferred out of the Executive Office of Health and Human Services, and all of the state's preschool, early childhood special education, and family support line items and functions were transferred out of the Department of Education. Those functions and funding streams were consolidated to form a new nearly $500 million department with 170 staff, organized in a mirror image of the state's Higher Education and K–12 systems. It was now an independent state agency run by a Commissioner, under the oversight of a public/private board appointed by the governor.[2] The "what" had been decided, and it was time to figure out "how" this new entity could embody the coordinated approach it was created to establish.

The transformational process had to start from within the agency first. Staffing decisions and reorganizations were announced as quickly and clearly as possible. The Director of the Head Start–State Collaboration Office and the manager of $8 million in supplemental grants to Head Start programs, who had never met before, now sat next to each other and became a new team. A unit of "policy" staff who saw their job as primarily about supporting work for low-income families was merged with "policy" staff who saw their job as primarily about educating children. A consolidated fiscal division began reconciling a philosophy of strict adherence to state fiscal requirements with a strong belief in flexibility at the local level.

Ongoing organizational meetings were held to learn about new colleagues, and understand how their work and skills connected to one another and to a new common mission and set of guiding principles. To help the staff process their real and understandable feelings of loss and fear of the unknown, the management team did their best to acknowledge the difficulty of change, share as much information as possible, answer questions honestly, and create a positive culture of openness and enthusiasm for the new opportunities ahead. Organizational consultants and other professional resources provided additional support over time to effectively establish a culture of "one EEC."

Building rapport within the agency was essential to be able to effectively take on the work ahead—untangling the deeply embedded, yet disconnected, policies and programs that now sat under one roof. As internal staff came to understand the new mission, there was more capacity to connect in a positive way with providers, advocates, and other related agency personnel, who were similarly wary about what the new agency would do. Finding leaders among the existing internal and external ranks, learning from and with the naysayers, and recruiting new talent all helped build the relationships necessary to address complex policy and program challenges.

The agency convened an Advisory Committee of external stakeholders to vet decisions, shared detailed information at monthly board meetings that were open to and well attended by the public, and met with a Parent Advisory group regularly to learn from their perspective. On every issue, the first step was to analyze commonly recognized and reliable facts, and to communicate them clearly, publicly, objectively, and repeatedly to make the case for change. Then the conversation about new solutions could begin from a more solid base. While it was never easy to meet the expectations of every stakeholder, the routine of sharing as much information as possible, and carefully incorporating feedback from all corners, began to create a deeper understanding of how the new department would approach decisions. The organizational culture—internally and externally—slowly started to shift from competitive to collaborative.

PUTTING CHANGE TO WORK FOR CHILDREN AND FAMILIES

With the fundamental building blocks in place—legislative authority, a data-driven, decision-making process, and strong relationships based on open communication—the agency's ability to initiate and implement effective change grew. Internal teams, made up of a deliberately representative mix of staff from every division of the agency, working with external subcommittees, began rethinking existing policies, programs, and procedures, and designing a new universal pre-K program.

The work was driven by the new department's guiding principles, most important, the one at the top of the list—"put children and families first." Initial changes focused on streamlining the convoluted processes that families had to navigate to obtain and maintain financial assistance for child care and early education. The goal was to make it easier for families to access aid, and to improve stability and consistency for children enrolled in programs. This included centralizing hundreds of waiting lists for parents needing financial assistance into a single online system, aligning eligibility rules that varied from program to program, and identifying new ways to prioritize the neediest children and ensure they remained eligible even when funding streams changed. Armed with the knowledge that 86% of families remained eligible following their 6-month "reassessment," the department's governing board voted to lengthen the redetermination period for financial assistance to 1 year for most families, providing greater predictability and less administrative burden all around.

Federal funding from Head Start and the Child Care and Development Fund was used more coherently with state funding to create stability in programming for children and commonsense transitions. Homeless children could remain in their programs as their fragile families became housed, children involved with the child welfare system could continue a stable relationship with their child care providers even if their abuse or neglect case was closed, low-income preschoolers could automatically qualify for before- and after-school programs when they transitioned to kindergarten, and 12-year-olds wouldn't lose their eligibility in the middle of an after-school program or summer camp on the day they turned 13.

As these changes began improving access to financial assistance for early education and school-age care, the agency started taking on the bigger challenge of improving the quality of the programs that families had access to, striving to keep equal focus on both the "education" and "care" in the department's name. Licensing regulations were revamped to better reflect that balance, workforce standards and policies were re-examined and strengthened, and funding for scholarships, training, and accreditation was reconfigured to better align across initiatives.

Funding to launch the Massachusetts Universal Pre-Kindergarten (UPK) program provided the first opportunity to apply the emerging systems approach to designing something new. The data showed that nearly 70% of preschool children were already enrolled in some type of program outside their home, but that the quality varied significantly—especially for low-income and educationally at-risk children—as did the length of the program's day and year. Rather than creating a parallel structure, the new program was designed to address what the data showed were the gaps. New resources were targeted to existing programs in underperforming school districts that could serve the needs of low-income working families. Quality grants could be used by programs to improve and implement early childhood assessment, build teacher skills, and/or increase compensation. The UPK strategy was consistent with, and central to, both the legislative intent of the new governing structure and the systems approach of the new department.

THE NEED FOR GREATER CHANGE

By establishing a new governance structure and changing how services were governed, Massachusetts made significant progress in moving toward a more comprehensive and systemic approach to improving services for young children and their families. A new organization was established; external stakeholders were engaged differently; data were analyzed and presented to support decisions; policies were revamped to put families ahead of bureaucracy; and resources were reconfigured to achieve greater efficiency for staff, providers, and policymakers.

As these changes began taking hold, and the agency looked ahead, it became clear that the next steps led to even further integration, and a new set of higher order challenges and opportunities. To more effectively support teachers in building their skills, higher education had to not only accept EEC scholarships but also actually engage in building pathways for early educators to seek and attain degrees. To have a sustainable impact on the lives of the most vulnerable children, the leaders of other state agencies serving children and families had to not only support greater access to quality child care, but also work at the same table on common goals and strategies. And, to deliver on the promise of UPK and improve the impact of after-school programs, the K–12 system would need to recognize that "care" was part of its mission too.

Creating the opportunity for that level of change—across and at every level of our child-serving systems—will require returning to the beginning: building the will for change.

NOTES

1. An additional legislative proposal, An Act Relative to Early Education and Care, which significantly added to the department's original enabling statute and further defined the Massachusetts Universal Pre-Kindergarten (UPK) Program, unanimously passed the House and Senate in Spring 2008 and was signed into law by Governor Deval Patrick on July 31, 2008.

2. Three years after being established as an independent agency, the department was clustered within a new Education Secretariat as a separate *and* equal agency to the state's Departments of Higher Education and Elementary and Secondary Education.

CHAPTER 17

Governance in
Early Childhood Systems
The View from Pennsylvania

Harriet Dichter

Pennsylvania is a large state that, in 2008, had 886,097 children age 5 and under (KIDS COUNT Data Center, 2008). Taking audacious steps to support young children and their families, the commonwealth created a new governance approach that aimed to significantly advance the achievement of positive outcomes for all children. Although the approach was broadly designed and included both the expansion of existing services and the generation of new services, its innovative and integrated approach to governance was the platform from which dynamic changes and a systemic approach to early education were spearheaded. This chapter is the story of the evolution, nature, and contributions of an integrated approach to governance.

THE NEED FOR COORDINATED GOVERNANCE

Like those of many states in the nation, Pennsylvania's policies and services to young children were multifaceted and fragmented. And, although bound by good intentions and a dedicated workforce, Pennsylvania fell behind many other states on assessments of school performance. Just adding new early learning programs would not go far enough. Several opportunities converged. In 2003, Pennsylvania, through its state government, became a BUILD state (www.buildinitiative.org); this encouraged consideration of governance strategies as part of improved learning opportunities for young children. In 2004, Governor Ed Rendell created the Office of Childhood Development (OCD) at the Department of Public Welfare to manage all of the state's child care initiatives, early childhood home-visiting programs, and infant–toddler early intervention services. In 2007, Governor Rendell authorized a second phase of this work through the creation of the Office of Child Development and Early Learning (OCDEL) that established a single, consolidated office, organizational structure, and staff designed to integrate the work of OCD with the early learning work being developed at the Department of Education. With dual accountability to the Secretary of Public Welfare and the Secretary of Education, OCDEL was well positioned to bridge the gap between welfare and education that had long characterized services for young children.

The rationale for Pennsylvania's decision to pursue an outside-the-box organizational and governance structure emanated from the commitment to the twin goals of equity and quality for all children, irrespective of background, economic status, home community, or ability. Unifying governance was regarded as a means to the end of improved learning experiences and outcomes for Pennsylvania's children. Moreover, the rationale was premised on the reality that many Pennsylvania families can and do enroll their children in more than one program, and that families expect any publicly available program to be of appropriate quality and support. Without a coordinated governance structure, the heavy lifting needed to achieve these ends was not deemed feasible. With the goal of creating a system and building the capacity for excellence, governance becomes a critical part of the work and is a core strategy to achieve sustainable success.

The decision to take on governance occurred as part of the strategy for better meeting the needs of young learners. Governance became a focus because of the state's goals for an integrated, efficient, and effective approach to maximizing its public investment to best meet the needs of children. In short, the decision to pursue governance was contextual and based on the goals set forth for the early childhood programs.

WHAT IS OCDEL AND HOW DOES IT WORK?

OCDEL's mission is to promote opportunities for all Pennsylvania children and families by building systems and providing supports that help ensure access to high-quality child and family services. Rhetorically ambitious, the effort was grounded in an operational framework that positioned positive outcomes for children and family at its core. Surrounding the core is a set of functions that needed not only to be in place, but also to be coordinated across early development and learning programs. These functions included system planning, monitoring, and accountability; standards for programs and practitioners; supports to meet and maintain standards; engagement and outreach; and financial supports. The framework is presented in Figure 17.1.

FIGURE 17.1. Pennsylvania's Early Learning System Framework

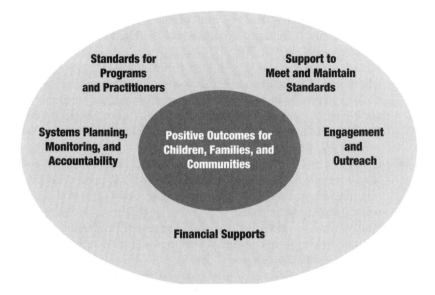

Not a mere framework on paper, this conceptualization was used to guide OCDEL's structure and organizational elements as it became a single, consolidated office and took on the responsibility for financial, policy, program, and implementation oversight, and accountability for all early learning programs in Pennsylvania. These programs include: (a) child care (i.e., child care certification/licensure; Child Care Works Subsidy; Keystone STARS Quality Rating and Improvement System/Keys to Quality; and Keystone Babies); (b) early intervention (i.e., services for children with delays and disabilities, birth through preschool); (c) family support (i.e., Nurse Family Partnership, Parent Child Home Program); (d) full-day kindergarten; (e) Head Start (i.e., Early Head Start, Head Start Supplemental Assistance Program, Head Start–State Collaboration); and (f) prekindergarten (i.e., PA Pre-K Counts, Head Start Supplemental Assistance Program). Within a context of collaboration and working to advance the framework, several firsthand examples clearly demonstrate the importance of a unified approach to governance.

Leveraging Unified Governance to Create Progress in Alignment

Central to the premise of advancing an integrated approach to early development, OCDEL has supported the development and implementation of early learning standards for all young children. OCDEL regards the standards as a pivotal core of quality enhancement. It has committed to the development, analysis, and implementation of standards within and across programs, grades, funding streams, and pedagogical approaches. Armed with a clear vision and a solid governance structure, OCDEL created a cadre of efforts that include:

- Alignment of Learning Standards for Early Childhood—Based on an independent horizontal and vertical evaluation of the early learning standards from infant–toddler through 3rd grade, OCDEL made necessary modifications to ensure appropriate vertical and horizontal alignment.
- Cross Systems Technical Assistance—Defined core competencies for all technical assistance initiatives for OCDEL programs and ongoing shared professional development for those providing technical assistance.
- Pennsylvania Inspired Leadership Educational Leadership Training—Established an innovative new component to the state's mandated professional development for school system instructional leaders (e.g., principals and superintendents) through the Early Childhood Executive Leadership Institute, which brings together leaders from both the K–12 and early childhood systems to build mutual understanding and strengthen the alignment between early education and traditional public education.
- Alignment of the early education Professional Development Record with new teacher certification requirements—Used the base for Pennsylvania's new teacher certification requirements (which remove the K–6th-grade omnibus certificate and substitute P–4th-grade and 4th-grade–8th-grade certificates) as the baseline for Pennsylvania's professional development record.
- Title I Transition to Kindergarten Grants—Focused on early education and basic education transition strategies involving Title I elementary schools and the Community Engagement Groups.

Leveraging Governance for Assessment and Accountability

Assessment and accountability is another area in which the governance structure helps to drive a systematic approach. To make best use of public resources that produce positive outcomes for Pennsylvania's young children, OCDEL developed a system of accountability across all programs. Program and fiscal monitoring, along with supportive technical assistance, underlie the state's approach to assessment and accountability. Using a common basis of standards and measures, staff monitor adherence to performance standards and fiscal requirements, and provide technical assistance and supports for programs to continue to improve their quality. Through this approach, programs work with OCDEL and its representatives to develop and implement improvement plans. Customer satisfaction surveys from both parents and providers also are included in this approach.

OCDEL BENEFITS

The benefits of OCDEL and its governance structure are many and are continually emerging. Two of particular importance will be highlighted here.

Advancing Policy and Practice Through the Effective Use of Data

A key to creating a quality early education continuum is the seamless transfer of information between programs and the ability to effectively use data collected on OCDEL's programs and services. To that end, integrated and cross-cutting information systems—known as Pennsylvania's Enterprise to Link Information Across Networks (PELICAN) and the Early Learning Network (ELN)—have been implemented. PELICAN's goal is to have a single integrated information system that allows OCDEL to track how Pennsylvania children and families use OCDEL programs, and, with a focus on quality, to provide easily accessible information for parents about early learning programs and services. Moreover, by centralizing demographic and enrollment information for children, teachers, and families, PELICAN is streamlining data management across OCDEL programs and, ultimately, will provide unprecedented aggregated data on children and families served. Over time, PELICAN will help Pennsylvania measure program, service, and provider performance as it relates to progress and outcomes for children participating in early childhood programs.

Supporting the PELICAN system, Pennsylvania's ELN tracks outcomes for children who participate in OCDEL's programs from birth until they enter kindergarten. Using the data collected, OCDEL can document how the state's quality early learning system is contributing to positive outcomes for children. Plans include the ability to link the information about children's participation in, and outcomes from, their early learning programs to their school-age participation and outcomes. In addition to providing fiscal and outcomes data for OCDEL administration, parents and teachers will have access to information about children's progress, which will help guide curriculum and will support children's progress at home. ELN also will track teacher education levels and experience, with the goal of providing information on how teacher education affects child outcomes. Although K–12 programs have already developed similar longitudinal data systems, the concept is relatively new for early childhood education. The development and implementation of ELN would not have been possible without the OCDEL governance and support structure.

Advancing Connections to Education and Public Welfare

OCDEL's experience creating a new organization that brings together all of the resources, expertise, and staff in an integrated structure connected to both the education agency and the human services/health agency is a net positive. These connections have proven important in several areas. For example, OCDEL has successfully leveraged Medicaid financing for several of its programs and has led an initiative for all child-serving programs within the human services and health agency to adopt a coherent approach to early childhood screening. On the education side, the critical work of having a sound continuum and connection between early education and basic education is aided by the organizational link between OCDEL and the state's education agency. Early education stands next to K–12, but it is not the same as K–12. OCDEL's interconnectedness with both education and human services helps everyone to understand this.

THE VALUE OF A CONSOLIDATED AND INNOVATIVE GOVERNANCE EFFORT

In Pennsylvania and around the country, early education is coming of age. Nonetheless, we are still early in developing acceptance within the basic education community of many of the unique aspects of early learning and child development. To many, early education remains a confusing array of scatter-shot programs. Across financing and program streams, significant fragmentation and isolation exist within the early learning community. And yet, the early learning field stands to benefit from the comprehensive child development philosophy and fundamental funding sources that exist in health and human services. The field also needs the education focus and investments offered by the public school system. These are important connections for early learning.

The burgeoning acceptance of early childhood, the extensive fragmentation of existing programs and policies, and supportive governmental leadership converged in Pennsylvania and influenced the consolidated approach to governance that led to the establishment of OCDEL. This approach to governance has helped early education become a better recognized and more vital contributor to positive child and family outcomes and to the state's economic productivity. The OCDEL experience in Pennsylvania demonstrates the value added by a consolidated, innovative governance effort.

REFERENCE

KIDS COUNT Data Center, Annie E. Casey Foundation. (2008). PA KIDS COUNT Indicators. Retrieved from http://datacenter.kidscount.org/data/bystate/stateprofile.aspx?state=PA&group=Grantee&loc=40&dt=1%2c3%2c2%2c4

CHAPTER 18

Building a High-Performing Early Childhood Professional Development System

North Carolina

Sue Russell

The key to producing good outcomes for young children in early care and education settings is the knowledge and skill of their teachers. A well-designed, high-quality, seamless, and integrated professional development system is crucial for ensuring that prospective and practicing teachers with all levels of education have access to the professional development they need in order to be effective. Building high-performing state early childhood professional development systems requires a combination of standards and regulation, investments, planning, cross-sector collaboration, and leadership. A set of core values should guide the development of these systems, including:

- All young children have a right to a highly educated, culturally and pedagogically competent, well-compensated teacher.
- Teachers of young children have a right to an accessible, high-quality, and well-financed professional development system.
- Teachers of young children can participate in well-defined and articulated education and career pathways as early childhood professionals.

This chapter describes North Carolina's approach to developing a professional development system, by tracing the state's recent efforts, examining key components of the system, and reviewing lessons learned in this process.

252

The leadership of two governors, Jim Hunt (1993–2000) and Mike Easley (2001–2008), focused North Carolina's attention on young children. Their efforts brought a large infusion of state dollars to two statewide early childhood efforts, Smart Start and More at Four. Smart Start supports the development of local partnerships designed to improve health, family support, and early education outcomes for children from birth to age 5. More at Four is a state-funded prekindergarten initiative, available to 4-year-olds who are at risk for school failure, with high teacher education and program standards. At the state level, child care subsidy, licensing, and the administration of quality dollars available through the Child Care and Development Block Grant (CCDBG) are consolidated into the Division of Child Development within the NC Department of Health and Human Services. The division developed a rated license system that links better program standards and higher levels of staff education to higher star ratings. Programs at the highest levels, four or five stars, receive better child care subsidy rates and are allowed to become More at Four sites. Smart Start measures the success of local partnerships by the percent of young children in four- or five-star programs.

Since 1992 North Carolina has had a loosely but consistently organized group of people developing an early childhood professional development system. Participants come from the higher education system, child care resource and referral agencies, state and local Smart Start partnerships, state government agencies, workforce initiatives, and the workforce itself. Called the North Carolina Institute for Child Development Professionals, they have spearheaded a collaborative effort of planning and development, including the creation of materials, assessment tools, trainings, and advocacy that have promoted a systemic approach to early childhood professional development. Key elements of their efforts are described next.

DATA AND ACCOUNTABILITY

North Carolina's system has been shaped and reshaped by collecting and using data on the teaching workforce and the effectiveness of various strategies designed to improve the quality of and access to professional development. Multiple studies have been conducted over time at the county and state levels to profile the education, compensation, personal demographics, workplace supports, professional development needs, and turnover of the early childhood workforce. These data have influenced both local and state professional development strategies and allowed examination of system-wide improvements in education, compensation, and retention over time. For example, in the early 1990s a statewide early childhood work-force study found low levels of education and wages, with high turnover; respondents cited they left or planned to leave their classrooms because of poor compensation. At the time, the turnover rate for teachers in early care and education (ECE) settings was 42% annually. After a number of local and state strategies were employed, the statewide turnover rate dropped to 24% by 2003.

ACCESSIBILITY

Ensuring all young children have teachers with degrees in early childhood education begins with an affordable and accessible higher education system. In 1990 the T.E.A.C.H. Early Childhood® (T.E.A.C.H.) Project was created to help individuals working in ECE settings to afford college. While it started small and focused its efforts on coursework leading to an associate's degree in early childhood education, it has grown significantly, with scholarships now available for coursework to earn credentials, 2- and 4-year degrees, and the birth to kindergarten (B–K) license. There is even a loan forgive-ness program under T.E.A.C.H. for full-time juniors and seniors majoring in early childhood education that provides a per-semester stipend in exchange for agreement to teach in prekindergarten classrooms with at-risk children upon graduation. In 2009 almost 5,400 individuals had a T.E.A.C.H. schol-arship and worked in 2,000 different public and private ECE centers and homes across the state. Most scholarships cover partial costs for tuition, books, travel, and paid release time; require a bonus or raise upon comple-tion of a minimum number of credit hours; and mandate that the individual remain in her sponsoring early care and education program for an addi-tional year. T.E.A.C.H. early childhood scholarships are central to North Carolina's professional development system; they increase access to higher education for practitioners and provide resources to augment the supply of early childhood coursework and degree programs.

Because of the perception that early childhood education is not a vi-able career, other states' higher education systems often fail to offer widely dispersed degree programs in early childhood education at the associate's, bachelor's, and master's degree levels. North Carolina is different. In 1993 only 28 of the state's 58 community colleges offered the associate's degree in early childhood education. By 1998 all 58 colleges offered this degree, making coursework available within a reasonable distance to anyone in the state. Using funding from local Smart Start partnerships, colleges were given one-time grants to build their programs, thus increasing the supply of available coursework. T.E.A.C.H. scholarships enabled the "demand" side to work, because cost no longer was a barrier. For the first time, individuals working in early care and education could realize their dream of going to college. Since its inception, more than half of scholarship recipients have been women of color. Similar growth has taken place in the number of 4-year institutions both offering a bachelor's degree in child development or early childhood education and being approved to offer the state's B–K licensure program. With 20 colleges and universities across the state offering bachelor's degrees, students have many options for continuing their education.

Accessibility also means that sufficient courses are offered at times and in places that meet the needs of working students. Community colleges in North Carolina offer about 21 early childhood courses per semester per college; this varies greatly by size of program. Community colleges offer an average of eight online early childhood courses per semester; only one does not offer any online ECE coursework. The beauty of both online coursework and wide dispersion of early childhood degree programs is that North Carolina's community college system has a common course catalog, ensuring that courses have the same name, course description, and learning goals across the entire system. As a result, students can take courses at community colleges beyond the one that is closest to them. There is real choice about when, where, how, and what courses are taken. Unfortunately, the 4-year system does not do this, even within the state's public universities. With North Carolina's large and increasing Latino population, coursework in Spanish is an unmet need, with only five community colleges offering early childhood courses in Spanish.

ARTICULATION

As more and more individuals earned 2-year degrees from the community college system, the articulation of that education into the university system became critical. It often took teachers 5 years to earn their 2-year degree, going to school part-time. Not being given credit for the work they had done, a 4-year degree was not obtainable for much of the workforce. Recognizing the need for a fully articulated system, a statewide articulation conference was convened by state leaders in the mid-1990s. At about the same time, T.E.A.C.H. scholarship funds for working students to earn bachelor's degrees were made available only to students who attended universities that had articulation agreements with area community colleges.

Soon thereafter, the University of North Carolina–Greensboro offered meaningful articulation agreements to every community college in the state, allowing students who graduated with their associate's degree to enter as juniors. In addition, a North Carolina study found that junior transfer students in early childhood education did as well as native students in terms of grades and graduation rates. These data helped convince other universities to develop flexible articulation agreements. Efforts to create a statewide articulation agreement between all 2- and 4-year schools continue.

QUALITY

In North Carolina, 50% of a program's score on its star-rated license is determined by the education of its teachers and directors. With high stakes like subsidy and More at Four payments tied to the star rating, the quality of education within community colleges must be high. It is no surprise that when NAEYC unveiled its early childhood associate degree accreditation, many of the state's community colleges quickly applied. The state has used CCDBG funds to provide incentives to support colleges to complete the process, with the expectation that all will become accredited.

In addition, all community college programs have completed a Curriculum Improvement Process in Early Childhood Education. This effort provided faculty with training and tools to improve their knowledge and practices, redefined and strengthened 65 early childhood courses in the common course catalog, developed or revised course competencies for all of the core courses that must be offered in early childhood statewide, created nine new courses, and set prerequisites for basic reading and writing skills for most of the courses. This process greatly improved the quality and consistency of instruction for students within the community colleges' early childhood degree programs.

COMPENSATION

As North Carolina has pushed its workforce to become better educated, it has invested millions of dollars annually to support compensation incentives to encourage retention. Using state Smart Start and More at Four funds as well as federal CCDBG funds, individuals working in more than two-thirds of North Carolina's counties are eligible to receive Child Care WAGE$® salary supplements tied to the level of their attained education. Supplements are paid every 6 months as long as the individuals stay in their programs. The education levels of those receiving supplements continue to rise, with many also taking advantage of T.E.A.C.H. scholarships. The annual turnover rate for WAGE$ participants is 12%, closely mirroring the turnover rate for public school teachers. The T.E.A.C.H. Early Childhood® Health Insurance Program also has helped subsidize health insurance costs in eligible sites.

When the state created More at Four, it mandated that all teachers with a B–K License, regardless of work setting, receive compensation comparable to that of teachers working in public schools. Because about half of children receiving More at Four funding are served in child care or Head Start programs, this requirement has had substantial impact on compensation practices. For the first time, teachers with a B–K license in child care settings have compensation parity with their public school teaching peers, breaking the glass ceiling for what teachers can earn working in child care programs.

PROFESSIONAL RECOGNITION

North Carolina is creating a system of certification and licensure for the entire early childhood workforce. The North Carolina Institute for Child Development Professionals is the certifying body. Beginning with those who work directly with young children, it eventually will include both those who administer programs and those who provide technical assistance and training in classrooms. Certification includes a review of the individual's transcript and the assignment of a level as an Early Educator. This allows teachers to be recognized for their achieved education, even if they do not have a birth to kindergarten license, and it encourages them to continue to go to school to advance their certification levels. Continuing professional development is required for renewal, either with college coursework or continuing education units (CEUs). Recent legislation has made certification mandatory. Plans are underway for individual licensure, building on certification status.

LESSONS LEARNED

Building on these successes, North Carolina continues to work on its early childhood professional development system. In addition to individual certification, next steps include renewed focus on the quality of training, both its content and the individual trainer's qualifications and competence. We continue to build on lessons we have learned from the past 20 years of work, including:

- Weaving each piece of the system together, ensuring balance, quality, and access;
- Focusing on formal education in early childhood as the foundation on which to build continuing professional development;

- Providing meaningful incentives to individuals, early childhood programs, and higher education institutions to leverage change;
- Using data to assess the needs and challenges of the workforce, profile the professional development system, and evaluate the effectiveness of strategies;
- Continually raising expectations for the workforce; and
- Incrementally but consistently addressing compensation parity for the workforce.

Building a high-performing early childhood professional development system requires vision, leadership, commitment, resources, and systemic integration, with the recognition that it is a long and continuing process.

CHAPTER 19

Building an Early Childhood Budget to Support a Comprehensive Early Childhood System in Louisiana

Geoffrey Nagle

The federal initiative, the state Early Childhood Comprehensive Systems (ECCS) grant program, administered by the U.S. Department of Health and Human Services, Maternal and Child Health Bureau, is designed to assist states in building comprehensive early childhood systems. These federal grants are available to each state's Maternal and Child Health program.

In Louisiana, this ECCS initiative is known as BrightStart and is administered by the state Office of Public Health's Maternal and Child Health program. The focus is specifically on children prenatal until age 5. In December 2009, Governor Bobby Jindal designated BrightStart to serve as Louisiana's Early Childhood Advisory Council.

BrightStart is focused on building a truly comprehensive early childhood system, with a system defined as including both infrastructure and services. The two primary goals of BrightStart are: (1) to develop, support, and maintain systems integration and partnerships to enhance children's ability to enter school healthy and ready to learn; and (2) to build an early childhood system that addresses the following priority areas: access to medical care; early care and education; family support and parenting education; and mental health and social-emotional development.

STARTING TO BUILD THE SYSTEM

When setting out to build an early childhood system, an obvious question is, "Where do you begin?" The answer for BrightStart was to begin with the state budget. This is because the state budget is the most important policy document used in decision making by governmental leaders. As Richard Nathan (2000) writes, "The budget process is the spinal column of public policymaking" (p. 42). Therefore, to be able to influence policy, one needs to influence the budget by getting involved in the budget process.

To do this, a deep understanding of the budget is needed. Such an understanding requires two essential steps. The first is a shift in thinking, or perspective, about what a budget is. Many people think that a budget is simply a series or arrangement of numbers identifying sums of money. However, if the perspective shifts to thinking of the budget as a policy document, then some reticence to examining the information may be minimized, and instead replaced with an attitude that the budget necessitates a deep review. This examination of the budget, at a minimum, will help in providing an understanding of the priorities the state has chosen to invest in and the financial commitments the state is undertaking.

Now, with a new perspective on the budget, the second step can be pursued, which is much more difficult. This step is to find the information needed to gain deep knowledge of and insight into the budget. Often, the budget information regarding particular issues lives in supporting state budget documents, perhaps even scattered in pieces throughout several different documents. Fortunately, it is not uncommon in this day of government "transparency" for much of the budget documentation to be accessible via the internet. The challenge is to find and compile all of the relevant pieces from different sections. This is very much the case in the area of early childhood, as the budget detail of interest may span two, three, or even four state departments (e.g., education, health, social services, workforce development). In addition, budget details may not exist as specific line items or programmatic entries, thereby failing to provide the needed specificity.

For this reason, BrightStart proposed that an early childhood budget be created. The need was clear: A deep understanding of the budget resources allocated to early childhood was the essential starting point to building an early childhood system. Our mantra was, and continues to be, "A cross-system plan without a cross-system budget is difficult to implement."

THE EARLY CHILDHOOD SYSTEM INTEGRATION BUDGET

The proposed budget document was named the Early Childhood System Integration Budget (ECSIB). The ECSIB was designed as a platform for integrating financial and programmatic information relevant to an early childhood system. This information would be organized around the defined priority areas of BrightStart as opposed to being organized by state department. Therefore, there would be four sections of the ECSIB named for these priority areas: (1) access to medical care; (2) early care and education; (3) family support and parenting education; and (4) mental health and social-emotional development.

Within these four areas, each state department would categorize program-specific information, including the lead contact person, a very brief program description (one to three sentences), the population served, the sources of funding for the program, and the parishes (counties in Louisiana) being served. For each line item, actual state and federal dollars invested in the program would be detailed.

For example, the early care and education section would include programs from the state's Department of Social Services, such as the child care subsidy program and the Head Start–State Collaboration office, alongside the Department of Education's prekindergarten programs, which include several separate funding sources that are involved in providing distinct prekindergarten programs. Once this information was compiled in the ECSIB (along with any other early care and education programs administered by other state departments), a policymaker or advocate could answer the practical question, "How much money are we spending on early education programs to prepare children for school?" The ECSIB provided the answer in one location, eliminating the need to dig through each separate department budget section trying to tease out which programs were providing relevant services.

It should be noted that the ECSIB does not make any judgment or assumptions about what is the proper amount of spending in any specific area. Instead, it simply provides the information to policymakers and other interested parties so that they can make whatever judgments they feel are warranted. With this big picture information, which does not provide any sort of per-child calculation, appropriate action can be proposed, debated, and/or pursued. In other words, the ECSIB is not about determining the appropriate amount to spend in any particular category or even overall on early childhood. Instead, the ECSIB builds a greater understanding of the resources allocated to support young children and, of those funds, how they are allocated.

The ECSIB also is intended to foster better collaboration across state departments with programs that share common goals or objectives. By organizing the budget by BrightStart priority area rather than by department, different departments can see more easily the other services being provided with goals similar to their own programs. In this way it becomes clear where there are opportunities for collaboration through the blending of funding streams or other resources, or even possibly where state dollars in one department can be used as a match for federal dollars in another department.

Once completed, the ECSIB will offer policymakers, state leaders, and advocates a greatly enhanced ability to examine the adequacy of funding in each priority area, opportunities for enhanced collaboration, and greater ease at identifying areas ideal for the blending and/or braiding of funds.

Fortunately, the concept of the ECSIB was embraced universally in Louisiana, as the utility of such a budget document was widely appreciated. Legislation to institutionalize the ECSIB was developed and introduced by state Senator Lydia Jackson in time for the 2008 regular session of the legislature. Introduced as Senate Bill 615, the legislation extended the existence of the Governor's Children's Cabinet, which was scheduled to sunset that summer. As the existing Children's Cabinet legislation included the call for a children's budget, the ECSIB was a natural extension of these responsibilities. The proposed legislation directed the state division of administration, which oversees all aspects of the state budget, to implement and update the ECSIB, which is described in detail in the bill.[1] The bill passed both chambers of the state legislature unanimously and was signed by Governor Bobby Jindal. The ECSIB became a legally required budget document on August 15, 2008.

A PRELIMINARY DRAFT OF THE ECSIB

A final draft of the first ECSIB is nearing completion. Although still not finalized, the ECSIB presents valuable information about resource allocation for young children. The current working draft shows that 61% of all dollars spent on early childhood in Louisiana are related to the access to medical care priority.[2] This large percentage would be expected due to the size, scope, and long history of the Medicaid program compared with many of the new initiatives. In fact, Medicaid accounts for 89% of all dollars spent in this priority area.

Early care and education, comprising primarily prekindergarten programs and child care programs, represents 20% of the total ECSIB.[3] Similarly, the dollars in the family support/parenting education priority[4] account for 19% of the ECSIB. This section includes the Supplemental Nutrition Assistance Program, Temporary Assistance for Needy Families cash assistance, and child support enforcement. While this section combines parenting education and family support initiatives, a large disparity is apparent as dollars spent toward specific "parenting education" programs represented less than 5% of this entire priority area, with the majority of these funds for just one program, the Nurse Family Partnership (NFP). Without the NFP program in the budget, only 0.4% of funds for early childhood are spent on parenting education.

**FIGURE 19.1. FY11 Draft Early Childhood System Integration Budget–
Distribution of Dollars in the BrightStart Priority Areas**

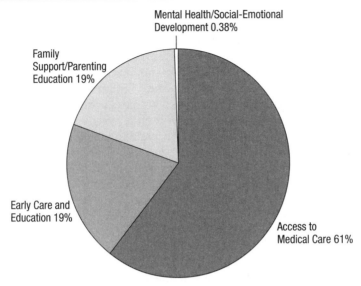

Mental Health/Social-Emotional
Development 0.38%

Family
Support/Parenting
Education 19%

Early Care and
Education 19%

Access to
Medical Care 61%

The mental health/social-emotional development section is perhaps most interesting due to the sheer lack of resources in this priority area.[5] In its current draft, only 0.38% of all funds in the ECSIB are dedicated to this category. Figure 19.1 provides a summary of the percentage breakdown in each priority area of the ECSIB. Again, the ECSIB makes no judgment about the distribution of these financial resources. However, it is difficult to view this chart and not conclude that insufficient funds are being allocated to support the critical area of social-emotional development.

There are certainly limitations of the current ECSIB in Louisiana. To begin with, the information includes only resources that the state is responsible for allocating. Therefore, there is no information about local government spending or private or philanthropic support. Furthermore, some specific programs are not detailed as they are subsumed under larger line items. For instance, the current ECSIB has only one line item for Medicaid. However, there are many different types of programs and services paid through Medicaid, and it would be more informative to list these as separate program items. It may be that some of the Medicaid-funded programs in fact belong in the mental health/social-emotional development category. Unfortunately, in the ECSIB's current form, Medicaid, and a number of other large programs, are listed simply as single items.

The creation of an early childhood budget in Louisiana has evolved from a concept to a statutory requirement. The resulting ECSIB has garnered much enthusiasm, but the full utility of the tool has yet to be realized. The good news is that the ECSIB that Louisiana has today does provide a fairly detailed understanding of the investments the state is making in early childhood. Not surprisingly, the bulk of the money is currently in the "medical" category, with very little being spent to support the social-emotional and mental health needs of young children. The ECSIB has enough information in its current standing to be used as a tool both to nurture collaboration and to provide policymakers and advocates with a fairly clear picture of how resources are being directed toward early childhood. With this information now available as part of the most important policy document in state government, more informed decision making and advocacy are possible for all those willing to jump in and gain a deep understanding of the budget.

NOTES

1. Senate Bill 615 from the 2008 Regular Session of the Louisiana legislature is available at www.legis.state.la.us. Once the bill was passed and signed by the governor, it became known as Act 774.

2. Access to medical care for the ECSIB was defined as programs with the primary goal of addressing the medical or physical health needs of children ages 0–5.

3. Early care and education for the ECSIB was defined as programs that have a primary goal of addressing the early care and educational needs of children ages 0–5.

4. Family support/parenting education for the ECSIB was defined as the programs that have a primary goal of addressing family support or parenting education needs of children ages 0–5.

5. Mental health/social-emotional development for the ECSIB was defined as programs that have a primary goal of addressing the social-emotional needs of children ages 0–5.

REFERENCE

Nathan, R. P. (2000). *Handbook for appointed officials in America's governments.* Albany, NY: Nelson A. Rockefeller Institute of Government.

Part V

LOOKING TOWARD THE FUTURE: FINDING COMMON GROUND ON SYSTEM BUILDING

CHAPTER 20

Beyond Systemic Structures

Penetrating to the Core of an Early Care and Education System

Stacie G. Goffin

The definition of an early care and education system as programs plus infrastructure (Kagan & Cohen, 1997) has been broadly accepted. General consensus also exists around professional development, financing, and governance as central components of the system's infrastructure. Additionally, program effectiveness, equity, coherence, and sustainability are widely recognized as desired systemic effects.

Missing from this accord, however, is clarity regarding the focal point of the early care and education (ECE) system being constructed. Using common parlance, what is the "it" that unambiguously explains the crux of early care and education? Because strong differences co-exist regarding basic and foundational field-defining constructs such as purpose, identity, and responsibility, a response to this question has eluded the ECE field for decades (Goffin & Washington, 2007).

Lacking field-wide agreement on what signifies early care and education, the substance of ECE's emerging system/systems,[1] along with their various subsystems, has been idiosyncratic, with decision-making responsibility delegated to a diverse array of state- and community-based, system-building groups from across the country. As a result, these system-building efforts easily become mired in what often is construed as insider fighting, as participants deliberate possible answers and struggle for inclusion of valued elements, skirmishes shaped in part by states' political, cultural, and policy frames for early care and education.

These struggles represent the challenge of determining what the ECE system's various structural components should encompass and toward what end. As prominent systems thinker Peter Senge (1990) has noted, systemic structure is crucial but by itself is insufficient. "By itself, it lacks a sense of purpose. It deals with the *how*, not the *why*" (p. 354, emphasis in original). This precept underscores that an effective ECE system should be grounded in a clear understanding of what it is expected to nurture, monitor, and sustain.

Although recognizing that no single entity has total autonomy in this regard, this chapter takes the stance that the ECE field should be a prominent source for answers to these questions. Being able to answer them with precision, however, requires the ECE field to have a shared response to what constitutes the purpose, identity, and responsibility of early care and education.

CALLING THE QUESTION

In contemplating this void in the field's system-building efforts (i.e., what is being systematized and for what purpose), something deeper than conceptual variety regarding systemic structures and functions and ECE's programmatic and funding fragmentation is at play. In *Ready or Not: Leadership Choices in Early Care and Education*, Goffin and Washington (2007) argued that "it's time to call the question. What defines and bounds early care and education as a field?" (p. 16). Drawing on terminology from parliamentary procedure, this call was not a rhetorical ploy. Pressing beyond the field's usual deflection to external circumstances, the call draws attention to the field's culpability for current inadequacies in early care and education and asserts that its indecision regarding purpose and responsibility has gone on for far too long.

Expanding beyond the ideas presented in *Ready or Not*, this chapter attends more fully to the systemic implications of the field's indecision. While aware of the personal risks involved in raising issues that make some uncomfortable, I attempt to make the case that the ECE field's cohesion regarding its purpose, identity, and responsibility provides the foundation for an effective ECE system. In the absence of collective and authoritative agreement on what defines and bounds early care and education as a field, the challenge of building a coherent system for early care and education takes on added complexity and difficulty; it also assumes the risk of instituting systemic structures limited by current arrangements and disconnected from a unified vision for early care and education.

The types of questions that will be posed in this chapter typically provoke still more questions, none of which have obvious or self-evident answers. Consequently, this chapter leaves many questions unanswered. This is intentional. Such is the nature of trying to open new space for examination.

Facing the Need for Internally Focused Change

Exponential growth in ECE programs during the 1980s and 1990s catalyzed recognition of the need for consistent quality across programs, equitable access, and financial and performance accountability, providing the impetus for thinking beyond discrete programs and contemplating a more systemic approach for early care and education (see, for example, Kagan & Cohen, 1997; Sugarman, 1991). In the context of growing appreciation from state and federal policymakers, business, education, civic, and philanthropic leaders, early care and education has become the beneficiary of growing public support and expanded financial resources. ECE advocates, often powered by philanthropic strategy and support, have propelled this growth through public awareness campaigns, marketing efforts, targeted state and federal advocacy, and relentless relationship building with "unlikely messengers" (a phrase credited to Margaret Blood; see, e.g., Bruner, 2004; Ludtke, 2004).

Largely missing from this exhilarating rise in status over the past decade, however, has been an accompanying focus on the changes required *within* the ECE field to ensure its capacity to fulfill the promises made on its behalf (Goffin, 2009; Goffin & Washington, 2007). Unless field-wide leadership emerges to assist the early care and education field in confronting the internal issues holding back its movement toward a shared, but different, future, an unsettling system-building question becomes unavoidable: *Can a cohesive and effective system be built in the absence of early care and education's formation as an organized field of practice? Field-wide leadership* refers to internally based leadership directed to a particular field of practice. It is defined by four characteristics:

- Inwardly focused on the field's need to change
- Directed toward transforming the discipline as a field of practice
- Focused on moving forward the overall field as a more viable, coherent, accountable, and respected field of practice
- Usually systemic and adaptive in nature (Goffin, 2009, p. 2)

A field's work is about collective versus individual action and responsibility, which is a central orientation of field-wide leadership. The term *field of practice* makes clear that the field in question revolves around performance of a specialized and shared competence.

While ECE system elements are largely known, still in question are the specific results we want facilitated by the field's system-building efforts. Too often unacknowledged in system-building debates is the reality that a significant contributor to this unknown is indecision regarding the question of what defines and bounds early care and education as a field of practice.

While the consequences of ignoring this quandary have intensified, this is not the first time this dilemma has been encountered when seeking to formulate a new architectural feature for the field. When, for example, in response to growing demands for ECE leadership, Kagan and Bowman (1997) attempted to offer a comprehensive set of recommendations for a leadership development agenda, they concluded, "Most fundamentally, leadership in early care and education cannot be defined until the field defines what constitutes early care and education" (p. 6).

Similarly, constructing a cohesive ECE system demands definition of what constitutes early care and education as a coherent field of practice with regard to its purpose, identity, and responsibilities. The field's inability to provide this definition undercuts system-building efforts, holds back attempts to advance the ECE field to the next level of field-wide development and performance, and jeopardizes its ability to effectively participate in efforts to coordinate with other systems as part of a comprehensive early childhood system (regarding the latter point, see Kagan, Goffin, Golub, & Pritchard, 1995).

While it can be argued that the current multiplicity of co-existing visions for early childhood systems are natural artifacts of the field's multiple histories and the seismic shift currently underway, it as easily can be claimed that this variety denotes and is augmented by the absence of clarity regarding the ECE field's purpose, identity, and responsibility. Unless this conceptual ambiguity is resolved, the winning vision will likely emerge from the strength of individual voices and/or forces outside of the field's desired intentions, even in the context of its present, scattered form.

The Quest for Collective Intentionality

Answering the overarching and fundamental question, "What defines and bounds early care and education as a field?" requires *collective intentionality*. Achieving collective, field-wide intentionality that is, joining together around a unified answer to the issues of purpose, identity, and responsibility depends on the ECE field's willingness and capacity to engage in the internal work required to coalesce and advance itself as a connected field of practice.

Applying insights from complexity theory to the realm of leadership, Margaret Wheatley (1992) defined a "field" as an "invisible world filled with mediums of connections, an invisible structure that connects" (p. 8). A connected field of practice typically is characterized by specialized competence (Dreeben, 2005; Freidson, 2001) that distinguishes it from other organized fields of practice.

Thus, a field's work is about collective (versus individual) performance and responsibility. Responding to the fundamental question of what defines and bounds early care and education as a field of practice requires shared intentionality that supports creation of common identity. Efficacy emerges from accepting shared responsibility for the field's overall competence.

To state the obvious: Early care and education is not a "connected" field of practice. This reality typically is described in terms of the field's diverse program standards, regulations, delivery systems, and funding steams. System-building efforts are accompanied by hopes and expectations that these discontinuities will be addressed through the system-building process.

Yet, in the absence of a common definition for what constitutes early care and education in terms of purpose, identity, and responsibility, fulfilling this aspiration is doubtful. Consensus regarding these issues is needed to create the invisible structure that bounds us as a unified field of practice. A coherent and functional system for early care and education, in turn, depends on the presence of an organized field of practice for its parameters.

At present, no common boundaries connect us. What, by way of example, is the name for this field? What is the age range served by the field's practitioners? What does one need to know and be able to do to claim inclusion in the field? What, if anything, is accepted as common responsibility? And to whom do answers to these field-defining questions apply?

These are the questions, among others, embedded in the issues of purpose, identity, and responsibility. Their answers provide connections that can coalesce the field's disparate parts. In their absence, early educators and caregivers mostly think of their programs and roles as existing outside of a broader, shared field-wide context.

This incoherence is further revealed in the field's oft-bemoaned need for definitional and conceptual clarity, as well as lack of functional precision regarding roles and responsibilities associated with the field's varying programs. Kagan, Kauerz, and Tarrant (2008) were sufficiently frustrated by this state of affairs to propose that an outside group, the National Academy of Sciences, assist with finding a way out of this morass. Their petition to an outside group to serve as convener is telling. It highlights not only the field's struggle with determining its own nomenclature but also the dearth of ECE institutions recognized as providing field-wide leadership (Goffin, 2009).

Cohesion as a field of practice is unlikely to emerge from focusing solely on nomenclature, however, unless, as part of the process, early care and education confronts what, in fact, it means to be a *field* for early care and education. In the absence of this internally driven work, ECE systems will continue to be customized by the people and states that construct them, with distinct intentions and unequal results.

Acquiring Collective Intentionality

Summoning collective intentionality and ensuring a strong underpinning for system building involves finding answers to six field-defining questions. These questions, organized by the three overarching issues of purpose, identity, and responsibility (Goffin & Washington, 2007, pp. 12–13), lay the groundwork for defining what bounds the field's work as a shared endeavor.

Purpose

1. What is the early care and education field's defining intent?
2. Does the field's intent vary by setting or by auspice (e.g., centers and schools, regulated family child care, license-exempt family, friend, and neighbor care)?
3. What chronological span describes the ages of children served (e.g., birth to the start of kindergarten, birth through kindergarten, birth to age 8, prekindergarten through grade 3)?

Identity

4. What is the field's distinctive contribution and competence as a collective entity?
5. Is early care and education a single/unified endeavor or a field comprising subfields or specialties (as is health care, for example)?

Responsibility

6. To what extent are members of the field willing to hold themselves accountable to one another and to be held publicly accountable for results in return for the autonomy to deliver programming based on the field's knowledge base?

The unifying core of an ECE system and its subsystems will vary depending on answers to these six questions. Currently, the presence of multiple and often conflicting answers to these field-defining questions delays and sometimes even derails system-building work. What usually is described as the complexity of system building more often should be portrayed as turmoil generated by the field's lack of consensual responses. This inconsistency, in turn, contributes to the mixed design of system-building efforts across the country.

As the intensity around system-building work escalates and financial incentives become more available, ambiguities and frictions embedded in these six field-defining questions are becoming more visible and the (sometimes overlapping, interlocking, and contradictory) implications for system building more discernible. For example:

- Consistent with historic linkages between the field's expansion and social reform efforts (Lazerson, 1971, 1972), public dollars increasingly are being directed toward children identified as at risk for school failure. As a result, the function of early care and education more and more is expressed in terms of early intervention, begging the field-defining question, "Who is the primary 'client' served by the early care and education field?"
- The rise in poverty among young children and concern for their overall well-being has led to increased focus on children's physical and mental health and specialized learning needs. What does it mean for early care and education to maintain its "whole child" focus in this context? Should the field's historical focus on the whole child continue primarily as an informant to pedagogical practices or should it be expanded to define the scope of the field's overall responsibilities? Should the purpose of the ECE field encompass all of young children's developmental needs—in effect, adopting more of a social welfare orientation—or be more narrowly defined a distinctive and specialized contribution to children's overall healthy development?
- To the cheers of many, the U.S. Department of Health and Human Services is recognizing the central role healthy child development plays in supporting community and economic development, broadening the construct of child development to encompass the multiple positive consequences generated by successful ECE programs (see Bruner, 2007; Golden & Lombardi, 2008). This lens prompts the question of how ECE's purpose should be construed: primarily in terms of the field's efficacy in relation to an overarching purpose or as a strategic lever for creating an economically viable community of caring adults and organizations that, in turn, will support children's learning and development?
- System-building efforts have focused greater attention on programmatic funding streams and regulations. Considerable attention has been given to transcending these differences and their bureaucratic complications so programs can provide more-seamless services to children and their families. Will better synchronized regulations and funding also lead to increased conformity across ECE programs? What might be lost by reducing the distinctive intentions of separately conceived ECE programs?

These field-defining questions are not easy to answer. Nor can possible answers be understood in rigidly either/or fashion. Yet, failing to pinpoint the field's primary intent dodges the question of what defines and bounds early care and education as an organized field of practice, leaving open the core focus of ECE system-building efforts to those individuals willing to step forward with answers.

Taking Responsibility

Pre-existing answers are not available for the field-defining questions being raised here. Nothing inherently right or wrong, for example, exists in defining the chronological scope of early care and education as birth through age 8 or birth to age 5. Goffin and Washington (2007) therefore framed these field-defining issues as adaptive challenges, thereby creating a conceptual and functional framework for the work being advocated.

As its name implies, adaptive work becomes necessary when external circumstances are sufficiently altered to provoke a need for change. Based on the work of Ron Heifetz and his colleagues, adaptive challenges are defined as "the gap between the values people stand for (which constitute thriving) and the realities they face (their lack of capacity to realize those values in the current environment)" (Heifetz, Grashow, & Linsky, 2009, p. 303). The extent to which the ECE field's lack of clarity contributes to the uneven quality of and access to ECE programs makes evident that the ECE field is hampered by multiple adaptive challenges (Goffin & Washington, 2007).

From systems thinking we learn that no "outside" exists (Senge, 1990, p. 67). The people with the problem *are* the problem; those of us who associate ourselves with early care and education plus those external sources contributing to the field's evolution are part of the same system (Heifetz, 1994; Senge, 1990).

Absent pre-existing solutions, those with an adaptive challenge, in this instance the ECE field, must identify bedrock values without which an identity as early educators would be lost. The field then needs to choose which longstanding values to discard because their continued presence undermines the field's ability to adapt to new realities. Finally, fresh answers to thorny, field-defining questions will need to be discovered and/or invented, thereby enabling the field to thrive in its new context (Heifetz et al., 2009; Linsky & Heifetz, 2007).

Dealing with loss is an integral feature of adaptive work (Heifetz, 1994; Heifetz et al., 2009). Choices will be required, often heart-wrenching ones that necessitate "letting go" based on having prioritized some values over others. Avoiding the hard choices, however, will signal the field's evasion of what is required to self-define its purpose and responsibility.

As Senge (1990) makes clear in describing a crucial decision point for system-oriented leaders, "Only through choice does an individual come to be the steward of a larger vision" (p. 360). We, the field of early care and education even in its present state can become stewards of a larger vision by engaging in the hard work of collective adaptation, formulating choices, and making decisions about the 21st-century definitions and boundaries that will delineate early care and education. Thus, responding to the call of what defines and bounds early care and education as a field of practice offers tremendous opportunity.

MOVING FROM INDIVIDUAL TO COLLECTIVE RESPONSIBILITY

Concerns regarding the field's vagueness about purpose are not new. In 1967, in the midst of heated debates about the most effective early childhood education program models, Caldwell noted, "While a great deal of attention is currently being given to fostering concept formation in young children, there appears to be relatively little concern with concept formation *about* the field most intimately concerned with child development. Why can we not be more explicit about our goals and objectives?" (p. 348, emphasis in original).

With dramatic growth in the number of children being served by ECE programs, Spodek (1973, 1977), Haberman (1988), Silen (1987), and the "reconceptualists," among others, raised questions regarding the purpose of early childhood education, attacking, in particular, the field's overreliance on child development theory for its answers (see Swadener & Kessler, 1991, for the reconceptualists' first "volley" in this regard). In 1987, Executive Director Marilyn Smith marked the 60th anniversary of the National Association for the Education of Young Children by identifying three challenges blocking a shared vision for the new millennium. The most troublesome, she suggested, was the field's lack of internal unity. "We MUST unify the field of early childhood education. The greatest obstacle, and yet the one that could have the most powerful impact on services to children and their families, is to find ways to negate the dichotomies that split our field apart" (p. 38, emphasis in original).

In continued pursuit of an integrated professional identity, Caldwell (1990) noted 23 years after her earlier lament that "the many names we call ourselves are evidence of our confusion about our profession. Just what is our field, anyway?" (p. 3). Then, a decade later, in 2001, concluding a review of six volumes focused on early childhood education from 1907 to 1991, published by the National Society for the Study of Education, Goffin resolved that the time had come to address the central purpose of early care and education and the elements essential to its achievement.

These expressions of concern largely paralleled the field's rise from a relatively inconspicuous field of practice to one increasingly visible nationally, spurred by the dramatic growth of early intervention programs, renewed interest in kindergarten as a result of children's increased participation, and the ever more prevalent presence of child care as increasing numbers of women entered the labor force. Despite their frequency, appeals to the overall field for critical self-examination were too sporadic and disconnected to engender the level of dialogue needed for change. Thus, they largely have been ignored, despite Kagan's hopeful forecast in 1991 that "early childhood education . . . is at the brink of a major shift in how it conceptualizes and defines it mission" (p. 237).

Field-Wide Inertia No Longer Can Prevail

Beyond proclaiming it as a primary rationale for system-building, limited attention has been given to the side effects of the field's internal disunity for system-building efforts. During the 1990s, as interest in system building mounted, attempts to launch field-wide change floundered (Goffin & Washington, 2007), curtailing system-building gains. During the past decade, however, the impact of the field's internal disunity has become more consequential. Participants in system building in states and communities now are regularly subjected to the confusion, frustration, restricted actions, and sometimes even embarrassment that come from seemingly unending and circular debates, often in rooms populated by individuals interested in the field's work from the business, policymaking, and philanthropic communities.

Now, in the century's second decade, public and federal expectations have risen regarding "deliverables" from early care and education. Ignoring the call to answer what constitutes early care and education in this context will likely reduce the field's options for influencing system-building efforts. Some might argue it already has, as external stakeholders gain greater influence and inject their solutions into the process.

Determining the purpose, identity, and responsibility of early care and education can provide the basis for generating a shared vision for early care and education, which, in turn, is central to framing the functions and responsibilities of an effective ECE system. A shared vision also fosters a longer term orientation (Senge, 1990). Sustained commitment to high-quality early care and education and to the system that supports it will come from an organized field of practice—one that defines its collective identity by the work ethic required to create the programs and results wanted for children and families. It will be the early care and education field that continues to care about systemic outcomes beyond the inevitable moment when early care and education no longer represents a popular public policy issue, thereby mitigating the field's continuous rotation between cycles of abundance and scarcity (Lazerson, 1972; Spodek & Walberg, 1977).

Mobilizing Field-Wide Adaptive Work

Presently, the field's change agenda is driven by advocates effectively speaking on the field's behalf, implementation of philanthropic strategy, and federal incentives and mandates. Following recent attendance at several economic-oriented early childhood summits, *Exchange* publishers Roger and Bonnie Neugebauer (2007) exclaimed, "At times, it feels like our field is being consumed by friendly fire" (p. 4). Nor can it be otherwise. Absent consensus regarding purpose, identity, and responsibility, the field lacks the ability to bring collective intentionality in response to the changes underway.

The quest for collective intentionality as an organized field of practice should not be confused with a grab for power or self-protection. To the contrary: It represents pursuit of increased efficacy on behalf of children borne of greater competence and opportunity in relation to self-determined commitments, goals, and outcomes.

Change is not an option. Adaptive work occurs in the context of trends and events compelling change. These trends and events, now well underway for early care and education, also help define possible outcomes of adaptive work. As Heifetz (1994) cautions, "To produce adaptive change, a vision must track the contours of reality; it has to have accuracy, and not simply imagination and appeal" (p. 24).

Shaking the ECE field from its apparent inertia demands a sense of urgency (Heifetz, 1994; Kotter, 2008). Toward this end, using phrases common to adaptive work, this chapter has attempted to "ripen the issue" and "turn up the heat" (Heifetz, 1994; Heifetz et al., 2009). If the field chooses to recognize the urgency of taking action, the strength of its commitment to young children provides a solid base for mobilizing attention to internal contradictions and defining the future it wants to create through its work with children and families.

When posing the question, "What defines and bounds early care and education as a field?" Goffin and Washington (2007) branded their call for action a leadership manifesto, stating that

> because of the nature of adaptive work, we will not be able to rely on the wisdom of a few leaders from the field. Resolving the field's adaptive challenges, especially in the context of new realities, necessitates moving beyond reliance on individual leaders and toward creation of a field-wide community of diverse leaders. (p. 3)

A recent study of five other fields of practice and their approaches to issues of field-wide import, such as those identified in this chapter, confirms the importance of field-wide leadership for addressing adaptive change (Goffin, 2009).

The study found that field-wide leadership typically is facilitated by membership organizations that provide a holding environment for the work. A holding environment, as defined by Heifetz and colleagues (2009), "consists of all those ties that bind people together and enable them to maintain their collective focus on what they are trying to do" (p. 155). Creating a "container" for the work underway, holding environments tend to be characterized by shared language, shared orienting values and purposes, a history of working together, and trust in authority figures and the authority structure (Heifetz et al., 2009). Yet no widely accepted aegis for field-wide leadership work seems to exist in early care and education (Goffin, 2009).

COMING TOGETHER TO CALL THE QUESTION

A telling example of the pervasive need for field-wide, adaptive work was revealed by Neugebauer's (2009) recent review of trends in ECE quality assurance efforts. Focused in particular on program accreditation, Neugebauer identified ten separate ECE program accreditation systems. Program accreditation systems, found across almost all fields of practice (e.g., museums, higher education, hospitals), represent an important structural element of fields wishing to be characterized by consistent levels of performance and wanting responsibility for defining requisite performance levels.

In this instance, the presence of ten different ECE program accreditation systems demonstrates the ECE field's disparate thinking regarding the definition of its work and its collective responsibility. Attempting to bring an upbeat prognosis to the situation, Neugebauer concluded, "It is the American way to 'let a thousand flowers bloom.' Instead of decreeing one right way of doing business, we let the market work things out" (p. 17). This approach to the ECE field's turbulence, however, delegates decision-making responsibility to the free market and absolves the field from resolving its internal contradictions so that more consistent and competent services can be provided to children and families.

It's time to call the question. What defines and bounds early care and education as a field?

Early care and education as an organized, cohesive field of practice can provide the guiding framework for ECE system-building efforts. It would imbue systemic structures with their fundamental core, ensuring that the *what*, as well as the *how*, is present (Senge, 1990). Without it, system-building efforts inevitably will be weakened, both in the near and long term.

"Calling the question" requires the field to acknowledge its adaptive challenges, build adaptive capacity, and move into a mode of exploring new and different possibilities since answers to the questions of most significance are not self-evident (Heifetz, 1994; Schwartz, 2003; Senge, 1990).

Although resolving the field's adaptive challenges would advance more effectively within the context of a field-wide leadership infrastructure, steps still can be taken to engage with field-defining questions and spur the field's adaptive work, even though, ultimately, sustained stewardship will be required.

First, groups across the country should engage with the field-defining questions raised by *Ready or Not* (Goffin & Washington, 2007). These efforts accord with Margaret Mead's well- known quote, "Never doubt that a small group of thoughtful, committed people can change the world. Indeed, it is the only thing that ever has." Initial efforts are already underway (Goffin Strategy Group, www.goffinstrategygroup/first_responders) and should be expanded. Their proposals can be used by the field as a platform for catalyzing field-wide consensus building.

Second, following the example of the emerging field of social entrepreneurship, a report from a respected, neutral group could be prepared and widely disseminated (Center for the Advancement of Social Entrepreneurship, 2008). Based on extensive interviews, focus groups, and review of field-defining documents, recommendations for potential next-step strategies could be proposed and used as a centerpiece for debate and action.

Third, membership organizations from the ECE field could come together as a coalition based on shared stewardship and commitment and agreed-upon operating principles to create a holding environment for this work. The coalition could choose to orchestrate and/or commission one or both of the two options first identified or invent other possibilities.

Regardless of approach, this work will not be easy, and it will not be quick—but nothing will happen absent a willingness to take a first step. Unless its internal contradictions are confronted, the ECE field cannot continue to grow in stature. Engaging in adaptive work will demonstrate the field's readiness to lift the stature and effectiveness of its work by becoming a "connected" field of practice.

NOTE

1. At this point in the field's system-building efforts, it remains unknown whether one or multiple systems are being constructed. For the purposes of this chapter, the singular term (system) will be used, but should be understood as open regarding its singularity or plurality.

REFERENCES

Bruner, C. (2004). *Beyond the usual suspects: Developing new allies to invest in school readiness.* Des Moines, IA: State Early Childhood Policy Technical Assistance Network.

Bruner, C. (with Wright, M. S., Timizi, S. N., & and the School Readiness, Culture, and Language Working Group of the Annie E. Casey Foundation). (2007). *Village building and school readiness: Closing opportunity gaps in a diverse society.* Des Moines, IA: State Early Childhood Policy Technical Assistance Center.

Caldwell, B. M. (1967). On reformulating the concept of early childhood education—Some whys needing wherefores. *Young Children, 22*(6), 348–356.

Caldwell, B. M. (1990, Summer). "Educare": A new professional identity, *Dimensions,* pp. 3–6.

Center for the Advancement of Social Entrepreneurship. (2008, June). *Developing the field of social entrepreneurship.* Durham, NC: Center for the Advancement of Social Entrepreneurship, Duke University: Fuqua School of Business.

Dreeben, R. (2005). Teaching and the competence of organizations. In L. V. Hedges & B. Schneider (Eds.), *The social organization of schooling* (pp. 51–71). New York: Russell Sage Foundation.

Freidson, E. (2001). *Professionalism: The third logic.* Chicago: University of Chicago Press.

Goffin, S. G. (2001). Whither early childhood care and education in the next century? In L. Corno (Ed.), *Education across a century: The centennial volume* (pp. 140–163). One Hundredth Yearbook of the National Society for the Study of Education, Part 1. Chicago: National Society for the Study of Education.

Goffin, S. G. (2009). *Field-wide leadership: Insights from five fields of practice.* Washington, DC: Goffin Strategy Group. Retrieved from www.goffinstrategygroup.com

Goffin, S. G., & Washington, V. (2007). *Ready or not: Leadership choices in early care and education.* New York: Teachers College Press.

Golden, O. A., & Lombardi, J. (2008, November 12). Department of Health and Human Services: Improving services for children and families (Research report). Retrieved from http://www.urban.org/UploadedPDF/1001233_improving_services_for_children.pdf

Haberman, M. (1988). What knowledge is of most worth to teachers of young children? *Early Child Development and Care, 38,* 33–41.

Heifetz, R. A. (1994). *Leadership without easy answers.* Cambridge, MA: Belknap Press of Harvard University Press.

Heifetz, R. A., Grashow, A., & Linsky, M. (2009). *The practice of adaptive leadership: Tools and tactics for changing your organization and the world.* Boston: Harvard Business Press.

Kagan, S. L. (1991). Excellence in early childhood education. In S. L. Kagan (Ed.), *The care and education of America's young children: Obstacles and opportunities.* Ninetieth Yearbook of the National Society for the Study of Education, Part 1. Chicago: National Society for the Study of Education.

Kagan, S. L., & Bowman, B. T. (1997). Leadership in early care and education: Issues and challenges. In S. L. Kagan & B. T. Bowman (Eds.), *Leadership in early care and education* (pp. 3–8). Washington, DC: National Association for the Education of Young Children.

Kagan, S. L., & Cohen, N. E. (1997). *Not by chance: Creating an early care and education system for America's children.* New Haven, CT: Bush Center in Child Development and Social Policy.

Kagan, S. L., Goffin, S. G., Golub, S. A., & Pritchard, E. (1995). *Toward systemic reform: Service integration for young children and their families.* Falls Church, VA: National Center for Service Integration.

Kagan, S. L., Kauerz, K., & Tarrant, K. (2008). *The early care and education teaching workforce at the fulcrum: An agenda for reform.* New York: Teachers College Press.

Kotter, J. P. (2008). *A sense of urgency.* Boston: Harvard Business Press.

Lazerson, M. (1971). Social reform and early childhood education: Some historical perspectives. In R. H. Anderson & H. G. Shane (Eds.), *As the twig is bent* (pp. 22–33). Boston: Houghton Mifflin.

Lazerson, M. (1972). The historical antecedents of early childhood education: Some historical perspectives. In I. J. Gordon & H. G. Richey (Eds.), *Early childhood education* (pp. 33–53). Seventy-first Yearbook of the National Society for the Study of Education, Part 2. Chicago: National Society for the Study of Education.

Linsky, M., & Heifetz, R. (2007). Foreword. In S. G. Goffin & V. Washington, *Ready or not: Leadership choices in early care and education* (pp. ix–xi). New York: Teachers College Press.

Ludtke, M. (2004, January). *Early education for all: A strategic political campaign for high-quality early education in Massachusetts.* New York: Foundation for Child Development.

Neugebauer, R. (2009, March/April). Where are we headed with center accreditation? Trends in quality assurance. *Exchange*, pp. 14–17.

Neugebauer, R., & Neugebauer, B. (2007, November/December). Friendly fire. *Exchange*, p. 4.

Schwartz, P. (2003). *Inevitable surprises: Thinking ahead in a time of turbulence.* New York: Penguin Group.

Senge, P. M. (1990). *The fifth discipline: The art and practice of the learning organization.* New York: Doubleday.

Silen, J. G. (1987). The early childhood educator's knowledge base: A reconsideration. In L. G. Katz & K. Steiner (Eds.), *Current topics in early childhood education* (Vol. 7, pp. 17–31). Norwood, NJ: Ablex.

Smith, M. M. (1987). NAEYC at 60: Visions for the year 2000. *Young Children, 42*(3), 33–39.

Spodek, B. (1973). What are sources of early childhood curriculum? In B. Spodek (Ed.), *Early childhood education* (pp. 81–91). Englewood Cliffs, NJ: Prentice-Hall.

Spodek, B. (1977). What constitutes worthwhile educational experiences for young children? In B. Spodek (Ed.), *Teaching practices: Reexamining assumptions* (pp. 5–20). Washington, DC: National Association for the Education of Young Children.

Spodek, B., & Walberg, H. J. (1977). Introduction: From a time of plenty. In B.
    Spodek & H. J. Walberg (Eds.), *Early childhood education: Issues and insights*
    (pp. 1–7). Berkeley, CA: McCutchan.
Sugarman, J. M. (1991). *Building early childhood systems: A resource handbook.*
    Washington, DC: Child Welfare League of America.
Swadener, B. B., & Kessler, S. (Eds.). (1991). *Early Education & Development. Re-
    conceptualizing early childhood education* [Special issue], 2(2), entire issue.
Wheatley, M. J. (1992). *Leadership and the new science: Learning about organiza-
    tion from an orderly universe.* San Francisco: Berrett-Koehler.

CHAPTER 21

Looking Forward
Four Steps for Early Childhood System Building

Sharon Lynn Kagan and Kristie Kauerz

As noted in Chapter 1, one of our major goals for this volume was to advance both our own and collective thinking regarding early childhood systems. Consequently, this final chapter presents our efforts to coalesce our thoughts and reflections with those from the contributing authors and to move forward by offering recommendations that have been both informed by and prompted by the diversity of ideas herein. We summarize both conceptual and practical challenges presented by early childhood systems by, first, sharing our reflections on this work, based on our own experiences and consideration of the contributions to this volume. Next, we describe our efforts to engage a group of early childhood practitioners, policymakers, and researchers in a deliberative Delphi process to discern the degree to which consensus exists on key system issues. We close the chapter by presenting four recommendations for the future of early childhood system building in the United States.

OUR REFLECTIONS

While we are unabashedly enthusiastic about the wisdom and strategies of the range of systems work presented throughout this volume, we simultaneously are struck by the wide variation in how systems are defined and what they are expected to accomplish. As we reflect on the compelling collection of chapters that constitute this volume, we highlight two observations.

First, as we note in our opening chapter, the field in which the systems work is taking hold, is defined by different labels and constructs. "Early care and education," "early education," "early childhood," "comprehensive early childhood," "early childhood education," and other terms often are used interchangeably. Similarly, various systems efforts clearly are targeted to programs and services for children from birth to age 5, while others are explicit about embracing children from birth to age 8. Still others advocate for systems to address primarily children from ages 3 through 8. Some argue that systems work should consider prenatal care and services; others argue that systems work should consider school-age children.

Second, and related to our first observation, we recognize the existence of two perspectives about early childhood systems—one perspective focuses on describing an *ideal* or *visionary* system, a system that stretches the imagination, engages multiple already-functioning systems and subsystems, and identifies a fully comprehensive set of services and programs needed to support every aspect of young children's growth and development from birth through age 8. Another perspective focuses on a more *practical* or *operational* system, one that has more definitive boundaries, legitimizes a range of hodge-podge programs and services as a unified sector itself, and can be implemented by instituting a discrete set of policies.

When these two observations are coupled, the variety of definitions and the difference in scope becomes problematic. For example, while many in the field hold a vision for a comprehensive early childhood system that embraces early care and education, health, mental health, family support, early intervention, child protection, and other sectors of services to young children, many of the on-the-ground systemic strategies (e.g., QRIS, professional development systems) are designed and intended to be applicable and beneficial to only one domain—early care and education.

Given these challenges, there is a need to be more explicit about which strategies are intended for which part of the system at which time. For example, when discussing professional development systems, is the intent to include all professionals who work with young children—child care and preschool teachers, elementary school teachers, home visitors, pediatric medical personnel, mental health specialists, and family support workers (what we would term the "early childhood" workforce)? Or, is the intention to focus the professional development system on a particular subset of professionals who work with young children—those who fall within the domain of early care and education and work primarily in prekindergarten, Head Start, child care, and school-based programs (what we would term the "early learning" workforce)? Similarly, when discussing quality rating and improvement systems, is the intention to focus on the full range of learning-based programs that children encounter from birth through age 8—including prekindergarten, Head Start, child care, and elementary school (what we would term "early learning" programs)? Or, is the intention to focus on the learning-based programs that children encounter prior to school entry (what we would term "early care and education" programs)? While the various labels may sound interchangeable, the actual work and implementation behind them is meaningfully different.

ENGAGING THE CONTRIBUTING AUTHORS TO REFLECT

In addition to our own thoughts and reflections, we were intrigued by the idea of gathering the collective responses of our contributing authors regarding the issues raised across and among their chapters. Given the time and cost to convene a meeting of busy people spread across the country, bringing together all of the authors for a face-to-face meeting was deemed impractical. Undeterred, however, we undertook a consensus methodology called a Delphi, a research method that is desirable when, for example: (a) the problem does not lend itself to precise analytical techniques but can benefit from subjective judgments on a collective basis; (b) more individuals are needed than can effectively interact in a face-to-face exchange; (c) time and cost make frequent group meetings infeasible; and (d) the heterogeneity of the participants must be preserved to ensure validity of the results (Linstone & Turoff, 2002). Further, the Delphi avoids many of the pitfalls of more traditional group processes, namely, dominance by a quantity or strength of personalities in the room, as well as reluctance of some participants to abandon previously stated opinions. We believe this method for exploring consensus—both where it exists and where it does not—provides a unique look at the collective wisdom of leading practitioners, policymakers, and researchers in the field. We further believe that the Delphi results serve as a compelling basis for reflecting on what the field needs in order to further instantiate consensus.

The Delphi Method

The Delphi may be characterized as a kind of virtual focus group, a method for structuring an effective group process that allows a number of individuals, as a whole, to deal with complex issues. The method comprises a series of questionnaire–analysis–questionnaire–analysis. In the first questionnaire, participants are asked to respond to a small number of issues. The group's responses are aggregated, analyzed, and presented back to the participants in the next questionnaire; in this way, participants have knowledge of others' collective thoughts and perspectives and can use the group think to inform their individual responses to the second questionnaire. The Delphi method maintains anonymity of the participants, permits a manageable volume and scope of feedback to be shared among participants, and allows for simple statistical analyses to be conducted in order to identify clear areas of agreement.

For our Delphi process, we invited all of this volume's contributing authors to participate; including the two of us, this number totaled 31 invitees. While there is variety in adaptations of the Delphi, we used a two-phase design where we sent two questionnaires and undertook two sets of analyses. The first questionnaire presented all contributing authors with a series of questions probing some of the more provocative issues raised across the chapters. We then analyzed the collective responses, distilled key lessons and salient areas of consensus, and presented our analysis back to the authors along with a second questionnaire. In the second questionnaire, we asked participants to review our summary of the first questionnaire's responses and then respond to a follow-up set of questions. Twenty-nine of the authors completed the first questionnaire and, of those, 28 completed the second questionnaire. In our analyses, we defined consensus in accordance with emerging convention in other Delphi processes (Ager, Stark, Akesson, & Boothby, 2010; Kauerz, 2009), using 90% agreement as the threshold for deeming a statement as having "clear consensus" and 80% as the threshold for "emerging consensus." Next, we summarize the more pertinent and interesting information from the Delphi.

Identifying Consensus

The two rounds of the Delphi process posed questions related to our compiled observations and reflections regarding the many perspectives on early childhood system building. We posed questions to see whether consensus existed on the ages of children to be served by an early childhood system, the scope of an early childhood system (e.g., which domains and sectors to include), the elements of an early childhood system, and the degree to which finding consensus on these issues is even desirable.

Extending from Goffin's chapter, we asked the panel about the extent to which they believed the early childhood field needs to reach consensus in the next 5 years on a range of issues (see Figure 21.1). Eighty-six percent of respondents felt that reaching consensus on a definition of results is absolutely essential, and 79% felt that reaching consensus on definitions of quality is absolutely essential.

The Delphi panel did not reach even emerging consensus on the age of children to be served by an early childhood system. Ten percent felt that, in an ideal world, the system should address children prenatal to age 5; 62% felt the system should address children prenatal through age 8. Interestingly, reaching consensual agreement on this issue was not deemed to be essential.

FIGURE 21.1. To What Extent Do You Think the Early Childhood Field Needs to Reach Consensus on the Following Issues in the Next 5 Years?

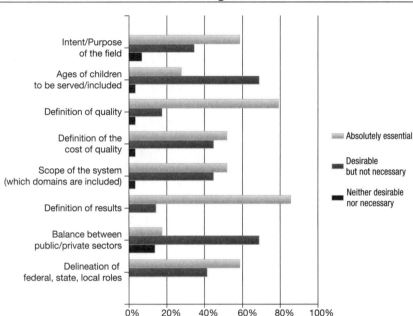

Only 27% of the Delphi panel felt that it was absolutely essential to gain consensus on the age of children to be included; another 69% felt it to be desirable, but not necessary.

The Delphi panel, however, did almost reach emerging consensus on the scope of an ideal early childhood system. Seventy-nine percent felt that the system should be comprehensive and incorporate multiple domains (i.e., early learning, health/mental health, family support, special needs/early intervention). Another 17% felt the ideal early childhood system should include those domains just listed, but also felt there were others not listed (e.g., child protection, parent education) that should be included. At the same time, only 52% felt that it was absolutely essential to gain consensus on this issue; another 45% felt it to be desirable, but not necessary. This perspective perhaps is explained best by one respondent who said, "The ideal comprehensive system should be fluid. It should include all domains to some degree, when and where appropriate."

Finally, the results from the Delphi shed light on who should hold responsibility for various aspects of system building (see Figure 21.2). The bulk of responsibility for most functions was ascribed to states, with the

FIGURE 21.2. Which Entity Should Have Primary Responsibility for Each Systems-Building Function?

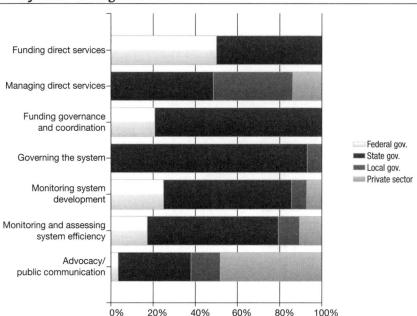

exceptions of funding and managing direct services, and leading advocacy and public communication efforts. With 50% of respondents believing the federal government, and the other 50% believing states, should have primary responsibility for financing direct services, there is an obvious role for increased investment by the public sector. Regarding the funding of governance and coordination efforts, 21% of respondents believe the federal government has primary responsibility, while 79% believe states hold primary responsibility. At the same time, the Delphi panel reached clear consensus, with 93% of respondents agreeing, that states should have primary responsibility for actually governing the system. Clearly, there is a sense that the federal government should provide funds to support system building, and that states themselves need greater capacity for leading and managing multiple aspects of the work.

In accordance with the methodology's purpose, and based primarily on the small number of participants, we considered the results of our Delphi to be exploratory and therefore used them as just one of the factors on which we base our recommendations. Nonetheless, the Delphi data were instructive and pointed to promising areas of consensus to be addressed and prioritized. In particular, and coupled with our own experience, we identified several key take-aways. Specifically, there is a need for:

- More vision and more precision about what we want to accomplish on behalf of young children so that they will thrive.
- Intentional and increased focus and investment to design and build an early care and education system for children from birth to age 5.
- More specific and consensual thinking about what progress in system building looks like. We need more capacity for defining the results of system building itself, with clear and more precise benchmarks of progress.
- Increased leadership and leverage from the federal government in order to propel better funded and more strategic systems work.

Throughout the remainder of this chapter, we discuss and offer recommendations for addressing these issues.

LOOKING FORWARD BY LOOKING TO OTHERS

As we and others have noted throughout this volume, and as the Delphi results above clearly indicate, ambiguity regarding the precise nature of an early childhood system may be its one unifying characteristic. The early childhood field, including the contributors to this volume, continues to wrestle with issues related to early childhood systems, despite a palpable need to pursue their development. As this volume clearly attests, systems efforts are moving forward aggressively as states and localities strive to unify, expedite, and improve the quality, accessibility, and continuity of services for young children.

The United States is not alone in this pursuit. Worldwide, many other countries also face systemic challenges. For countries that are developing new policies, debate centers on the appropriate role of the public and private sectors, the appropriate government entity to administer and oversee the services, and how to honor population diversity while maintaining standards of quality and efficiency. For countries that have long histories of investment in young children, debate centers on service consolidation and, in many cases, their decentralization. Moreover, even countries that traditionally have invested deeply in early education services are contemplating how to best link their services with other institutions, notably public primary education and health services; by contrast, countries that have offered health services to the young, often through maternal and child heath auspices, are considering how to infuse or augment their services with an early education focus. Whatever the pretext, expansion yields systemic challenges.

It is for these reasons that in October 2008, UNICEF published a report by the Innocenti Research Center that proposed internationally applicable benchmarks for early childhood care and education. Designed to serve as a blueprint for what economically advancing societies owe their young children, the document provides ten benchmarks that denote basic minimum standards for comprehensive service provision in early care and education. The first benchmark addresses paid parental leave; the second addresses whether a national plan with priority for disadvantaged children exists. The third and fourth benchmarks target access issues, focusing on child care provision for children under age 3 and accredited early education services for 4-year-olds. The next four benchmarks address quality issues: benchmark 5 focuses on training for staff, benchmark 6 on the education levels of staff, benchmark 7 on staff/child ratios, and benchmark 8 on the level of public funding directed to early care and education services. The last two benchmarks address wider social and economic factors that influence early care and education—the level of child poverty rates and the degree to which basic health services are universally offered to young children. Although not addressing the broadest range of comprehensive early childhood services (e.g., social welfare, home visiting, parent education, and family support), these benchmarks propose a clear systems metric.

Not simply conceptual, the benchmarks were used to gauge the status of 25 nations, spanning Nordic, Western European, Asian, and North American countries. Sadly, out of the 25 countries included in the analysis, the United States ranked 22nd, meeting only three of the standards: (1) benchmark 3, which related to the provision of care and regulated child care services for 25% of children under age 3; (2) benchmark 6, indicating that at least 50% of teaching staff in accredited early childhood programs have been educated at the tertiary (college) level and meet minimum qualifications; and (3) benchmark 7, which noted that preschool education programs have minimum child/staff ratios of 15:1. Although one expects Nordic and many Western European nations to rank well on such metrics, this analysis shows that the performance of Mexico, Slovenia, Hungary, and Portugal surpassed that of the United States, with only Australia, Canada, and Ireland trailing behind.

At one level, these findings are important because they indicate how poorly the United States ranks when compared with other nations. At another level, the study is important because it indicates the repertoire of services and supports that international experts deem important to the development and well-being of young children and to a system that supports that development. Moreover, in establishing specific ranking criteria, it renders precision to the levels of accomplishment necessary to mark achievement of each benchmark. As such, the UNICEF framework both resembles and stands in marked contrast to the "four ovals" that have guided much early childhood work in the United States. It resembles the ovals in that it is comprehensive and clearly attends to an array of services. It is distinguished from the ovals framework in that it explicitly denotes access levels and evaluation criteria: for example, 25% of children under age 3 should have access to child care (benchmark 3), and 80% of 4-year-olds should have access to publicly subsidized and accredited services for a minimum of 15 hours a week (benchmark 4). It also acknowledges the importance of the infrastructure to the existence of quality services and a quality system. The criteria, for example, call for a national plan for disadvantaged children (benchmark 2), minimum levels of staff training for those who have significant contact with young children (benchmark 5) and minimum levels of staff with higher level education and training (benchmark 6), minimum child/staff ratios (benchmark 7), and minimum levels of public funding (benchmark 8). While the report does not allude to governance or accountability, elements that we deem critical to an early childhood system, it does advance a comprehensive notion of services for young children and establishes a clear framework for their documentation and measurement.

A FOUR-POINT PLAN

Our purpose in sharing the UNICEF framework is neither to pedestal it nor to deny the important contributions of the four ovals and other conceptual models in advancing systemic thinking in the United States. It is, however, to set the stage for recommendations that we believe will advance early childhood systems work in the United States and, in so doing, improve the visibility, accessibility, quality, continuity, and equity of service provision and distribution. We use the remainder of the chapter to discuss a plan that first posits the feasibility and desirability of defining a comprehensive vision for young children's services (much like the UNICEF document) and then addresses a strategic piece of that vision systematically over time.

Our four-point approach is simple: As a country and as a field, we first need a comprehensive vision that is hallmarked by clear definitions and a clear conception of what young children need in order to thrive, prenatal through age 8. Although there have been many efforts to establish such a vision, we call for a rethink that is characterized by a greater level of specificity. Second, within that vision, we need an operational focus to strategically achieve elements of the vision. We believe that a focus on the early care and education domain, from birth to age 5, is crucial. Third, we need an operational model or a theory of change that engenders more-strategic thinking about how to sequence reform efforts. Fourth, we need to merge the vision and the focus to produce a set of workable benchmarks that both guide and measure our systemic successes.

Step One: A Comprehensive Vision for the Services Children Need in Order to Thrive

There is little disagreement among child experts regarding the general conditions that promote optimal development for young children. Most would agree that young children need a healthy start to life, a safe and healthy environment in which to grow, loving and caring relationships, experiences that foster their development, and supports that are necessary in times of need. For children with special circumstances, including experiencing disabilities, poverty, unsafe environments, or exploitation, or even speaking a language in their homes different from that spoken in the public discourse, extra supports are needed. Moreover, such a vision would include that young children live in a society where adults honor the unique period of childhood and provision for it accordingly.

Beyond such global statements, ambiguities and arguments arise when the discourse moves from a discussion of what young children need to the services that must be provided to meet those needs, and who should provide them. Such ambiguities take several forms. First and most basic, there are conceptual and definitional ambiguities regarding how such services are "held" (Goffin, this volume). Definitionally, for example, there is little agreement on the terminology the field uses to describe itself and little agreement conceptually on what should be included and excluded from such a "field." The Delphi results reconfirmed this. Moreover, there is little agreed-upon conceptualization of what "governance" and "system" really mean within the early childhood context and what elements are essential for inclusion (Kauerz & Kagan, this volume; Goffin, Martella, & Coffman, 2011). Not trivial matters, such ambiguities beg for clarification.

As important as they are, definitional issues become clouded by a second confounding factor—the decided lack of consensus on the conditions under which, and by who, such services should be provided. Values, attitudes, and resources come into play when discussing the role of government to address these needs, rendering the waters murky, if not treacherous. Different perspectives on the roles of government and different capacities of different governments arise. Moreover, there is vast confusion regarding not only whether and when government should intervene, but at what level: Does the federal, state, or local government have primary jurisdiction for service provision? For infrastructure support? What is an effective balance between public- and private-sector provision? Which entities should carry out primary and secondary responsibilities for which services? These questions, just the barest list, suggest that a vision of what is needed for young children differs dramatically from an operational discussion of the services needed to address that vision. These are two distinct constructs and need to be addressed as such.

Unfortunately, discourse about what young children need and the services to be provided for them often become entwined. In part, this is logical because the needs of young children should predict the services offered them. The goal should be to let the ideal contour the real. Yet, this interlacing of intention and operations has hampered clarity and the important distinctions between the two. To alter this, we suggest that a consensus vision be determined concerning what young children need in order to develop. Building on such efforts as KIDS COUNT and Policy for Results, this should not be a list of services; rather, it should be developmentally driven and describe the dynamic physical, social, health, emotional, and educational stimuli needed for optimal development, regardless of who delivers them.

To address this we recommend that the National Academy of Sciences create a panel, involving multiple disciplines, to establish more precision and consensus about what young children need to thrive. Using empirical research and practitioner judgment as a basis, we suggest that such a panel concentrate on children from prenatal through 8 years of age. Such an effort would provide the rationale and the definitive explication of the comprehensive needs of young children in a consolidated visionary document.

Step Two: Bringing Strategic Focus to ECE Services

Coming to consensus on what services young children need in order to grow and thrive opens the door for difficult decisions regarding the nature of the services needed, who should meet these needs, and how service providers can function most effectively and efficiently. Several things are clear. The overall needs of young children will not be met by one discipline and they will not be exactly the same for all children. Since most service delivery in this nation is aligned with a single discipline, so that we have departments of health, departments of education, and departments of social services, it is axiomatic that multiple departments will need to be involved in service delivery. Just how these various departments/disciplines come together is a matter that distinguishes states from one another. The goal, therefore, should be to provision for maximum flexibility in how services are organized and minimum variation in the elements embraced, with elements including governance, quality improvement, and data systems.

While we unequivocally endorse the importance of conceptualizing a comprehensive, multidomain early childhood system, we also believe there needs to be renewed intention and specificity around designing and implementing an early care and education system for children from birth to age 5. System building in the early childhood field should be more discerning about the difference between the need to link and align already-functioning systems and the need to legitimize a range of programs and services as a unified system itself. To us, the former refers to the goals of building a comprehensive early childhood system; the latter refers to the need to build a focused and functional early care and education (ECE) system. The ECE system is a central and necessary part of the comprehensive system. In the current state of affairs, however, the lack of an ECE system makes aligning early care and education programs and services with other services and sectors (e.g., health, mental health, family support) a messy, if not altogether improbable, endeavor. Important work was begun on this in the 1990s (Kagan & Cohen, 1996, 1997), and many states have made impressive progress on this front (see Kershaw & Reale; Dichter; Thornburg & Mauzy; Russell, this volume), but ECE system building needs to be reinvigorated and made more explicit as a necessary precursor to achieving a comprehensive, multidomain system.

Specifically, we recommend that a collaborative group of foundations fund, and a neutral body convene, a panel of early care and education systems thinkers to develop a template for the elements of such a system and to devise funding strategies to put such systems in place. This group would draw from the lessons of states already undertaking this kind of work (e.g., Georgia, Massachusetts, Washington, Maryland), addressing the current array of publicly and privately funded direct service efforts (e.g., Head Start, child care, state-funded prekindergarten, family child care), as well as the many efforts to improve the infrastructure (e.g., quality rating and improvement systems, resource and referral efforts, accreditation). Moreover, the group would consider the needs of children with disabilities, children living in poverty, and children for whom English is not the dominant language.

Step Three: Adopt a Strategic Theory of Change for an ECE System

Throughout this volume, there has been a recurrent focus on the construct of change. Kershaw and Reale remind us that change is part of the process and therefore must be attended to constantly. Similarly, Goffin suggests that change is not an option; adaptive work occurs in the context of trends and events compelling change. Those engaged in systems work often suggest they are "building a plane while flying it" or constructing the "foundation of a house that lacks a blueprint." Both analogies highlight that change is occurring, although the specific direction is largely uncharted.

Change is fast and multifaceted. Part of the reason for the rapidity of change relates to the shifting context that influences children and families. Floundering test results place more burdens on schools and, in turn, more demands for productivity and outcomes on early childhood programs. These demands hasten calls for quality, which bump against the fiscal woes of now-bankrupt states that, in many cases, are making cuts to state-funded programs and services. At the federal level, the picture is mixed. Federally funded literacy programs are being eliminated, funding for Head Start and child care subsidies remains level, and the Early Childhood Comprehensive Systems grants administered by the Maternal and Child Health Bureau of the U.S. Department of Health and Human Services were allowed to expire. At the same time, as this volume went to press, the Obama Administration announced a $500 million competitive grant allocation for the Early Learning Challenge. This unsteady and somewhat inconsistent political picture, along with new demands on systems work that continues under a variety of auspices (e.g., Early Childhood Advisory Councils, QRIS, and state systems work), contributes to an early childhood world that is marked by near-frenetic change.

As noted above, part of the challenge of change is dealing with its untidiness and lack of prescription. Nothing could be truer of early childhood system-building efforts. Springing up in states and the federal government, these efforts have taken many forms, with diverse outcomes. Accordingly, ongoing work represents a laboratory for learning. We have been fortunate to either witness or be part of such efforts in a large number of states and internationally. We have seen examples of stellar systems efforts, and examples of those that, however well intentioned, have been derailed by unexpected events, personnel turnover, budget cuts, or organizational burn-out. We have studied institutional and organizational change, written about systems integration, and lived through countless systems meetings and visioning sessions.

As a result of these experiences, we have amassed ideas that, when aggregated, form a theory of systems change or a logic model for early care and education systems development. We offer this for consideration and debate; it is not intended to be the definitive or final word, but rather one conception of how system-building efforts might evolve more strategically and with greater spread, credibility, durability, and efficacy. We offer our theory of change with the hope that it will inspire conversation and action that render early care and education a functioning system in and of itself.

The basis for this logic model is rooted in systems work of the past; our ideas are more about sequencing than redefining basic understandings of ECE systems. In 1993 and 1994, a group of 15 early childhood thinkers and doers came together for a Carnegie-funded effort entitled Quality 2000 to form the Essential Functions and Change Strategies Task Force. The group was tasked with the development of a list of elements that, when aggregated, would constitute the early care and education system. Articulated in working papers and in the *Not By Chance* report (Kagan & Cohen, 1997), the essential functions recommended were: (a) quality programs; (b) results-driven systems; (c) parent and family engagement; (d) individual licensing; (e) professional development; (f) program licensing; (g) funding and financing; and (h) governance, planning, and accountability. While these elements or functions have been tweaked by many, including the original authors, very few system schematics have veered dramatically from these core functions. In fact, most principles enunciated then have remained constant. For example, infrastructure has become more widely accepted both in its nomenclature and as an essential component of the system. It is widely understood that the infrastructure and the direct service programs, together, yield a system. Indeed, it is this call for multiple elements/functions existing simultaneously that makes the design and implementation of ECE systems so complex.

In offering a refreshed theory of change, we accept the premise of essential functions, the principles of direct services and infrastructure, and the need for all elements. Above all, experience tells us that there needs to be more integration and some guidance on sequencing implementation of the elements so that they can be accomplished in concert.

To that end, we offer the following key elements as our essential functions: (a) governance, (b) finance, (c) data systems, (d) program quality improvement, (e) professional development, (f) family and public engagement, (g) accountability, and (h) linkages to other systems. In our theory of change, we see that while efforts in all areas can and do take place simultaneously, there are efficiencies that can be realized by sequencing the prioritization of the essential functions. To portray our theory of change, we suggest that these eight essential functions belong to three distinct categories: *foundational functions*, which includes governance and finance; *subsystem functions*, which includes data systems, program quality improvement, and professional development; and *pervasive functions*, which includes family and public engagement, accountability, and linkages to other systems. Graphically, we portray our theory of change as follows.

Foundational Functions. We regard the foundational functions as just that—foundational; without them, there can be no system. By placing governance first, we do accord it primacy, sensing that it is the first and most essential function of the early care and education system. It is important to note that we do not use the nomenclature lightly. A true governance system must be hallmarked by the properties of authority and accountability (Kagan & Kauerz, 2009). Such authority and accountability must pertain to all programs in the system. In other words, a governance structure that has authority for a pre-K program alone is not equivalent to a governance structure with authority for the full ECE system. Early Childhood Advisory Councils, even if they address all of the early childhood programs in a state, frequently do not meet a governance standard because they hold neither the operational authority over programs nor the accountability for their effectiveness (see Chapter 5).

FIGURE 21.3. Theory of Change for an Early Care and Education System

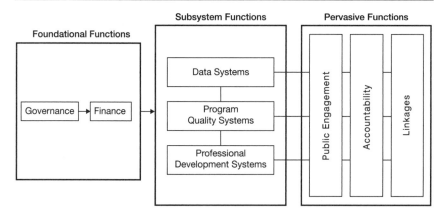

The second foundational function is finance. We believe that an early care and education system must be financed; that is, in addition to the direct services that are funded, we underscore that funds must be set aside to handle the elements of the infrastructure discussed (see chapters by Stebbins, Nagle, and Brodsky, this volume). Whether this is accomplished through set-asides, or through dedicated dollars from private philanthropy, the ECE system must have funds to operate. Ideally, we welcome private/public partnerships that spur innovation and, taking its lessons, provide for ongoing support.

Subsystem Functions. Subsystem functions are those that depend on the governance and finance systems but may be freestanding. That is, they should address the same direct service programs as those addressed by the governance and finance functions. Each may evolve as a separate subsystem, but needs to be linked with the others. A comprehensive data system is essential to planning and monitoring functions (see Gruendel & Stedron, this volume). It should be provisioned for, using the work of the Data Quality Campaign as a basis for consideration. Data elements should be specified, along with the periodicity, and data collection mechanism. We urge the parsimonious collection of data, with each data element meeting a usability standard before it is inserted into routine data collections. The quality of ECE programs is central to their effectiveness. As a result and given the overall poor quality of many early care and education programs, efforts to enhance program quality must be mounted. Joining accreditation and accreditation facilitation efforts, the quality rating and improvement (sub) systems that are being developed warrant attention and support as an essential function of the overall ECE system (see Schaack, Tarrant, Boller, & Tout; Thornburg & Mauzy, this volume). Finally, no ECE system would be complete without the existence of a professional development (sub)system bolstered by innovative incentive systems that result in improved compensation (see Hyson & Vick Whittaker and Russell, this volume).

Pervasive Functions. Hard to classify and yet hard to live without, the last three functions should permeate all of systems work; thus, we call them pervasive functions. These pervasive functions intersect consistently with the three subsystems discussed above, and their depth and meaningfulness rely on the existence of successful foundational governance and financing mechanisms. The first, family and public engagement, refers to the need for vibrant involvement of families and communities in the creation and the implementation of ECE systems. Not only is family involvement a canon of early childhood pedagogy and practice, but parents and the public are needed as supporters and advocates influencing ECE policy. Accountability is receiving so much attention that its presence as an essential and pervasive function of an early care and education system is also axiomatic.

The second pervasive function, accountability, needs to be built in to each element of the system, with data systems provisioned to accommodate the accountability needs generated by other parts of the system. Accountability also characterizes effective governance and financing systems. Every element and subsystem of the ECE system must have meaningful, understandable, and publicly available metrics that demonstrate its effectiveness.

Finally, the third pervasive function, linkages between the ECE system and other domains of a comprehensive early childhood system (e.g., health, welfare, K–12 education), will not occur unless it is intentionally planned for and deliberately implemented. Efforts to create linkages with K–12 education are robust and expanding under the rubric of many P–20 (or variations thereof) initiatives. Similar linkages must be strengthened among ECE, health, mental health, child welfare, and other key service sectors.

Our theory of change suggests that governance and finance mechanisms are foundational to an effective ECE system. With sustained focus on the development of data, QRIS, and professional development subsystems, the ECE system has structures that function to improve and align the quality and accessibility of services, programs, and personnel. Neither the foundational nor the subsystem work can unfold without attention to family and community engagement, accountability, or linkages. This theory of change suggests a sequence for considering the development of early care and education systems. It also suggests that certain key functions—characteristic of many systems—must exist if early care and education is to both meet its potential as a potent social elixir and deliver on the expectations placed upon it.

We recognize that the starting point for our theory of change, governance, has pragmatic limitations. In a time of severe budget cuts with countless states eliminating major initiatives and offices, it may seem audacious to recommend an entity or a subentity devoted to young children. We acknowledge that this may not be the most propitious time to create a new governance entity. We also acknowledge that there will be start-up costs incurred in the short term in any transfer of governance. Further, we know that if an ECE system is established, it will no doubt generate requests for future funds. It is precisely because of these realities that the time is ripe for strategic consideration of the early care and education system. We assert that a system will reduce duplication of both effort and expense. Take, for example, the case of standards and assessments; rather than having them developed (a costly enterprise) for different early care and education programs, one set of high-quality standards and assessments germane to the diversity of programs in a state could be developed. We further believe that investing in the ECE system will yield greater quality in the delivered programs and hence even greater overall cost effectiveness.

We acknowledge that other aspects of our theory of change may be controversial; we encourage others to review and discuss it. In addition, we offer the following policy recommendations for greater federal leadership. We recommend that the reauthorization of the Elementary and Secondary Education Act include provisions for early childhood and, moreover, that a portion of those funds be devoted to the development of early care and education systems. Given the competitive nature of the Early Learning Challenge, we call for intentional and timely effort—from both federal and national organizations—to disseminate key lessons and strategies learned so that *all* states can benefit. We recommend the establishment of a national clearinghouse on systems, a repository for innovative systems work, by which states can learn from one another's challenges and accomplishments. We also recommend establishing research on systems as a routine part of the early childhood research agenda funded by the federal government. Research that examines the comparative efficacy of diverse systems, and the differing conditions under which it is achieved, should be funded as well. Finally, the federal government should fund Early Childhood Systems Fellowships that give provocative thinkers the opportunity to examine and consider systems work; such work could be conceptual, scholarly, and/or research focused.

Step Four: Linking Vision and Practice into Workable Systems Standards

As chronicled in Kagan's earlier chapter on early learning standards, the development and use of standards as a tool to advance action are not new. Within early care and education, there has been much focus on the development of standards that specify what young children should know and be able to do as a means of enhancing children's learning. Interestingly, and despite a near-universal call for standards, there has been scant attention accorded the development of systems standards, or standards that specify what *systems* should look like and be able to do. If the presence of standards lends specificity and benchmarking capacity and acts as an elixir to desired results, then systems standards could be helpful in advancing systems efforts.

To that end, we suggest that the field needs concrete standards that identify, measure, and evaluate the quality and effectiveness of systems work itself. Specifically, standards for effective *systems* should be established and contain data that measure the degree of system accomplishment. Elements of such accomplishment might address systemic efficiencies, cost savings, and the elimination of service redundancies. To determine the range of such metrics, the development of systems standards should build on extant work (see Coffman, this volume; UNICEF, 2008) and from the three prior steps we propose in this chapter. Having consensually developed standards would enable a systems vision to be quantified and rendered clear. It would publicize with precision what it takes to develop and maintain both an ECE system and an early childhood system. And it would provide measures of accomplishment that are clear to parents, the public, and policymakers.

In recommending a movement toward specification, we understand that there are some serious limitations. Most serious among them is the lack of agreement in the early childhood field regarding what constitutes a system. We suggest that much of the ambiguity associated with this challenge could be mitigated by concentrating on our Step Two above. A second concern revolves around the idea of standards themselves. It is often suggested that the presence of standards promotes too much uniformity and inhibits creativity and diversity. Given the state of early childhood systems work, work that currently is characterized by tremendous lack of specificity and by diversity, we suggest that some standardization regarding society's obligations to young children is necessary and timely. A third concern emanates from questions about whether we have the technical expertise to develop a set of standards and related indicators that transcends the breadth of the field and that addresses its interconnections with other already-functioning systems. While we do agree that there are technical challenges inherent in the development of systems standards, we do not see them as significantly more problematic than those in developing other kinds of standards.

Such technical feasibility would need to address the content of the standards themselves. They could, for example, address the degree to which the early care and education system reduces costly redundancies. Administering and monitoring several public early care and education programs can be costly for a state; consolidation within a single department, while exacting start-up costs, is likely to save funds over time. Presently, however, data do not exist in any state to attest to cost savings accrued by the elimination of these administrative redundancies. A second content example might pertain to transparency for families. Presently, families have a very difficult time navigating the ECE system, often being confused by numerous programs. By setting up systemic standards that commit to parental clarity through, for example, better information provision, greater transparency could be advanced and hopefully secured. Not limited to content alone, feasibility also is determined by the process: Just how would the field go about establishing systemic standards? Although there is limited precedent for this in early childhood, other fields are developing standards that transcend individuals or an individual institution. Building on processes used in other fields and the knowledge of early childhood, the development of systems standards is both doable and timely. It should be remembered that when the ideas of setting individual and programmatic standards were introduced, they too were met with skepticism regarding their feasibility.

Beyond technical feasibility, there is an important moral imperative for developing early care and education systems standards. Given that so much information is collected on the accomplishments or the outputs of young children in early childhood programs, it only seems just to have some metric that assesses the inputs and the processes. To date, program quality often has been that metric. Yet, it is clear that program quality itself is an output, conditioned on the systemic inputs that enable programs to achieve quality rankings. Such inputs and processes (e.g., finance, governance, professional development) are functions of an effective system, yet we do not measure them. In measuring only child outcomes and program quality, we are sustaining a clear injustice, one that is quick to blame the child and the program for deficiencies, without assessing the degree to which the system supports either. In calling for the clarification of the vision and for the specification of systemic standards, we advance both quality and equity.

Given the technical nature of standards work, we recommend that a team of specialists, with some from early care and education and some from other fields where systems standards have been established, convene to develop standards for the early care and education system. Once such standards have been developed, they should be piloted in several states to determine their efficacy and the actual supports needed for their implementation. Once the pilot has been evaluated and the standards revised, if necessary, they should be made available for states to use on a voluntary basis.

CONCLUSION

This volume has proffered various ideas about what might constitute an early childhood system, bringing particular focus and strategy to thinking about early care and education systems. It has offered theoretical and practical chapters on the elements that are necessary to support systems development. And it has offered the perspectives of many, all of whom believe that developing an early childhood system is timely and necessary. We designed this book because we agree. Continuing piecemeal approaches to funding an enterprise so essential to the national good will continue to yield piecemeal accomplishments. This entire volume, and specifically the recommendations contained in this chapter, underscores the pressing need to alter our strategies, our work, and our policies. Early childhood providers, policymakers, and scholars know what needs to be done; that our professional sisters—to whom this volume is dedicated—warrant political and economic support is undeniable. Yet, ultimately the development of an early childhood system transcends politics and economics: It beckons us because it is nothing less than the moral obligation of society and the social right of young children.

REFERENCES

Ager, A., Stark, L., Akesson, B., & Boothby, N. (2010). Defining best practice in care and protection of children in crisis-affected settings: A Delphi study. *Child Development, 81*(4), 1271–1286.

Goffin, S. G., Martella, J., & Coffman, J. (2011). *Vision to practice: Setting a new course for early childhood governance.* Washington, DC: Goffin Strategy Group.

Kagan, S. L., & Cohen, N. (Eds.). (1996). *Reinventing early care and education: A vision for a quality system.* San Francisco: Jossey-Bass.

Kagan, S. L., & Cohen, N. (1997). *Not by chance: Creating an early care and education system for America's children.* New Haven, CT: Bush Center in Child Development and Social Policy.

Kagan, S. L., & Kauerz, K. (2009). Governing American early care and education: Shifting from government to governance and from form to function. In S. Feeney, A. Galper, & C. Seefeldt (Eds.), *Continuing issues in early childhood education* (3rd ed., pp. 12–32). Upper Saddle River, NJ: Pearson.

Kauerz, K. (2009). *The early childhood and elementary education continuum: Constructing an understanding of P–3 as state-level policy reform.* New York: Teachers College, Columbia University. ProQuest Dissertations and Theses, Retrieved from http://search.proquest.com/docview/304870194?accountid=11311

Linstone, H. A., & Turoff, M. (2002). *The Delphi method: Techniques and applications.* Newark, NJ: New Jersey Institute of Technology. Available at http://www.is.njit.edu/pubs/delphibook/index.html. (Original work published 1975)

UNICEF, Innocenti Center. (2008). *The child care transition: A league table of early childhood education and care in economically advanced countries* (Report card 8). Florence, Italy: Author.

About the Editors
and the Contributors

Sharon Lynn Kagan is the Virginia and Leonard Marx Professor of Early Childhood and Family Policy and Co-Director of the National Center for Children and Families at Teachers College, Columbia University, and Professor Adjunct at Yale University's Child Study Center. Author of 225 articles and 13 books, Kagan currently consults domestically with federal and state agencies, Congress, governors, and legislatures, and is a member of numerous national boards and panels. Internationally, she is working with UNICEF, the World Bank, UNESCO, and the Inter-American Development Bank, and 35 countries globally. Recipient of honorary doctoral degrees domestically and internationally, Kagan is past president of the National Association for the Education of Young Children and Family Support America and a fellow of the American Educational Research Association (AERA). She is the only woman in the history of American education to receive its three most prestigious awards: the 2004 Distinguished Service Award from the Council of Chief State School Officers (CCSSO), the 2005 James Bryant Conant Award for Lifetime Service to Education from the Education Commission of the States (ECS), and the Harold W. McGraw, Jr. Prize in Education.

Kristie Kauerz is program director for PreK–3rd Education at Harvard Graduate School of Education (HGSE). Kauerz specializes in early care and education and elementary school reform, comprehensive early childhood system building, and the linkages between policy, research, and practice. Her experience includes working in two different gubernatorial administrations in Colorado (Governor Bill Ritter, Jr., and Governor Roy Romer); working at the national level—across states—as program director for early learning at Education Commission of the States; and working in academia at the National Center for Children and Families (Teachers College) and at the Center for Human Investment Policy (University of Colorado–Denver).

She has authored or co-authored numerous articles, book chapters, and reports on topics ranging from state kindergarten policies to early childhood governance to P–3 policy alignment. She co-authored Washington State's Early Learning and Development Benchmarks and a book on improving the early care and education teaching workforce. Kauerz earned her B.A. in political science from Colorado College, her M.A. in international development from American University, and her Ed.D. in early childhood policy from Teachers College, Columbia University.

Kimberly Boller is a senior research psychologist at Mathematica Policy Research. She holds a Ph.D. in developmental and cognitive psychology from Rutgers University. Dr. Boller studies the effects of early childhood care and education policies and programs on children, parents, and the quality of early childhood services.

Andrew Brodsky is a senior associate at Augenblick, Palaich and Associates, a Denver-based educational research firm. His research interests include early childhood finance, cost estimation, and system building; teacher assessment and alternative compensation systems; and K–12 finance and school reform. He received his B.S. in psychology from the University of Massachusetts, his teaching certificate from the University of Southern Maine, and his Ph.D. in educational research methods and policy from the University of Colorado.

Charles Bruner is founding director of the Child and Family Policy Center, established in 1989 to better link research and policy on issues vital to children and families. He served 12 years as a state legislator in Iowa and holds a Ph.D. in political science from Stanford University. Dr. Bruner also manages the State Early Childhood Policy Technical Assistance Network and is the Research and Evaluation Director for the BUILD Initiative.

Dean Clifford provides consultation to local and state organizations working to improve early childhood services, both through her individual firm and as a member of the Smart Start National Technical Assistance Center. She was the founding director of the Forsyth Early Childhood Partnership, a Smart Start partnership in Winston-Salem/Forsyth County; was founder of Great Beginnings, a family support program; and has been a public school teacher and counselor and family child care provider. She holds a Ph.D. in child development and family relations from the University of North Carolina in Greensboro; an M.Ed. in counseling from Wake Forest University; and a B.A. from Salem College.

Julia Coffman is founder and director of the Center for Evaluation Innovation. She specializes in the evaluation on systems change, advocacy, and communications efforts. She received her B.S. in psychology from the University of Illinois at Urbana–Champaign and her M.S. in justice studies from Arizona State University.

Jeanine Coleman is an early childhood specialist at Denver Public Schools. She specializes in authentic assessment practices for children birth to 5 years and has worked at both the state and local level on early childhood systems in Colorado. She received her M.S. degree from Southern Illinois University and her Ph.D. from the University of Denver.

Harriet Dichter works at the First Five Years Fund, serving as national director. Previously, she served as secretary for the Pennsylvania Department of Public Welfare and as the state's founding deputy secretary of the Office of Child Development and Early Learning. Dichter is a summa cum laude graduate of Yale University and a cum laude graduate of the University of Pennsylvania Law School.

Sangree Froelicher is deputy director for Thrive by Five Washington, a public/private partnership in Washington state that mobilizes long-term statewide commitment to early learning by bringing together key public and private resources and stakeholders to ensure that all families with young children have access to proven, high-quality programs, information, and support. She specializes in early learning, with particular interest in state policy and systems change. She received her B.A. in political economy from The Evergreen State College.

Eugene García has published extensively on language teaching and bilingual development, authoring or co-authoring more than 200 articles and book chapters as well as 14 books and monographs. Dr. García is conducting research in effective schooling for linguistically and culturally diverse student populations and is presently Vice President for Education Partnerships at Arizona State University, a post he has held since 2006.

Stacie G. Goffin is the principal of the Goffin Strategy Group, established in 2004 to build the capacity of the early care and education field to provide effective programs and services to young children through system building and leadership. Prior to this, Goffin led the 5-year effort to reinvent the National Association for the Education of Young Children's early childhood program accreditation system. She is a former senior program officer at the Ewing Marion Kauffman Foundation, higher education faculty member, and preschool educator.

Janice Gruendel currently serves as deputy commissioner for the Connecticut Department of Children and Families and is the founder of Gruendel & Associates, a nonprofit and government consulting firm. She has worked in senior leadership positions in the governmental, nonprofit, and business sectors, and is involved in organizational change based on the science of children's development. She received her B.A. in sociology from the University of Maryland, her M.Ed. in educational psychology from Rutgers University Graduate School of Education, and her Ph.D. in developmental psychology from Yale University.

Jodi Hardin is director of Early Childhood Systems Initiatives in the Office of the Lt. Governor in Colorado. She uses a public health approach to identify and implement strategic linkages across health, human service, and education systems in order to achieve positive outcomes for young children and their families. She received an M.P.H. from the University of North Carolina at Chapel Hill, with a focus on maternal and child health.

Karen Hill Scott is president of her own consulting firm and an Adjunct Professor of Public Policy at UCLA. She has been actively involved in the development of early education systems, particularly in California where she chaired the State Master Plan for Early Education and incubated the state's largest existing system in Los Angeles County. She received her Ed.D. in learning and development from UCLA and is on the Board of the Foundation for Child Development.

Marilou Hyson is a consultant in early childhood development and education and Affiliate Faculty in Applied Developmental Psychology at George Mason University. Formerly editor of *Early Childhood Research Quarterly* and NAEYC's Associate Executive Director for Professional Development, she advises on professional development issues for early childhood projects in Indonesia, Vietnam, and Bangladesh. Hyson holds a B.A. from Boston University, an M.A. from the University of North Carolina at Chapel Hill, and a Ph.D. from Bryn Mawr College.

Amy Kershaw is a senior project manager at the Massachusetts Department of Children and Families, where she oversees an internal systems change effort designed to transform and improve the way children and families involved in the state's child welfare system receive services. Previously, Kershaw served as deputy, and then acting, commissioner, for the Massachusetts Department of Early Education and Care. She received her B.A. from Williams College and her M.P.A. from the Maxwell School of Citizenship and Public Affairs at Syracuse University.

Lisa G. Klein is executive director of the Birth to Five Policy Alliance. Prior to that, she served as Vice President of Early Education and Manager of Research and Evaluation at the Kauffman Foundation and worked in the not-for-profit community, specializing in emotional and behavioral treatment and policy advocacy for children and adolescents. She received a B.A. in psychology from Occidental College, an M.S.Ed. from the University of Kansas, and a Ph.D. in psychology with an emphasis in child development from the University of Missouri–Kansas City.

Denise Mauzy is director of the Opportunities in a Professional Education Network (OPEN) Initiative at the Center for Family Policy and Research at the University of Missouri. She focuses on state-level systems development, including early childhood and youth development workforce data collection and evaluation of early childhood before- and after-school program quality. Mauzy received an M.S.W. from the University of Missouri and is a licensed clinical social worker in Missouri.

Geoffrey Nagle is director of the Tulane University Institute of Infant and Early Childhood Mental Health and an Associate Professor of Psychiatry at the Tulane University School of Medicine. He also is a policy fellow at the Reilly Center for Media & Public Affairs at Louisiana State University. He received his B.A. in political science from Duke University, his M.S.W. and M.P.H. from Tulane University, and his Ph.D. in mental health policy research, also from Tulane University.

Karen Ponder is a consultant in state policy and program development with Ponder Early Childhood, Inc. She has a special interest in creating and maintaining local coalitions on behalf of young children. She has worked in all areas of early education, as a pre-K and kindergarten teacher, center director, teacher educator, and state policy and program developer. She is the former president of Smart Start and Smart Start's National Technical Assistance Center. She received her A.A. from Anderson University and her B.A. from North Carolina State University, and completed additional studies at the University of North Carolina at Chapel Hill.

Ann Reale is a principal in the Education Division at ICF International, co-ordinating state and local initiatives, and previously provided consultation and managed system-building projects at the National Child Care Information and Technical Assistance Center. She has more than 12 years of senior budget and policy experience in education and child care at the state government level, including serving as the first commissioner of the Massachusetts Department of Early Education and Care. Reale earned a bachelor's degree in economics from the University of Massachusetts at Amherst and a master's degree in public administration from Syracuse University's Maxwell School.

Sue Russell is president of Child Care Services Association, a nonprofit agency committed to improving access to high-quality early care and education in North Carolina and across the country. She has focused much of her life's work on improving the education, compensation, retention, and recognition of the early care and education workforce.

Diana Schaack is an independent research and early childhood policy consultant. She specializes in quality rating and improvement systems particularly as they relate to measuring early care and education program quality and evaluating their impact on children's school readiness skills. She received her B.A. in psychology from Hobart and William Smith Colleges, her M.S. in early childhood and elementary education from Bank Street College, and her Ph.D. in applied child development from the Erikson Institute/Loyola University Chicago.

Helene M. Stebbins is president of HMS Policy Research, an early childhood policy and research firm specializing in the coordination of the health, education, and care of children from birth through age 5. By tracking state initiatives and best practices, she works to promote the exchange of good ideas among policymakers to improve state policies. She received her M.A. in public affairs and policy analysis from the University of Wisconsin–Madison, and her B.A. from Carleton College in Minnesota.

Jennifer M. Stedron is Policy Director for Early Childhood Education, Health and Human Services for the Hickenlooper-Garcia administration and executive director of Colorado's Early Childhood Leadership Commission. Prior to this, she served as program director in the Education Program at the National Conference of State Legislatures, where she specialized in the policy areas of early childhood, time and learning, school finance, and data systems. She received her B.A. from Michigan State University and her master's degree and Ph.D. from the University of Denver in child clinical psychology with a specialty in developmental cognitive neuroscience.

Kate Tarrant earned a doctorate in education from Teachers College, Columbia University, where she also served as a graduate research fellow at the National Center for Children and Families. She received her B.A. from Emory University and her M.P.A. from Columbia University's School of International and Public Affairs. Her research and policy interests focus on early childhood systems, workforce development, and quality improvement.

Kathy R. Thornburg currently holds two half-time positions: Director of the Center for Family Policy and Research at the University of Missouri and Assistant Commissioner of Early and Extended Learning at the Missouri Department of Education. Her career has spanned more than 40 years teaching, directing early childhood/after-school programs, conducting research, and working toward policies that support young children, their families, and the professionals who work with them. Her graduate degrees are in child development/early childhood from the University of Missouri.

Kathryn Tout is Co-Director of Early Childhood Research at Child Trends. She specializes in research on quality rating and improvement systems, professional development initiatives, and how families make early care and education decisions. She received her Ph.D. in child development from the University of Minnesota and her M.A. in public policy from the University of Chicago.

Fasaha Traylor spent the past 2 decades at senior levels in philanthropy, first at the William Penn Foundation in Philadelphia and then at the Foundation for Child Development in New York City. Her tenure with both organizations focused substantially on improving early education through changes in policy and practice. She currently consults on issues in public education.

Jessica Vick Whittaker is a research scientist at the University of Virginia's Center for Advanced Study of Teaching and Learning. Her areas of expertise include early childhood classroom processes and teacher–child relationships that promote children's positive academic and social-emotional outcomes. She is currently the co-investigator on two randomized controlled trials of professional development interventions aimed at improving the quality of teacher–child interactions. She received her B.A. in psychology from Duke University and her Ph.D. in human development from the University of Maryland.

Index